D1601542

Church on the Way

CHURCH
ON THE WAY

Hospitality and Migration

NELL BECKER SWEEDEN

PICKWICK *Publications* · Eugene, Oregon

CHURCH ON THE WAY
Hospitality and Migration

Pickwick Publications
An Imprint of Wipf and Stock Publishers
199 W. 8th Ave., Suite 3
Eugene, OR 97401

www.wipfandstock.com

ISBN 13: 978-1-4982-0916-8

Cataloguing-in-Publication data:

Becker Sweeden, Nell.
  Church on the way : hospitality and migration / Nell Becker Sweeden ; foreword by Miguel A. De La Torre.

  xiv + 174 p. ; 23 cm. Includes bibliographical references and indexes.

  ISBN 13: 978-1-4982-0916-8

  1. Hospitality—Religious aspects—Christianity. 2. Church work with immigrants—United States. 3. Sanctuary movement. I. Title.

BV640 S85 2015

Manufactured in the U.S.A.   07/14/2015

Contents

Foreword

Miguel A. De La Torre

DANIEL NEYOY RUIZ AND his family sit with me in their new living quarters, a former office of a church pastor. For several weeks, Southside Presbyterian Church, in Tucson, Arizona, has become their home. Daniel, along with his documented wife Karla and their thirteen-year-old, U.S. born son Carlos, moved into the church because Daniel is undocumented. For fourteen years he has worked in this country, paying taxes and raising a family, until a minor traffic violation turned his life upside-down. Lacking proper documentation, he was turned over to the immigration authorities. For three years, he has been fighting his deportation orders; however, he has run out of options. To be deported will mean separation from his love ones, making his wife and son, according to Southside pastor Alison Harrington, into a "widow and orphan." Even though the Hebrew Bible calls followers to take care of society's most vulnerable members, "the widow, the orphan, and the alien within our midst," our immigration policies, which has disappeared tens of thousands, is devastating communities, turning our neighbors who have undocumented relatives within their families into "widows and orphans." By taking sanctuary, Daniel is asking the federal government not to continue splitting up families, specifically his family. This is why they now sleep in bunk beds in a church office, a desperate attempt to uphold the family value of remaining united.

Historically, hospitality has been the virtue spouted by many Christians, called to love and care for the stranger in their midst, because, as the biblical text reminds us, "you yourselves were once aliens" (Lev 19:34). The Bible can be read as a book of immigration testimonies: from Adam and Eve being the first refugees forced out of the land that witnessed their birth; to the Patriarchs Abraham, Isaac, and Joseph who were wandering migrants in a land that was not theirs; to a forty-year trek in the wilderness; to an exile community in Babylon; to a Messiah who himself was a refugee in Egypt. Not surprisingly, hospitality and the care of the immigrant, plays an important role in the Scriptures. Nevertheless, providing hospitality is not what motivated Southside to grant Daniel sanctuary, for Daniel is no stranger—he is a neighbor. "Neighbors are disappearing," Rev. Harrington tells me. "They are snatched up from the streets, on their way to work, on their way to the store. Parents leave the house while children stay at home not knowing if their parents will return." The love of neighbor, specifically the undocumented neighbor, is becoming the primary religious motivation and spiritual justification of the New Sanctuary movement.

The attitudes and biases undergirding our immigration policies are not just destroying the lives of the undocumented; they are creating oppressive structures and situations in the lives of their documented families. Both Daniel who is undocumented and his wife and son who are documented are equally seen and defined as not belonging, for to be Hispanic is to be "walled off." For Latina/os to live on the borders moves the discourse beyond the physical border wall that acts, as Gloria Anzaldúa reminds us, as a bleeding scare where the First and Third World chafe against each other. The concept of border also encompasses the invisible wall that separates Hispanics from the rest of the dominant U.S. culture. Borderlands are more than just a geographical reality—they also symbolize the existential reality faced by all U.S. Latina/os—including those with proper papers. Most Hispanics, regardless as to which state they live in or how they or their ancestors found themselves in the United States, live on the borders. Borders separating Latina/os from other Americans exists in every state, every city, and almost every community, regardless as to how far away they may be from the southern international line. Borders are as real in the Dakotas, in Iowa, and in Minnesota, as they are in Arizona, in New Mexico, and in Texas. To be a U.S. Hispanic is to constantly live on the borders, that is, the border that separates privilege from disenfranchisement, that separates power from marginalization, and that separates whiteness from browness. Most U.S. Hispanics, regardless as to what city they reside in or which state they belong to, live on the borderlands.

Currently, over eleven million undocumented immigrants live in the United States, the vast majority being from Latin American countries. While Americans debates what course of action should be taken; few contemplate why they come in the first place. For some, they come searching for jobs and freedom; for others, they come to use up our social services and have their so-called "anchor babies." There are even those who, like former Colorado Congressman and 2008 Republican presidential candidate Tom Tancredo, believe "[illegal immigrants] are coming to kill you, and you, and me, and my children and my grandchildren." All of the reasons given as to why they come are wrong. The reason an immigration dilemma exists is complex and goes beyond simplistic sound-bite explanations. Nevertheless, one of the main reasons they are here is due to U.S. foreign policy. Because the present immigration discourse fails to consider why they come, multiple draconian legislations passed in states like Arizona are immoral, specifically because they do not consider U.S. historical complicity in creating the present immigration situation.

When we consider the invasion of Mexico in 1846 that resulted in the taking of half their territory including the gold of California, the copper of New Mexico and Arizona, the Silver of Nevada, and of course, the oil of Texas, the rich minerals that served as seed-money for the launching of the U.S. industrial revolution; or when we consider our own foreign policy rooted in gun-boat diplomacy that placed the entire might of the U.S. military apparatus at the disposal of U.S. corporations like the United Fruit Company, engaging in some 47 "regime changes" during the past century (boots on the ground and CIA covert operations); or when we consider the NAFTA trade agreement that have impoverish Mexico by flooding their markets with our subsidized agricultural goods; why then are we shocked that we have an immigration policy? We created, over the past century the very conditions that contribute to our current immigration crises. And yet, it is ironic that those who are the invaders, who massacred the indigenous people, who are the latest immigrants to this region, rewrite the national narrative so that they can be the victims of this immigration crisis.

To burn someone else's house down so that they are left hungry and homeless, and then offer him or her space in one's own home, calling it Christian hospitality, is at the very least, problematic. Our military ventures, our protection of corporate interests, and our appropriation of other peoples' cheap labor and natural resources is the flame that burns down the houses of our southern neighbors, leaving them homeless migrants. Only by ignoring U.S. colonial adventures south of the border, are we able to reimagine the crises we are responsible for causing, casting U.S. citizens as victims who, nonetheless, due to their Christians virtues, are providing hospitality. Maybe a new understanding of hospitality might be needed, for hospitality masks the history remembered by the subaltern. When one nation, builds roads into another nation, to extract its raw material and cheap labor, why should we be surprised when those people take those same roads following everything that has been stolen from them. Daniel and his family are forced to take sanctuary in a church, living out of a pastor's former office, because conditions have been created during the previous century that forced him to seek residence in the very country that economically and militarily benefitted from the ravishing of his own country of origin. If this is true, what then should be a proper hospitable response?

It deeply grieves me that all too often, the church is asleep in the light. We are at a moment in time that desperately needs churches to engage and offer support, protection, and sanctuary to the very least among us, to Jesus (the migrant traversing between divinity and humanity) who comes to us disguised as Jesús, the undocumented. Maybe a shift is needed in the rhetorical usage of the virtue of hospitality, moving our understanding of the term towards an inclusion of, or replacement by the concept of restitution. What is due to those upon whose sweat, tears, and blood we build U.S. global wealth and strength? The problem with hospitality is that it assumes *we* own the house, and out of the goodness of our Christian hearts, we are providing room for the so-called stranger to stay in our home. However, it is the cheap labor of the "stranger" that built the house in the first place. A radical form of hospitality is needed that moves away from some self-congratulating virtue called for by many liberals who refuse to explore their complicity with the deaths that are occurring at our southern border.

To assist us in our struggle in finding ways by which to respond to this immigration crisis, Nell Becker Sweeden provides a timely book geared to assist in formulating appropriate praxis through the act of solidarity. Her voice is important, and many more voices like hers are needed. Many of us who are Latina/os that speak out on this issue can easily be dismissed as simply being "angry Hispanics," and thus ignored because, after all, our concerns, according to the popular mythology, are not rooted in a call to justice, but based on our ethnicity. But when allies, who "do not have a dog in this fight," speak up in the name of justice, they move the issue beyond the tendency of making immigration simply into a Hispanic issue. But this call to justice through a reimagined radical hospitality is not just so we can become "good" Christians, but also "good" Jews, and "good" Muslims, and "good" Buddhists, and "good" Hindus, and "good" humanist, and "good" atheist. This is a human crisis that requires all of us who are human, regardless of faith or lack thereof, to step up to the plate and offer the solidarity of walking with the ones searching for sanctuary.

Acknowledgments

I WISH TO THANK the community that led me toward this book and the community that has supported me throughout. *Church on the Way* would not be possible without the loving support and encouragement of my family, friends, professors, mentors, and colleagues. I am grateful to my colleagues at Nazarene Compassionate Ministries, particularly Larry and Lynne Bollinger and Cort and Karen Miller, as well as the NCM international team who continue to inspire me and bring me much hope and joy in my work. I also wish to thank my professors who inspired my theological imagination and encouraged me to go on to further studies, particularly Michael Lodahl, John Wright, Ron Benefiel, John Knight, Doug Harrison, Jacque Mitchell, Herb Prince, and Jamie Gates as well as my pastors Steve Rodeheaver, Brian Postlewait, Matt Jenson, Tim Kauffman, Kaza Fraley, and Jason Veach. I am grateful for my colleagues at the BU School of Theology, particularly Xochitl Alvizo, Krishana Zuckau, Montague Williams, Adam Wallis, Kathryn House, and the theology students I have the privilege of learning from as a student and teaching assistant. I am indebted to my friends both near and far who continue to cheer me on, particularly Kelly Becker Tirrill, Karen Marshall, Cheryl Stone, and Cheryl Mittan. I wish to thank Claire Wolfteich for her guidance in teaching and in the field of practical theology and Roberto Goizueta at Boston College for how his teaching and theology inspired this book. Thank you especially to Shelly Rambo who continually inspires and challenges my theology and was an invaluable conversation partner in the development of this book. I wish to thank my doctoral advisor and friend, Bryan Stone, whose teaching and writing continues to inspire me and who graciously guided me in writing my first book. I am grateful to my current George Fox Evangelical Seminary community and their support in bringing this book to publication. Thank you especially to my writing partner, Leah Payne, and to Brice Larson whose

Acknowledgments

careful final edits of the book made it much more enjoyable for my readers. Finally, I am thankful for my family—especially Doug and Diana Becker, Sarah Becker Carrera, and Russell and Fanda Sweeden—who were constant encouragement during this process. Finally, thank you to my partner in life, Josh, who brings me joy in the journey.

1

Introduction

THE PRACTICE OF CHRISTIAN hospitality reaches back to the early centuries of Christian life as well as deep into Jewish history, life, and Scripture. This practice is alive today in Christian churches and parachurch organizations within the United States, but new contextual realities—in particular twenty-first century global migration patterns—have altered the conditions under which hospitality is practiced. The reality of migration and its effect on human lives disrupts static conceptions of hospitality and challenges ecclesial communities toward contextual appropriation of hospitality practice.[1] This book explores Christian hospitality practice in light of twenty-first century U.S. Latino/a migration and develops the notion of a journeying hospitality of accompaniment with and among persons migrating that fosters deeper relationships and formation. The shifting identities of persons "on the move" challenge assumptions about what it means to welcome another in hospitality and, ultimately, what it means to be church from within these new relationships. In turn, the new conceptions and expressions of hospitality I offer press how the nature and mission of the church will be oriented toward new ecclesial patterns and alternative forms of residing on earth.

1. I have employed the term "ecclesial communities" rather than "churches" or "congregations" to encompass the wider range of hospitality practice within intentional communities, para-church organizations, and/or multiple congregational groups gathering together all of which may or may not identify themselves specifically as a "church" or "congregation." I specifically address them as "ecclesial" rather than "Christian communities" because I wish to investigate how hospitality practice contributes to ecclesiology.

Christian practices of hospitality—theologically conceived as welcome of the stranger or alien within Judeo-Christian tradition and Scripture—often involve members of an ecclesial community inviting an unknown person in need into a home or congregation. This welcome often includes sharing a meal and an exchange of material assistance or providing care.[2] For Christians, this hospitality is broadly recognized as an ethical responsibility mirroring the welcome of God in Jesus Christ. Traditionally, such practice has been understood and embodied as an invitation for the stranger to come *in* rather than the community venturing *out*. In Christian communities in the United States, the practice often takes shape as an invitation into a community's own life and does not necessarily allow for a reciprocal invitation by the person welcomed. This relationship, therefore, is limited to a one-way exchange often excluding the full participation of marginalized persons. The practice does not allow for a (mutual) process of exchange in which the ecclesial community itself can be formed by this new relationship.

At the end of 2014, the International Organization of Migration (IOM) estimated 232 million international migrants worldwide, comprising roughly 3 percent of the world's population.[3] The reasons for migration vary, and many migrations are voluntary. This book explores hospitality practice pertinent to persons who have migrated out of economic necessity, however, it also has implications for persons forced to migrate as refugees and asylum seekers due to natural disaster, persecution, political unrest, war, and as itinerants. IOM estimates that there are about 33 million people internally displaced worldwide and the global number of refugees is today

---

2. Pohl notes: "For most of the history of the church, hospitality was understood to encompass physical, social, and spiritual dimensions of human existence and relationships. It meant response to the physical needs of strangers for food, shelter, and protection, but also a recognition of their worth and common humanity. In almost every case, hospitality involved shared meals; historically, table fellowship was an important way of recognizing the equal value and dignity of persons." *Making Room*, 6. Amy Oden writes: "While hospitality can include acts of welcoming family and friends, its meaning within the Christian biblical and historical traditions has focused on receiving the alien and extending one's resources to them. Hospitality responds to the physical, social, and spiritual needs of the stranger, though, as we shall see, those of the host are addressed here as well. . .On the face of it, hospitality begins with basic physical needs of food and shelter, mostly powerfully symbolized in table fellowship, sharing food and drink at a common table." *And You Welcomed Me*, 14.

3. See U.N. report of on "International Migration and Development," http://www.iom.int/files/live/sites/iom/files/What-We-Do/docs/SG-report-Intl-Migration-and-Development-2013-A_68_190-EN.pdf.

16.7 million.[4] Additionally, 48 percent of all global migrants are women.[5] The twenty-first century reality of bodies marked by wandering makes necessary an investigation and re-appropriation of the Christian practice of hospitality that reflect migrants' identity, spirituality and faith practice, reasons for their migration and journey, as well as the economic and political factors surrounding their migration. Because of the complexity of international migration and the distinctiveness of each individual context, the following pages focus specifically on *Latino/a* undocumented or unauthorized persons who migrate. Recent trends show that unauthorized immigrant population has leveled off nationally between 2009 and 2012.[6] In 2012, the population of unauthorized immigrants was 11.2 million, roughly the same as 2009.[7] Today this accounts for roughly 3.5 percent of the U.S. population.[8]

Bodies displaced through forced migration challenge traditional notions of home, belonging, and identity as they pertain to hospitality.[9] Persons who have migrated may have complex and varying memories of the home(s) they have left. Many continue to travel and are unable to settle

4. See recent statement by the IOM Director General, William Lacy Swing: http://www.iom.int/cms/en/sites/iom/home/news-and-views/press-briefing-notes/pbn-2014b/pbn-listing/iom-director-general-calls-for-a.html.

5. See UN report "International Migration and Development," available at: http://www.iom.int/files/live/sites/iom/files/What-We-Do/docs/SG-report-Intl-Migration-and-Development-2013-A_68_190-EN.pdf.

6. Passell and Cohn, "Unauthorized Immigration Totals Rise," available at http://www.pewhispanic.org/2014/11/18/unauthorized-immigrant-totals-rise-in-7-states-fall-in-14. Statistics show that from 2000 through 2004 an average of 800,000 undocumented immigrants per year entered the United States. While the average has dropped to 500,000 immigrants per year between 2005 and 2008, the undocumented immigrant population in the United States increased by 40 percent between 2000 and 2008. See Passell and Cohn, *Trends in Unauthorized Immigration*, iii. Cited in De La Torre, *Trails of Hope and Terror*, 2.

7. These totals are down from the peak in the unauthorized immigrant population in 2007 with 12.2 million.

8. Ibid.

9. I play with the language of "bodies on the move" and below "bodies marked by wandering" to signify the perpetual nature of migration and the mobile patterns of life that persons endure in transnational migration. I specifically utilize the word "bodies" to indicate the negative consequences of displacement in migration, in which persons out of their own control or will are forced to migrate in order to survive. I understand bodies forced to move as signifying how human lives are determined by global market forces. I employ this phrasing as a synonym to "migrants" or "migrations," as well as "displaced persons," as indicative of the negative consequences of migration.

into a new home. Some migrants may find that they have multiple homes. In such a context, a sense of belonging and identity formation take on complex forms depending on conditions such as a person's reason for migration, her or his journey to the United States, or her or his present residence and support community.

When migrants are welcomed into U.S. congregations, they encounter a variety of familiar and unfamiliar ecclesiological formations. An invitation *into* a community is also an invitation into this community's own socio-cultural context. For this reason the investigation of hospitality must take into account how cultural and socio-historical factors, in addition to models of worship, denominational politics, and theological differences, all contribute to this welcoming or non-welcoming environment. Furthermore, differences of race and ethnicity, gender, class, culture, and language within the congregation must be taken into account in how a community offers hospitality and the degree to which the person welcomed can participate in the life of the community.

Christian theology of hospitality also demands that the welcoming community be confronted by those it encounters and enter into deeper relationship. Hospitality compels the church to be continually shaped by relationships that involve risk and often demand change. Ultimately the church is faced with a pressing ecclesiological question: *How will the present context of migration form hospitality practices and inform the identity and mission of ecclesial communities?*

PRACTICES AND PRACTICAL THEOLOGY

Before moving forward, a few notes about my method are in order. I investigate hospitality practice, as well as the integrated relationship between ecclesiology and hospitality practice, building off of Alasdair MacIntyre's definition of practice and the practical theologians who draw from his work. For MacIntyre, practices arise out of communal formation toward teleological ends and involve a community's ongoing, cooperative appropriation of these ends. He defines practice as:

> a coherent and complex form of socially established cooperative human activity, through which goods internal to that form of activity are realized in the course of trying to achieve those standards of excellence which are appropriate to, and partially definitive of that form of activity, with the result that human powers to

achieve excellence and human conceptions of the ends and goods involved, are systematically extended.[10]

As a practice extended from the life of the church, I argue that Christian hospitality practice is theory-laden, rooted in Christian ecclesiology, Scripture, and tradition, and tied to the concrete performance of Christian hospitality in ecclesial communities.[11] Dorothy Bass nuances MacIntyre's definition from a Christian perspective, and I draw from her definition in understanding how Christian practice shapes the life of the church. Bass defines Christian practice as follows:

> Practices are born of social groups over time and are constantly negotiated in the midst of changing circumstances. As clusters of activities within which meaning and doing are inextricably interwoven, practices shape behavior while also fostering practice-specific knowledge, capacities, dispositions, and virtues. Those who participate in practices are formed in particular ways of thinking about and living in the world.[12]

Bass's definition is critical for uncovering how ecclesial communities negotiate and adapt hospitality practice (or any Christian practice for that matter) according to the contexts in which they find themselves. Additionally, Bass points to how hospitality as a Christian practice might shape behavior, knowledge, virtues, and understanding of the surrounding context within the life of an ecclesial community. Bass includes a teleological origination to Christian practice, noting, ". . .to be called 'Christian' a practice must pursue a good beyond itself, responding to and embodying the self-giving dynamics of God's own creating, redeeming, and sustaining grace."[13] The focus of Christian practice toward a *telos* in God will be central to how I

---

10. MacIntyre, *After Virtue*, 187.

11. For more information on practices as theory-laden, see Browning in *A Fundamental Practical Theology*, 9, 47, 139. Volf and Bass, eds., *Practicing Theology*, 1–12. Bass notes the distinction between MacIntyre's virtue ethics and the work of social theorist Bourdieu's *Outline of a Theory of Practice*. Bass writes, "MacIntyre's virtue ethics emphasizes that practice pursue a good in a coherent, traditioned way, while social scientists influenced by Marxist thought stress the constant negotiations over power that give particular shape to practice in specific social situations." Volf and Bass, *Practicing Theology*, 6. I build upon MacIntyre's virtue ethics, but argue that practices are continually negotiated as they are practiced in social situations where power dynamics are uncovered and challenged.

12. Bass, "Ways of Life Abundant," 29.

13. Ibid., 30.

point to the journeying ecclesial imagination of the people of God and how this journeying informs and is informed by hospitality with and among persons migrating.

Gustavo Gutiérrez's description of the theological task is helpful in my examination of hospitality as a practical theological and ecclesiological exercise. Gutiérrez defines theology as critical reflection on praxis in light of the Word of God.[14] A central theme in liberation theology, praxis points toward the indissoluble unity between action and reflection, and the ongoing discovery of praxis manifests itself in an action-reflection continuous spiral.[15] Gutiérrez presents the need for a recovery of historical praxis in light of the eschatological dimension of theology. In order to accomplish this task Gutiérrez and liberation theologians challenge traditional conceptions of theology and ecclesiology by uncovering critical perspectives and suspicion arising from the lived reality of the poor. They build off of Paulo Freire's process of "concientization," which refers to the form of liberating education by which the oppressed learn to perceive economic, political, and social contradictions and take action toward transforming this reality.[16]

ECCLESIOLOGICAL ORIENTATION

Throughout this study, I seek to hold in tension traditional conceptions of hospitality practice and the challenges posed by new contexts. Nicholas Healy's development of the church as a theodramatic performance and ecclesiology as a practical-prophetic discipline are instructive.[17] Healy adapts Hans Urs von Balthasar's theodramatic theory to describe the relations between God, world, and church as a dramatic play in which humans are participants and live entirely within the drama. Healy interprets this play through Augustine's articulation of Christian existence struggling toward the City of God and the church as a mixed body made up of members of

---

14. See Gutiérrez, *A Theology of Liberation*, 5–12.

15. Ibid., 10.

16. See Freire, *Pedagogy of the Oppressed*. Also see Segundo, *The Liberation of Theology*. Segundo articulates a methodology for liberation theology through a hermeneutical spiral in which persons 1) experience reality and expose ideological biases, 2) apply ideological suspicion to theology, 3) experience a new ideological reality and develop exegetical suspicion, 4) discover a new hermeneutic for understanding scripture.

17. Healy, *Church, World, and the Christian Life*.

both the city of God and the city of humanity.[18] Thus, Healy reads Augustine's ecclesiology as an open-ended narrative of the two cities "in their interwoven, perplexed and only eschatologically separable reality."[19] Through theodrama, Healy develops an alternative to what he calls "blueprint ecclesiologies" in order to focus more intently on the theological description of the context in which the church finds itself.[20] He defines "blueprint ecclesiologies" as ideal descriptions of what the perfect church should look like in its "true nature" or "essence."[21] In turn, these theologies often fall short at explaining the concrete church in the world in its broken and sinful state.

Thus, Healy focuses on theological inquiry as historical, ongoing, and open-ended, while blueprint ecclesiologies distort and often prevent theological reflection on the concrete church *in via*. Healy directs attention to how the church works out its theology within context. He writes: "The concrete church, living in and for the world, performs its task of witness and discipleship within particular, ever-shifting contexts, and its performance is shaped by them. Critical theological analysis of those contexts, and the present shape and activity of the church within them, should therefore be one of the central tasks of ecclesiology."[22] Healy does not treat the life of the church and cultural or sociohistorical context as different or separate spheres that need to be "correlated."[23] In fact, he notes that these two entities

18. Ibid., 55. Relying on Augustine's *City of God*, which he abbreviates as (CoG), Healy writes, "'The church proceeds on its pilgrim way in this world, in these evil days. Its troubled course began . . . with Abel himself. . .and the pilgrimage goes on from that time right up to the end of history' (CoG 18.51). The church is, indeed, 'even now the kingdom of God,' but, quite unlike the City of God, it is a 'kingdom at war' (CoG 20.9). Its task is therefore to gather those who have already been chosen for 'testing and training' so as to 'raise them from the temporal and visible to an apprehension of the eternal and invisible' (CoG 10.14)." Ibid.

19. Healy, *Church, World, and the Christian Life*, 56.

20. The theodramatic horizon can hold in tension a number of ecclesiological realities that otherwise may be confused, separated, or treated one-dimensionally. For Healy, "These tensive elements include the following: the church's identity is *fully* constituted by *both* divine and human agency, permitting *theological* reflection upon the *concrete* church; the church's role includes the *formation* of the individual disciple's *distinctive* identity; the church's orientation renders it *superior* to others, yet it is *dependent* upon others and is always more or less *sinful;* the church claims to be orientated to *ultimate* truth, yet it must acknowledge that our view of that truth is *limited* by our location within the ongoing drama." Ibid., 22; italics original.

21. Ibid., 35, 36.

22. Ibid., 39.

23. See ibid., 38–39 n. 48. He points to the distinction between two correlatable poles

cannot be described independently of one another, for the concrete church always finds itself residing within and formed by its context.[24]

Healy's practical-prophetic ecclesiology offers possibilities for guiding the concrete church in how it encounters both Christian and non-Christian "Others" and the extent to which the church allows itself to be confronted by difference.[25] This challenge cannot be met without the concrete church recognizing and self-critically reflecting upon its own sinfulness and shortcomings. He draws upon Kathryn Tanner's development of the theological work of *ad hoc bricolage* that concedes to a messier and conflictual ecclesiological reality.[26] Tanner's insights are valuable for focusing on the church *in via* particularly in light of cultural and contextual challenges. She writes: "the distinctiveness of a Christian way of life is not so much formed *by* the boundary as *at* it; Christian distinctiveness is something that emerges in the very cultural processes occurring at the boundary, processes that construct a distinctive identity for Christian social practices through the distinctive use of cultural materials shared with others."[27] Tanner's observations are fitting for examining hospitality practice in light of the global phenomenon of migration.

Tanner, as well as many feminist theologians, emphasize that churches are communities of faith *and* struggle. They caution against the church turning too hastily toward unity, because such unity can too easily become uniformity. Uniformity neglects the voices of margin and voices of opposition in community, which are necessary for a community of faith and struggle. I rely upon Letty Russell's imagery of the church for re-shaping hospitality practice in ways that demand honesty in relationship.[28] Russell focuses on new possibilities of unity and difference through her ecclesiology of "church in the round."[29] Stretching traditional conceptions of church,

---

as the basis of Niebuhr's classic work, *Christ and Culture.*

24. Healy, *Church, World, and the Christian Life*, 39.

25. Ibid., 153.

26. See Lindbeck, *The Nature of Doctrine*; and Hauerwas, "The Servant Community." Also see Tanner, *Theories of Culture.*

27. Tanner, *Theories of Culture*, 115.

28. Seeking to reform rather than discard hospitality, which some postcolonial theologians would protest, Russell draws upon hospitality as a way forward for the church in understanding how difference shapes the community in ways that resist uniformity.

29. See Russell, *Church in the Round*. Russell arrives at "church in the round" based on the notion that all are welcome *in the reign or household of God*. See ibid., 23. The ecclesial image of a round table comes from C.S. Song's description of Chinese culture

Russell presents new spatial and relational imaginations and focuses on community gathered around a round table. She writes, "Like the eucharist and like the church that gathers at Christ's table, the round table is a sign of the coming unity of humanity. It achieves its power as a metaphor only as the *already* of welcome, sharing, talk, and partnership opposes the *not yet* of our divided and dominated world."[30] She develops the notion of a table that challenges the church body toward back-and-forth movement and continual discernment between margin and center.[31] Russell calls for ecclesial communities to reread tradition and Scripture for new insight and in order to "talk back" to the tradition using the critical lens of marginality and power relationships.[32] Russell's understanding of hospitality derived from the "church in the round" concept builds upon what she terms "kitchen table solidarity," which reflects living with and among others and being drawn into a partnership of sharing and reflection amidst the sweaty tasks of daily living.[33] This imagery is important because it highlights the fact that community, relationships, and partnerships are born in difficult and often mundane tasks. Ecclesial communities continue to be shaped as all members perform life together in the ordinary that does not escape or separate out the chaos and difficulty of life.

While Healy is Roman Catholic and his work speaks back into this tradition and polity, Russell, a Protestant feminist ecclesiologist who worked in a variety of ecumenical contexts, develops intentionally relational and

---

and hospitality that has influenced Chinese paintings of Jesus and the disciples sharing a "last supper at the round table." Ibid., 12. In this sense, based on the celebration of the Eucharist and the church gathered together around the Lord's Table, Russell notes that "the round table is a sign of the coming unity of humanity." Ibid., 17. She continues, "If the table is spread by God and hosted by Christ, it must be a table with many connections. The primary connection for people gathered around is the connection to Christ. The church is the community of faith in Jesus Christ . . . Because Christ is present in the world, especially among those who are neglected, oppressed, both church and society, always welcoming the stranger to the feast to sharing the feast where the 'others' gather. Christ's presence also connects us to one another as we share in a partnership of service. . .The round table itself emphasizes this connection, for when we gather around we are connected, in an association or relationship with one another." Ibid., 18.

30. Russell, *Church in the Round,* 17.

31. Ibid. Russell notes, "Because Christ is present in the world, especially among those who are neglected, oppressed, and marginalized, the round table is also connected to the margins of both church and society, always welcoming the stranger to the feast or sharing the feast where the 'others' gather." Ibid., 18.

32. Ibid., 24–29.

33. Ibid., 75.

communal ecclesial imagery to expand notions of church. The following pages attempt to hold in tension a number of theologians' perspectives, social locations, and theologies that are not normally juxtaposed. My intention is to explore the dynamic nature of ecclesiology through various theological perspectives, in order to identify and explore alternative spatial imagination and hospitality praxis within the church in light of migration. The performative and contextual focus of Healy's practical-prophetic ecclesiology together with Russell's "church in the round," and others who suggest different manifestations of church in light of feminist and postcolonial critiques, provide unique vantage points—not to mention, formations—with which to reflect on how practices of hospitality challenge ecclesial communities to change and adapt with context.

U.S. Latino/a and postcolonial theologians challenge ecclesial communities to identify and act against various forms of exploitation and occlusion of difference in their communities and suggest alternative ecclesial imagery in light of migration. The intersectionality of race, class, and gender as well as factors of cultural, economic, and political suspicion must weigh into conversations regarding hospitality as an ecclesial practice. Postcolonial U.S. Latina theologian, Mayra Rivera, notes the dramatic reversal between the geographical representation of Christianity 100 years ago and today: "In 1900 approximately 65 percent of the world's Christians lived in Europe and North America," whereas today 60.3 percent of global Christianity resides in Africa, Asia and Oceania, Latin America and the Caribbean.[34] Postcolonial theology calls attention to the representation, identity, and influence of victims of colonialism and of those who continue to be marginalized in current systems of power.[35] Rivera's challenge to the church is fitting: "Must the 'white-washing' of Christianity continue to bleach out the colors of all of our lives?"[36] Confronted by the reality of a white dominant majority in the church, I intend to unearth and highlight the theological contributions of persons who journey on the margins and,

34. Rivera, "Alien/Nation, Liberation, and the Postcolonial Underground," 14–15. She notes Segovia's statistics of changes in global Christianity in "Interpreting beyond Borders," 21.

35. See M. A. Gonzalez, "Who is Americano/a?" Gonzalez draws from Sugirtharajah, *Asian Biblical Hermeneutics and Postcolonialism*, 16. Gonzalez adds that the theme of exile is not exclusive to Segovia's work, but appears of various Latino/a theologians' work, including: J. L. González, *Mañana*; Isasi-Díaz, *Mujerista Theology*, specifically her chapter "By the Rivers of Babylon."

36. Rivera, "Alien/Nation," 4.

because of their mobility, are often excluded from a valued place in ecclesial communities.

Fernando Segovia characterizes Latino/a theology as a theology of diaspora, born in exile, displacement, and relocation.[37] Roberto Goizueta challenges U.S. Hispanic ecclesiology toward accompaniment in light of many migrants' experiences of having no way forward and having to forge a way as they walk. He presents hopeful possibilities through the communal invitation—*caminemos con Jesús* (let us walk with Jesus)—in an adapted liturgical procession by the San Fernando Cathedral parish in San Antonio, Texas. U.S. Latino/a and postcolonial theological voices are central to my critical analysis of hospitality practice and ecclesiology. Their insights and imagination direct me in beginning to re-shape hospitality practice in ways that take into account displaced persons' participation in and exclusion from ecclesial communities. The constructive or strategic practical theological proposals I build are not intended as solutions or rules. Rather, I propose a new sensitivity in ecclesial communities to the displacement and mobility experienced by migrating persons and suggest alternative patterns of hospitality practice and ecclesial life that open the church up to the contributions of those "othered" in that their participation has been and/ or continues to be marginalized.[38] Additionally, the reform of hospitality and ecclesiology is ongoing and never-ending. My project is a movement toward new understanding, but by no means a complete or finalized plan.

Unique to this particular practical theological investigation is attention to concrete hospitality performance in lived ecclesial communities. Often practical theological projects direct readers toward strategic proposals as a final move but offer recommendations rather than return

37. Gonzalez, "Who is Americano/a?" 60. Gonzalez writes: "Segovia characterizes Latino/a theology as a theology of the diaspora, 'born and forged in exile, in displacement and relocation.' The traits of this theology are as follows: 'a self-consciously local and constructive theology, quite forthcoming about its own social location and perspective; a theology of diversity and pluralism, highlighting the dignity and values of all matrices and voices, including its own; a theology of engagement and dialogue, committed to critical conversation with other theological voices from both Margins and center alike." Ibid., 71–72. See Segovia "Biblical Criticism and Postcolonial Studies," 53.

38. See Nausner, "Homeland as Borderland." Discussing the tension between nomadic lifestyles and the sedentary culture of institutionalized religion, Nausner writes, "I am not proposing a solution to this tension. But I am suggesting that a new sensitivity to alternative ways of conceiving territoriality is important for Christian theology, if it does not want to align itself smoothly with imperial power." Ibid., 128.

to concrete examples.[39] Additionally, postcolonial theology, in its critical deconstructive moves, can be accused of paralysis in constructive thought and action.[40] My turn to concrete alternative practices of hospitality in the final chapters of this book draws postcolonial theology further into creative and constructive praxis.

Drawing from lived examples of hospitality on U.S.-Mexico borderlands, I describe how performative dimensions of ecclesiology, such as liturgies and rituals, help to shape the church community's hospitality practice, not to mention its broader discernment of faithfulness amidst ever-changing contexts. Again, these concrete manifestations span a variety of ecclesial traditions. Performative hospitality is demonstrated through creatively and intentionally contextualized practices of Roman Catholic parishes and movements as well as Evangelical, Mainline, and Free Church congregations and ecclesial movements. The variety of traditions represented reveals many possibilities for how performative expressions of hospitality can arise out of ecclesial communities. I also point to how communal and corporate partnership between congregations and non-profit organizations suggests how they can build relationships and form alliances in order to more expansively offer hospitality and advocate alongside and on behalf of migrants. I return to a wide span of ecclesial traditions as I explore the practices of baptism and eucharist in chapter 6. Offering two contemporary manifestations of hospitality through eucharistic celebrations at the U.S.-Mexico border, I point to Roman Catholic liturgy and theology in a Mass

39. For example, see the practical theological method of Browning in *A Fundamental Practical Theology*. See pp. 47–58 for an outline of his four step strategic practical method. His final strategic step offers recommendations and practical solutions for Christian churches (see chapters 3, 9, 10, and 11). My method, while it offers constructive proposals like Browning, also seeks to provide concrete embodiments where hospitality practice is already adapting to the contexts of global migration. This adds to the constructive element of my work.

40. Recognizing this critique, Susan Abraham directs attention toward the constructive side of postcolonial theology. She writes: ". . . the postcolonial context remains a contested but radically creative site for the continuing re-imagination of political, religious, and cultural communities. In particular, theological imagination in the postcolonial context is characterized by a marked distance from doctrinaire positions on identity, ethics, and liberation. In its stead emerge the heterogeneity of multiple (sometimes contrasting and contradictory) positions that remain an opportunity for creative revisioning. The practical context of postcolonial theology in view of globalization does not provide for the unifying and homogenizing visions of either liberal assimilation or conserving visions of "pure" or orthodox identity or ethics." Susan Abraham, "What Does Mumbai Have to Do with Rome?," 376.

celebration, as well as Free Church and Methodist traditions that shape a Christian worship gathering and Love Feast. U.S. Latino/a theologians, often drawing upon the Roman Catholic tradition, and the sacramental realist approach of Mennonite theologian John Howard Yoder, are important influences in this endeavor.

In discussing ecclesial practices, I rely upon Yoder's explanation of baptism and eucharist as two of five ways he proposes "in which the Christian church is called to operate as a *polis* . . . Our model in each case will be the practice of the early church as reflected in the writings of the New Testament."[41] Additionally, I present practices of the church as they relate to hospitality ecumenically. Yoder's explanation of ecumenical is helpful: "Our agenda is ecumenical, not in the modern organizational sense of arranging conversations among denominational agencies, or in the sense of comparing and contrasting the foundational documents of conflicting confessions, but in the simpler sense of being relevant to all kinds of Christians."[42] My intention is not to create rules, procedural guidelines, or a set of beliefs that pertain to hospitality practice or ecclesiology. Rather, indebted to Yoder's vision of church practice, I hope that my vision for hospitality practice reconceived in the life of congregations has "to do more with a style of approaching any question than with particular moral choices."[43] I seek to present how concrete practices shape the community toward particular ways of life together in the name of Christ. Thus, such practices

> foster flexibility and readiness to approach any new challenge. That frees them from bondage to any one cultural setting; it frees them for evangelical interaction into any new missionary context. They are all good news, all marks of the new world's having begun.[44]

I offer contemporary examples that point toward new patterns of journeying for hospitality practice, as well as strategic practical suggestions for congregations, to reveal how ecclesial practice cultivates an adaptability that is necessary for ongoing reform in the life of the church. Ultimately, the goal in this process is to inspire congregations to creatively manifest the gospel amidst ever-shifting contexts.[45]

41. See Yoder, *Body Politics*, ix.

42. Ibid., *x*.

43. Ibid., 46.

44. Ibid.

45. I use the terms "gospel" and "good news" interchangeably in reference to the *evangelium* announced and embodied by Jesus.

THE ROAD AHEAD:
MAPPING THE CHAPTERS

The chapter following this introduction, "Mapping Christian Hospitality: Place and Performance," examines the current literature on the practice of hospitality and surveys present understandings and embodiments in U.S. churches, denominations, and para-church organizations. Additionally, I explore current models of Christian hospitality and the ways in which they have dominated popular conceptions of this practice within the United States. Specifically, I investigate the Catholic Worker movement begun by Dorothy Day and Peter Maurin, intentional community models in what is commonly referred to as New Monasticism, and the L'Arche communities started by Jean Vanier. I unearth different dimensions of the practice as they relate to identity, place, gestures of welcome, gift and exchange, borders and boundaries, and journey or pilgrimage.

The third chapter, "Understanding the Complexities of Migration: Contextual Considerations in Hospitality," introduces the global phenomenon of transnational migration, as well as the context of migration in the United States. I narrow my focus to explore more thoroughly the context of Latino/a undocumented immigration. Drawing upon cultural studies and postcolonial theory in conversation with U.S. Latino/a theology, I begin to critically analyze Christian hospitality in light of the displacement and mobility of persons in migration. Several U.S. Latino/a voices—Ada María Isasi-Díaz, Carmen Nanko-Fernández, Miguel A. De La Torre, and Virgilio Elizondo—are central to my description of U.S. Latino/a migration and uncovering the challenges it poses to theology and ecclesiology.[46]

Chapter 4, "Objections to Hospitality and Possibilities for New Ecclesial Imagination," builds upon the contributions of various U.S. Latino/a and postcolonial theologians to challenge ecclesial communities' hospitality practice in light of the cultural, economic, political, religious, and social factors of migration, while taking into account the intersectionality of race, class, and gender in these factors. This chapter analyzes identity construction and how it relates to borders and boundaries in church and society. Postcolonial theological reflections regarding alternative forms of spatial imagination in migration, as well as the pervasiveness of empire in people's lives, become instrumental within a critical analysis of hospitality. Additionally, the power dynamics inherent within a guest/host binary together

46. U.S. Latino/a theology is more recently identified as U.S. Latin@.

with reconceived postures of encountering, accompanying, and fostering friendships with others arise as vital aspects to consider in re-imagining hospitality. Of course, surrounding the investigation of hospitality practice within congregations, it becomes critical also to address how communities discern and negotiate Christian identity amid changing circumstances and the differing perspectives of church members. In this middle chapter, I draw my critical analysis to a close allowing for constructive possibilities to begin rising to the surface. I point ecclesial communities toward new hospitality praxis focusing on themes of journeying and accompaniment, while also continuing to affirm the need for critical self-reflection in the church.

Chapter 5, "Re-imagining Hospitality and Ecclesiology: Practical Theological Embodiments," begins my practical theological movement toward re-imagining hospitality practice through lived examples. I address how the performance of hospitality takes on new shapes and forms in light of changing patterns of migration along U.S.-Mexico borderlands. To arrive at concrete and practical proposals, I present and analyze contemporary embodiments of the practice of hospitality through: 1) the performance of liturgy and ritual outside the walls of the San Fernando Cathedral in San Antonio, Texas, 2) simple acts of accompaniment through the Catholic Worker house Casa Juan Diego in Houston, Texas, and 3) the value of corporate and communal partnerships amongst organizations and churches in El Paso, Texas. These contemporary manifestations reveal a wide span of ecclesiological orientations, which I draw from in engaging my own ecclesiological commitments.

Chapter 6, "Eucharistic Formation of a Hospitable Community," constructively engages how hospitality practice arises from but also challenges the baptismal and eucharistic formation of the church. Here, I draw upon two expressions of hospitality through eucharistic celebrations physically shared across the U.S.-Mexico border. Through contextual manifestations of worship and hospitality—nurtured through Holy Communion shared across geopolitical lines—one can begin to question how nation-state borders and boundaries inform ecclesial identity and, in fact, shape bodies in the church. The continual practice of the eucharist in such spaces heightens the political and economic formation inherent within the eucharist. It is this formation that has the potential to guide self-critical reflection in the church and nurture renewed sacramental vision in how the church lives and acts in the world.

The concluding chapter, "Journeying Somewhere Through Hospitality: New Imagination and Praxis," reflects on how a re-conceived notion of hospitality furthers explorations in ecclesiology and migration. Specifically, I suggest ecclesiology is shaped by hospitality practice re-conceived in light of journey with and among persons who migrate. The church *on the way* is the church not only on an eschatological journey, but on a journey of discovering the unveiling Reign of God before us today. I reveal how hospitality practice as ecclesial ethics furthers the church's understanding of place, journey, and pilgrimage that are so central to its nature and mission.

2

Mapping Christian Hospitality
Place and Performance

INTRODUCTION

CHRISTIAN HOSPITALITY PRACTICE IS a growing concern for the church of the twenty-first century and there certainly is no scarcity of theological literature surrounding this practice in U.S. ecclesial communities. Yet, before diving into potential objections with regard to hospitality practice, it is important to identify the aspects of this practice that are shared in congregations today and at what points hospitality practice is being stretched and challenged to meet new contexts and developments in ecclesiology and culture. The challenges posed to hospitality practice directly influence how ecclesial identity continues to be discerned and negotiated amidst ever-changing circumstances. In other words, the work laid out here addresses how both hospitality *and* ecclesiology are stretched simultaneously in new contexts.

In order to survey the contemporary Christian hospitality landscape in the U.S., a brief introduction of ecclesiological resources on hospitality is in order. Then, I investigate three concrete manifestations of hospitality within Christian faith communities: the Catholic Worker movement and Houses of Hospitality, intentional communities within the New Monastic movement, and L'Arche communities. Building off of the origins and practices of these contextual embodiments of hospitality, I look deeper into the shared behaviors, gestures, and ways of life within ecclesial communities and begin to explore the relationship between boundaries and identity formation. Lastly, juxtaposing hospitality practice and ecclesiology, I explore how they may mutually inform one another as each responds to the context surrounding a local congregation.

Contemporary Christian scholars from a variety of ecclesial traditions have explored the historical, scriptural, and theological sources of hospitality practice to unearth hospitality as a moral category for contemporary practice in a U.S. ecclesial context. Christine Pohl's seminal work *Making Room: Recovering Hospitality as a Christian Tradition* brings together research from eight communities that incorporate hospitality as a way of life together. Pohl invites her readers to remember the Judeo-Christian heritage of hospitality, reconsider this tradition, and recover the practice in present-day embodiments. While Pohl brings together Christian voices from many traditions, her work is often considered the Protestant guide to hospitality as it stands alongside additional hospitality practices and resources from Roman Catholic history and tradition. Examples include monasticism and specifically the Benedictine tradition, the Catholic Worker movement of Dorothy Day and Peter Maurin, and Jean Vanier's writings on the L'Arche communities.[1]

In *And You Welcomed Me: A Sourcebook on Hospitality in Early Christianity*, Amy Oden presents a collection of early Christian texts about hospitality practice. Her excerpts include various literary genres spanning North Africa, Egypt, Palestine, and Syria, as well as Europe and covering the first through the eighth centuries, with the bulk arising from the fourth and fifth centuries. In 2008, Oden also published a guide to hospitality for congregations entitled, *God's Welcome: Hospitality for a Gospel-Hungry World*. This work addresses the foundation of Christian hospitality arising out of God's welcome and guides congregations in patterning God's welcome of others. Other notable ecclesial resources on hospitality practice surface in the *Practicing our Faith* series edited by Dorothy Bass as well as John Koenig's work *New Testament Hospitality*. Koenig's work is a historical-theological resource on hospitality practice in first-century Judaism and the early Christian church as it traces the teachings of Jesus. Each of these major works on hospitality practice can be used side-by-side as biblical, historical

1. Other notable Roman Catholic lay resources on hospitality include Richard's *Living the Hospitality of God* and Nouwen's *Reaching Out*.

and theological guides providing background for congregational practice and theological reflection on hospitality.

What these works do not specifically address—and what I aim to investigate—is how hospitality practice has adapted and been stretched to accommodate new contextual realities. These works also do not pose challenges to hospitality practice or directly address its abuse or misuse in ecclesial communities. As this chapter explores the practice of hospitality I build off these resources, while also identifying various nuances of hospitality expression within the contexts of: 1) offering hospitality to persons who are poor and without homes in primarily urban settings; 2) hospitality that arises out of an intentional community that shares living space and meals and seeks to build lasting relationships with strangers in its neighborhood; and 3) living out hospitality in caring for persons who have intellectual and physical disabilities. To begin this exploration and identify ways hospitality practice is being stretched, I turn to these three contextual manifestations of hospitality.

CONTEXT, PLACE, AND PERFORMANCE OF HOSPITALITY

The Catholic Worker Movement

The practice of Christian hospitality in the context of the twentieth century United States produced several important antecedents for the practice of hospitality in today's ecclesial communities. The Catholic Worker movement, cofounded by Day and Maurin in the 1930s in New York, is one notable example. Drawing upon the influences of the early church and its saints, contemporary French personalists, Benedictine and ancient Irish monasticism, and keeping company with those who were poor and without homes in society, Day and Maurin inspired a worldwide movement embodying a radical renewal of Catholicism.[2] Their movement challenged the social and economic order of the times, which Day continually referred to as "the filthy, rotten system," and inspired a faithfulness to the life and teachings of Jesus who walked with and among the poor and was himself poor.[3]

Day and Maurin began *The Catholic Worker* newspaper with writings that concerned faith and the situation of workers in 1933. They committed

2. Zwick and Zwick, *Catholic Worker Movement*, 1.

3. Ibid., 148.

their lives to voluntary poverty, hospitality, and works of mercy. Day and Maurin strove to live out the seven corporal and seven spiritual Works of Mercy based on Matthew 25:31:

> The Spiritual Works of Mercy are: to admonish the sinner, to instruct the ignorant, to counsel the doubtful, to comfort the sorrowful, to bear wrongs patiently, to forgive all injuries, and to pray for the living and the dead.
>
> The Corporal Works of Mercy are to feed the hungry, to give drink to the thirsty, to clothe the naked, to ransom the captive, to harbor the harborless, to visit the sick, and to bury the dead.[4]

Matthew 25: 31–46 would become the default mission statement of the Catholic Worker movement. As people began to read about hospitality in the newspaper, they arrived to be a part of this way of life. Their commitment to Works of Mercy, soon materialized into Houses of Hospitality, bread and soup lines for the hungry, and farming communities.[5] The moral imperative to be poor and care for those who are poor arises out of Jesus' own identification with the poor in Scripture and this Matthew 25 passage, thereby drawing a parallel between knowing and caring for the poor and caring for Jesus himself. Through this motivation, members of the Catholic Worker movement see Christ in their encounter with the poor. Mark and Louise Zwick explain:

> Dorothy spoke of the "long-continuing crucifixion" of the poor and the hope in sharing somehow in their poverty. As she said in her Easter meditation in the April 1964 *Catholic Worker:* "The mystery of the poor is this: That they are Jesus, and what you do for them you do for Him. It is the only way we have of knowing and believing in our love. The mystery of poverty is that by sharing in it, making ourselves poor in giving to others, we increase our knowledge of and belief in love."[6]

Day's and Maurin's writings continued to advocate for the poor, but perhaps more effectively, they also put their writings into practice through their Houses of Hospitality and Agricultural Centers. Life together in the Houses of Hospitality and farming communes was to be a witness to the gospel for the world, while also providing alternative, local economic models. As with monasticism, each House of Hospitality would stand as an

4. Ibid., 30.
5. Ibid., 25.
6. Ibid., 41.

autonomous community and pattern itself after the work schedule of the Benedictines in uniting labor, prayer, and meals.[7] Additionally, each of the Catholic Worker communities sought to provide an alternative to economic individualism in that properties were meant not for individual use, but communal sharing.[8] Brigid Merriman describes Day's purpose for Houses of Hospitality as "a center of Catholic action in all fields, to work for, teach and preach social justice, to form a powerhouse of genuine spirituality and earnest educational and vocational work, to dignify and transform manual labor, and to work for the glory and love of God and His Church."[9]

The Catholic Worker movement's core commitment to voluntary poverty arises from their welcome of brothers and sisters who are poor in Christ and their seeking an alternative to the economic system. From the movement's beginning, all workers went without a salary and were expected to share their work as gifts. Maurin describes the motivation of "going without luxuries in order to have essentials."[10] The property and possessions were understood to be for everyone in the house with a focus on meeting basic needs. The impetus for voluntary poverty arose from the harsh reality of involuntary poverty for so many: "Catholic Workers knew from experience how destitution ground people down, how difficult it was for those who had not chosen their poverty."[11] There was a responsibility of the workers toward those forced into poverty; such persons had a special place in the house. Day continually struggled with the notion of charity and its condescending tendencies. Charity, for her, could never be understood apart from justice or Christ's own identification with the poor. Charity must be distinguished from philanthropy. James Douglass's distinction of the two is fitting: "The condescending tone of the term 'charity' can be avoided only if we sink to poverty ourselves and continue to give from our poverty. . .The Catholic Worker counteracts these pressures [of the consumer, affluent society] by the protest of the poor giving to the poor, shattering the illusion of the billfold apostolate."[12] Hospitality and voluntary poverty must be held

7. See ibid., 45, 51.

8. Ibid., 138.

9. O'Shea Merriam, OSF, *Searching for Christ*, 87, quoted in Zwick and Zwick, *Catholic Worker Movement*, 42.

10. Zwick and Zwick, *Catholic Worker Movement*, 33.

11. Ibid.

12. Douglass, "Dorothy Day and the City of God," 42, quoted in Zwick and Zwick, *Catholic Worker Movement*, 35.

together; the volunteer is the object of reform rather than the poor.[13] Welcoming the poor is understood as a gift. Day's words clearly articulate the vision: "Too often we are afraid of the poor, of the worker. We do not realize that we know him, and Christ through him, in the breaking of the bread."[14]

Today, there are over 227 Catholic Worker communities committed to the founders' embodiments of voluntary poverty, prayer, nonviolence, and hospitality for the homeless, hungry, and marginalized.[15] They continue to be inspired to this work because of the belief in the God-given dignity of every human person. Additionally, in the same spirit as Day and Maurin, Catholic Worker communities are often known for their protest of injustice, war, racism, and violence of all forms.[16] Catholic Worker houses of hospitality may be most known for the acts of hospitality they offer to those in need; however, a commitment to confronting the unjust systems that often perpetuate poverty, homelessness, and exploitation of humans are intimately tied to this hospitality. This confrontation is wedded to hospitality because the economic and social system deeply affects the lives of those whom the Catholic Worker households welcome and with whom they share life. The Catholic Worker movement continues to advocate that the social and economic system needs to be changed and rebuilt.[17] They are particularly concerned with the dignity of labor for workers and caution against growing materialism in U.S. society.

Throughout the years Maurin and Day would be strong critics of industrial capitalism and investigated alternative economic models. In the December 1948 *Catholic Worker*, Day wrote:

> We, who witness the thousands of refugees from our ruthless industrialism, year after year, the homeless, the hungry, the crippled, the maimed, and see the lack of sympathy and understanding, the lack of Christian charity accorded them (to most they represent the loafers and the bums, and our critics shrink in horror to hear them compared to Christ, as our Lord Himself compared them) to us, I say, who daily suffer the ugly reality of industrial capitalism and its fruits.[18]

13. See Zwick and Zwick, *Catholic Worker Movement*, 34–35.

14. Miller, *Dorothy Day*, 166, quoted in Zwick and Zwick, *Catholic Worker Movement*, 36.

15. See Catholic Worker Website, http://www.catholicworker.org.

16. Ibid.

17. Zwick and Zwick, *Catholic Worker Movement*, 148.

18. Ibid., 162–63.

Those who comprise the Catholic Worker Movement today continue to communicate Day's and Maurin's motivations and actions within new contexts. The Zwicks, for example, place the earlier Catholic Worker movement emphasis on "refugees from ruthless industrialism" parallel to modern migrant "refugees" they receive at their house of hospitality in Houston, Texas.[19] More will be explored with regard to the Catholic Worker practice of hospitality in the remaining sections. For now, it should be said that the Catholic Worker's commitments to nonviolence and alternative forms of economics, arise from the movement's larger purpose to seek God's will on earth as it is in heaven.[20]

Intentional Communities in New Monasticism

Drawing from the Catholic Worker movement among other influences, more recent manifestations of hospitality houses and intentional communities have sprung up across the United States in what has been termed "New Monasticism." The shape and inspiration of these communities differ from the Catholic Worker movement due to the contexts, socio-economic make-up, and faith traditions of new monastic communities themselves. The "New Monastics" have identified as followers of Jesus who have committed to a new way of life in community.[21] The Rutba House in Durham, North Carolina is one such Christian community formed around hospitality, peacemaking, and discipleship. They self-describe:

> We are shaped by our common life and rule for living. We pray together daily, share meals, fast once a week, and worship together as a way of shaping our life around the gospel. These are important practices that form our identity as we try to be faithful disciples of Jesus. But it is our neighbors who ground the Rutba House and help us remember who we are.[22]

Inspired by the monastic communities manifested throughout Christian history, these newer communities are drawn toward unearthing authentic Christian witness from within forces of empire, nation-state, etc. The

19. Ibid., 315.

20. See ibid., 321. The language references vision-casting toward "a new heaven and a new earth, wherein justice dwelleth" and is from *The Catholic Worker,* February 1940.

21. See New Monasticism Website, http://www.newmonasticism.org.

22. Rutba House, ed., Editor's Preface in *School(s) for Conversion,* vii.

overarching "New Monasticism" movement seeks grassroots ecumenism and prophetic witness within the North American church and is characterized by 12 marks: 1) Relocation to abandoned places of Empire; 2) Sharing economic resources with fellow community members and the needy among us; 3) Hospitality to the stranger; 4) Lament for racial divisions within the church and our communities combined with the active pursuit of a just reconciliation; 5) Humble submission to Christ's body, the church; 6) Intentional formation in the way of Christ and the rule of the community along the lines of the Monastic novitiate; 7) Nurturing common life among members of intentional community; 8) Support for celibate singles alongside monogamous married couples and their children; 9) Geographic proximity to community members who share a common rule of life; 10) Care for the plot of God's earth given to us along with support of our local economies; 11) Peacemaking in the midst of violence and conflict resolution within communities along the lines of Matthew 18; and 12) Commitment to a disciplined contemplative life.[23] In exploring the new monastic communities as exemplars of hospitality practice, I will focus here on the first four marks as they relate to hospitality practice.

Drawn to what they call, "the abandoned places of empire," the New Monastics seek to pattern their lives after Jesus' own life and ministry as well as the voluntary relocation of early desert monastics, in order to understand anew that they are called to dwell and gather as the People of God, the Church, in places rejected and unwanted by broader society. One of these places is the inner city. It is here that New Monastic communities gather, make homes, and build communities with their neighbors and witness to the gospel of Jesus Christ. In a similar vein to the Catholic Worker movement, resistance to unjust systems and values is an important part of community life. The communities believe in confronting injustice and providing an alternative way of life in Christ together. They do this by addressing their context: "The issues of our time, such as militarism, nuclearism, poverty, homelessness, and ecological problems, as manifested on the margins, will call for personal and communal conversion in the form of disciplined resistance in lifestyle and engagement in the search for solutions."[24] They seek to live out this mission locally as they live and interact with their neighborhoods and surrounding communities and cities.

23. Ibid., xii–xiii.
24. Ibid.

New Monastic intentional communities share many aspects of life together, such as living space, prayer and worship, meals, and even finances. Moreover, their life together is built around the practice of hospitality. The Rutba House members find that "hospitality in the form of sharing food, roof and friendship with neighbors will foster both compassion and engagement and will be a form of holy communion with marginal cultures and poor populations."[25] The New Monastic communities describe the motivation for hospitality and shared life together as arising out of God's abiding love that draws humanity near. They see God as a God of welcome, and they live by the moral imperative that Christian identity ought to reflect this.[26] The God of welcome is most fully known in God physically drawing near to humanity and becoming human. They describe Jesus' incarnation as a "radical relocation"—God in Christ "took on flesh and moved into the neighborhood."[27] In the same way, they challenge Christians to draw near to the other and build community there.

The New Monastics understand hospitality as a discipline that needs to be cultivated and practiced by all. Though it takes many shapes and forms depending on context, food and sharing meals are central. Through sharing meals, their communities pattern their lives after Jesus' own meals with "sinners" and participate in the origins of the Eucharist.[28]

Maria Russell Kenney illustrates four different ways hospitality in New Monasticism takes shape. First, motivated by the moral imperative to "welcome strangers in the land" in Hebrew law, Mercy Street community in Houston, Texas welcomes Somalian refugees and helps them resettle and adjust to life in the United States. The second community, Solomon's Porch in Minneapolis, Minnesota, emphasizes a hospitality crafted around spirituality. Their practice includes sharing in regular meals, but also goes beyond them in emphasizing hospitality as a "way of drawing out and drawing in, of allowing people to share of themselves and their journeys with God, and then bringing them and their experiences together with others in the family of faith."[29] Thirdly, Russell Kenney highlights the L'Arche Communities founded by Jean Vanier, which is an international association of 146 communities in 35 countries comprised of "'people with a learning

25. Ibid., 21.
26. See ibid., 45.
27. Ibid.
28. Ibid., 47–48.
29 Ibid., 50. Also see Mercy Street's Website at: http://www.mercystreet.org.

disability and those who choose to share their lives.'"[30] The emphasis here is on friendship and mutual care for one another across lines of "ableness" in ways that move beyond a one-way relationship typical of a patient-assistant. Russell Kenney also describes the gift of being a stranger and receiving hospitality from another stranger. Here, she challenges the host toward recognizing the need to flip the guest/host relationship and relinquish control to another—true hospitality must be reciprocal and mutual. For Americans who "have largely forgotten what it's like to be a stranger," the recognition of inherent power found in the host role and deliberate repositioning is particularly important.[31] Tragically, as Russell Kenney aptly notes, "With our massive borders and relative isolation, we have lost touch with the sense of our own vulnerability."[32] Vulnerability is a necessary part of building human community. It is through such diverse manifestations of hospitality that New Monastics emphasize how strangers become friends, nurture mutual care and love for one another, and highlight the gifts found in each of the communities.

In seeking to plant themselves in "abandoned places of empire," specifically in the inner city, New Monasticism has focused on how hospitality practice relates to lament for racial divisions and seeking reconciliation. In many cities, particularly in the South, this racial divide may be more characteristically "white" and "black." At the same time, the complexity of race and racism also interfaces with questions of class, ethnicity, and minority status in society. New Monastic communities lament how racial segregation in many forms has divided the church body. The movement also seeks to uncover the painful ecclesial history and continued hiddenpresence of racism that has shaped the life of the church. Chris Rice's description of the "hidden wound" of racism in the South is instructive: "America's church patterns of 'us' and 'them' were and continue to be indelibly shaped by trajectories birthed in legal segregation and church schisms that had very little to do with housing preferences or worship styles, and everything to do with race, white supremacy, and slavery."[33] Lament is a necessary practice in refusing forgetfulness of this history and refusing complacency that

30. Ibid., 51. Also see the L'Arche Website at: http://www.larche.org. For reference to a number of communities and presence in countries, see Whitney-Brown, "Introduction," in *Jean Vanier: Essential Writings,* 13.

31. Ibid., 52.

32. Ibid.

33. Ibid., 59.

further allows racial division to be normalized in ecclesial communities. This lament, however, is not without the responsilbity to work toward effective change. Rice continues, "what comes into view is that as we pursue holiness, we are also called to do the hard work of social analysis. Behind faithful lament is theological and social discernment."[34] Practices of lament, remembering, and social analysis do not come easily, and it is necessary to move the community away from the tendency to gather among "people like us." Hospitality is a necessary practice that stretches a community "to people *not like us*"—to the neighbor who is difficult to get along with, to the outcast or marginalized in society, to the enemy across the divide, and as Scripture reminds us, to the alien, the least of these, the orphan, the widow, the prisoner.[35] Opening oneself and one's community to the stranger is "a check against culture (or cultural preference, or the church as a personal refuge) becoming an end in itself. Such openness puts our identity at risk, for we cannot remain the same in the exchange."[36] Hospitality is always a move away from sameness and pursuit of one's own self-interest. Hospitality challenges the church toward ongoing relationship-building with people not like us, that is, the stranger. Those who have been made "strangers" are more than those one does not know personally. Rather, New Monasticism recognizes how social and economic systems, history, society, and church have helped to define some people groups as "strangers" and perpetuated divisions across ethnic, class, and racial lines. Confronting the power differential in society and in churches and unlearning the habits of marginalization and exclusion begins with communities seeing differently and living together differently.

New Monastics continue to struggle with the challenge of difference because the majority of those who comprise the intentional communities are: "educated whites who came from family histories of social privilege, and had come to see the dead end of materialism and the 'rat race,' were now willing to mobilize downward."[37] In contrast, downward mobility is not necessarily the motivation of others with whom the community seeks to build relationships. Many persons made to be "strangers" in society— that is of minority, ethnic, and/or lower socio-economic status—may not identify downward mobility as a priority. New Monastics have felt the con-

34. Ibid., 60.

35. Ibid., 61.

36. Ibid.

37. Ibid., 65.

sequences of often not being able to bridge the race and class divide in their own community make-up. Despite the best intentions, the communities often remain largely white, middle to upper-middle class, and young adult. They continue to seek to build relationships across divides, unlearn the habits of racism, go to unfamiliar places, and practice lament so as to be challenged out of complacency and toward furthering God's intentions for reconciliation. They recognize, however, that the work of reconciliation is beyond their intentions, efforts, and desires, but is a work of the Holy Spirit. In light of these challenges, Rice concludes:

> It is exactly right to put "lamenting racial divisions" in front of "pursuing a just reconciliation." Lament reminds us that we are not God, that visions like the new monasticism do not capture the Kingdom, that true reconciliation is only in the eschaton, when all things are reconciled in Christ. We keep naming the 'not yet' of the coming Kingdom, keep praying to be interrupted by the unexpected, keep reaching out to the stranger, keep holding our hands outward for the gift of new people that the Holy Spirit may bring us tomorrow. Or not.[38]

L'Arche: Ableness, Growth in Community, Spiritual Journey

In searching for authentic community and friendship in response to societal discrimination and misunderstanding of persons living with disabilities, Vanier began sharing a small house in Trosly-Breuil, France with Raphaël Simi and Philippe Seux, two men living with severe intellectual disabilities, in 1964. This would be the beginnings of L'Arche, today a worldwide charitable foundation and network of nearly 150 communities. The L'Arche communities value shared living space among persons with differing ableness. Vanier describes this community as "groupings of people who have left their own milieu to live with others under the same roof, and work from a new vision of human beings and their relationships with each other and with God."[39] They focus on developing friendship, providing care, and nurturing trust among the community. This life is not easy, and those who have mental handicaps often come with considerable needs. Hospitality is here defined in the welcome of friendship and care that works through the difficulties between the relationships of "assisted" and "assistants." Vanier

38. Ibid., 67.

39. Vanier, *Community and Growth*, x.

encourages community members to persevere and find joy in the daily, mundane tasks, to spend spontaneous time with people, and to learn to recognize one's own weakness and need.[40] Vanier describes the community as follows:

> L'Arche is special, in the sense that we are trying to live in com-
> munity with people who are mentally handicapped. Certainly we
> want to help them grow and reach the greatest independence pos-
> sible. But before "doing for them," we want to "be with them." The
> particular suffering of the person who is mentally handicapped,
> as of all marginal people, is a feeling of being excluded, worth-
> less and unloved. It is through everyday life in community and the
> love which must be incarnate in this, that handicapped people can
> begin to discover that they have a value, that they are loved and so
> loveable.[41]

L'Arche, for Vanier, was not just about becoming responsible to others in the community, but rather, about developing relationships of mutual love and interdependence. What is most difficult and demanding in this com-mitment is less about the needs of others, and more about a revelation of one's own weakness.[42]

Vanier's journey was defined by coming to understand the weaknesses in himself and discovering what it meant to be human through relationship with persons living with mental handicaps. Upon visiting centers for people with mental disabilities before beginning L'Arche, he writes, "I was touched by these men with mental handicaps, by their sadness, and by their cry to be respected, valued, and loved."[43] This caused him to consider his own longings and to reflect on the course his life had taken. His was an interior spiritual journey found in building deeper community with persons often hidden away from society and by delving deeper into his own spiritual

---

40. After Vanier returned from being hospitalized after falling ill from exhaustion while traveling, "he highlights in a new way the importance of spending spontaneous, unscheduled time with people. His own experience of being assisted in his weakness underlies a new sensitivity to the problematic aspects of L'Arche's distinction between the assisted and the assistants: 'Everything I see here makes me really question our L'Arche communities and the double culture of the 'assistants' and the 'assisted' that can exist." Vanier, *Essential Writings,* 40–41.

41. Vanier, *Community and Growth,* xi.

42. Ibid., 27.

43. Whitney-Brown references Vanier's words in her "Introduction," to Vanier's *Es-sential Writings,* 29.

personhood to discover the mystery of God there.[44] Vanier's spiritual journey and his life with others caused him to turn inward. He reflected on solitude, on simplicity, on the body, on recognizing his own poverty, and on the meaning of real relationships. He encouraged listening to the anger, anguish, loneliness, and pain in one's own heart. Vanier discovered that if he listened to this, he would also hear something deeper—the voice of God, a voice that professes love.[45]

Vanier's writings emphasize the necessity of growth in "becoming human," something that he encountered in living with persons with intellectual disabilities. This attitude is not often found among the general public. He presents a progression of five attitudes in broader society toward people with intellectual disabilities: 1) persons in society may view disability as a sign of disorder and suppress it; 2) they may develop a so-called charitable attitude (that is in fact pity) toward those with intellectual disabilities, and the general public may glorify those who do such compassionate work; 3) the general public and professionals may begin to recognize, respect, and feel compassion toward persons with disabilities and see how they grow and progress; 4) stemming from the third, the public may develop relationships and friendships with persons with intellectual disabilities; 5) finally, persons may come to see their own humanness and that of their new friends who have recongnizable disabilities.[46] The love and care Vanier

44. Vanier writes: "Since I was a child, there have been three very distinct stages in my life. When I was thirteen, I joined the navy and spent eight years in a world where weakness was something to be shunned at all costs. We are required to be efficient and quick to climb up the ladder of success. I left this world, and another world opened up to me—the world of thought. For many years, I studied philosophy. I wrote a doctoral thesis on Aristotelian ethics, and I embarked on a teaching career. Once again, I found myself in a world where weakness, ignorance, and incompetence were things to be shunned—efficiency was everything. Then, during a third phase, I discovered people who were weak, people with mental handicaps. I was moved by the vast world of poverty, weakness, and fragility that I encountered in hospitals, institutions, and asylums for people with mental handicaps. I moved from the world of theories and ideas about human beings in order to discover what it really meant to be human, to be a man or a woman." Vanier, *Our Journey Home*, 33.

45. Vanier spoke of the value of slowing down. . ."Let us simply stop and start listening to our own hearts. There we will touch a lot of pain. We will possibly touch a lot of anger. We will possibly touch a lot of loneliness and anguish. Then we will hear something deeper. We will hear the voice of Jesus; we will hear the voice of God. We will discover that the heart of Christ, in some mysterious way, is hidden in my heart and there, we will hear, 'I love you. You are precious to my eyes and I love you.'" *Images of Love, Words of Hope*, 82. Carolyn Whitney-Brown cites this in her "Introduction," 40.

46. See Whitney-Brown, "Introduction," 48.

experienced from working with persons of varying intellectual abilities in L'Arche was a continual motivation to challenge societal perceptions of disability, as well as societal pulls toward elitism, strength, and competition. Vanier invites one to find humanity in growing downward, at the bottom of the social ladder. The hospitality and community he nurtures is one that concomitantly challenges the status quo because it calls for a Christian, alternative understanding of wholeness in humanity and recognition of the value of differing ableness in society. Vanier's teachings would have broader influence in society as well in promoting peace and love amidst racism, injustice, and violence throughout the world. As Vanier's teachings intertwined with his own journey of spiritual growth and life in community, he continually emphasized the need "to change the world, with love, one heart at a time."[47] This "changing the world" is realized in the simplicity of hospitality—welcoming others who are made strangers in society and discovering them as friends.

Vanier's motivation for L'Arche communities also led him to begin an international Christian ecumenical movement for people with disabilities, and their families and friends. Vanier met Marie Helen Mathieu in the 1960s, and they would later plan a pilgrimage to Lourdes for people with handicaps and their families. Vanier encouraged these pilgrimages with his own communities as well. He saw the importance of traveling together as a community in celebration and joy. Pilgrimages provided persons who often do not get to travel with new experiences and also presented society with the opportunity to encounter them. These pilgrimages for persons living with disabilities and their families have grown into a network of travel communities known as Faith and Light. In 2008, there were fifteen hundred Faith and Light communities in eighty countries.

The Catholic Worker, New Monasticism, and L'Arche communities reveal numerous ways in which various traditions have concretely interpreted Scripture and theology to shape their contextualized intentional practice of hospitality. Each *embodiment* of hospitality also reveals important aspects of the practice, such as how hospitality teaching is appropriated in context and adapts as circumstances change. Discernment, self-reflection, and social analysis, have been an important part of their practicing hospitality. Building upon these examples, I turn to discuss some of the behaviors involved in practicing hospitality.

47. Ibid., 42.

BEHAVIORS, GESTURES, AND WAYS OF LIFE TOGETHER

While several aspects may come to mind when one thinks about contemporary Christian hospitality, there are countless small moves—indeed "little moves against destructiveness"—that contribute to the breadth of hospitality practice.[48] This section will explore a variety of behaviors, gestures, and ways of life that ecclesial communities have developed as part of their hospitality practice. Here, it is important to begin to identify the parallels in hospitality practice between communities, as well as how their hospitality practice is uniquely stretched and challenged by contextual circumstances. I will begin to identify the various ways ecclesial communities encounter, are encountered by, and are formed by those that they welcome.

Eating Together

Preparing food and the practice of sharing meals together, is a hallmark of hospitality. Perhaps more than home ownership or shelter, food is central to welcoming others and building community. Eating together takes on heightened theological importance in Christian hospitality practice because of the emphasis on Jesus sharing meals with his disciples and others in the Gospels. Additionally, the ritual of the eucharist reenacts Jesus' final supper with his disciples before his crucifixion. Celebration of the eucharist, or the Lord's Supper, is a meal that defines the life of the church. The eucharist, of course, is much more than sharing a meal, but implies the significance of Christ's life, death, and resurrection ushering God's kingdom into the world. More will be discussed on the theology of eucharist in later chapters, but, for now, it is of note that early Christian communities celebrated the eucharist as a shared meal. Reflective of chapters 2 and 4 of Acts, early Christian communities understood that in this meal none were to go away hungry. The early practice of eucharist involved sharing a lavish meal, what came to be known as a love feast. While some traditions today partake of a wafer and wine in the celebration of eucharist, love feasts continue to be practiced today in many others. The practice of sharing a meal also has been adopted anew in intentional communities focused on hospitality. Shared meals may be celebrated in such communities as the *de facto* Lord's Supper or are often understood to be tied to the communities'

48. For further information on the language of "little moves against destructiveness" see Pohl, *Making Room,* 12. Pohl draws from ethicist Hallie, *Lest Innocent Blood Be Shed.*

additional celebration of eucharist during a worship service or Mass. Additionally, such shared meals may be understood less as a formal sacramental practice, and more as an act of welcome and fellowship, similar to gathering for a Sunday-afternoon "potluck."

Pohl notes in her article, "A Community's Practice of Hospitality: The Interdependence of Practices and of Community," that the Open Door Community in Atlanta, Georgia invites others to share meals daily throughout the week, while they also celebrate the eucharist together once a week as part of communal worship. Both the table fellowship and the celebration of the eucharist are understood as central to worship. At the same time, sharing meals daily draws the community deeper in friendship and fellowship and is an integral component of their hospitality practice. Pohl's description of the union that takes place in meal sharing is fitting:

> When the community's eating place is transformed on each Sunday afternoon in preparation for the sharing of the Lord's Supper, the connections between the common meal and the Eucharist become obvious. The two are so spatially and temporally proximate that daily meals literally flow into the feast Jesus shared with his disciples, the feast he now shares with those gathered in this place. One of the community's greatest strengths is that the flow between worship and daily life will continue, as the sacrament informs the convivial Sunday evening supper that follows and then all the other meals of the next six days. Ed Loring of the Open Door community writes, "We understand that every meal we eat is related to the Eucharist, to the eschatological banquet—that promise by which we live that there is enough for everybody, and that when we obey God's Spirit who is moving across the earth there will be no hunger."[49]

The Open Door community illustrates how the basis for eating together at all—in fact, the means of engaging in hospitality—originates in the theology of the eucharist. The life, ministry, and sacrifice of Jesus, as well as the joys of God's abundant provision in the eschatological banquet, bring meaning and moral value to hospitality practices of food and feasting. Pohl adds, "In the Eucharist, Jesus' sacrificial welcome is continually reenacted; in the daily meal, practitioners remember and recognize God's generous and gracious provision, as they enjoy one another's company and feed one

---

49. Pohl, "A Community's Practice of Hospitality," 135. See Loring, *I Hear Hope Banging at My Back Door*, 6.

another's bodies."[50] In celebrating the eucharist, community members learn to give of themselves to others because they have received God's gifts and trust in God's continued provision.

Pohl draws from the work of Jualynne Dodson and Cheryl Townsend Gilkes in their article entitled: "'There's Nothing Like Church Food': Food and the U.S. Afro-Christian Tradition: Re-Membering Community and Feeding the Embodied Spiritual(s)." Here, Dodson and Townsend Gilkes draw attention to the grand meals and the importance of sharing food as a way of drawing the community together during significant events like weddings, funerals, welcoming new pastors, etc. Such meals are also important for remembering the community's heritage and reaffirming the people's identity in a hostile world. Drawing from ethicist Peter Paris, Dodson and Townsend Gilkes make note of equality and siblinghood in black churches and how this relates to food. The sharing of meals echoes the call to feed the hungry and clothe the naked in Scripture, and together with "the tradition of Spirituals lifts up the story of the rich man and Lazarus in such a way as to make clear God's eternal displeasure at our failure to feed those who are laid at our gate."[51] Put simply, following God's commands to love and care for one another involves "feeding." Among many African American influences and denominational traditions, Dodson and Townsend Gilkes particularly point to the church movement associated with "Father Divine," an evangelist who made available meals, clothing, and shelter to the black community during the Great Depression. Emphasizing trust in God's provision in the great eschatological banquet, Dodson and Townsend Gilkes write,

> Father Divine's own religious vision indicated that his dining rooms were a microcosm of the Utopian vision articulated in the Gospels at the great eschatological banquet. The actions in the meals were signs of the actions of a better world to be actualized through his movement. He said: "So I Am glad to say that charity, or love, begins at home and spreads abroad; we are going to manifest this mighty love right here in this dining room and from here we are going to manifest this Truth from shore to shore and from land to land, and it all comes about through those who are willing to sacrifice." Throughout the Great Depression Father Divine furnished food, clothing and shelter to destitute blacks, but he

50. Ibid.

51. Dodson and Townsend Gilkes, "'There's Nothing Like Church Food,'" 534.

also provided a theology that promised a better life and a brighter future to anyone, regardless of economic status.[52]

The love ethic in sharing food as acts of hospitality reflects a counter-cultural identity evidenced in Jesus. Acts of hospitality remind the congregation that "they are pilgrims and strangers and that as they feed somebody one day, they may stand in need on another."[53] Dodson and Townsend Gilkes note how black congregations understand the need to gather and feast together so as to challenge the hostilities of the world by calling forth God's great eschatological feast. They conclude:

> The hyper-individualism endemic to American cultural values is challenged and overcome with the New World African "spirituality of interdependence" . . . And in a world of hatred and conflict, with its racism and deprivations, the saints are able to sit together at their welcome tables and remind one another in the giving and receiving of food, that they may continue to believe that "the greatest of these is love." There is nothing like church food.[54]

Not only are hospitality and love central to identity, but sharing meals as the church is an identity-forming practice.

Understanding Boundaries in Identity Formation

The Anabaptist tradition reflects a different heritage of oppression and persecution than the black church, but they similarly focus on a love ethic and being drawn toward God's eschatological banquet. Instead of formal sacramental eucharist celebration or even a "spirituality of interdependence," Anabaptist communities celebrate Love Feasts. Specifically an enactment of identity in Christ, Love Feasts embody an identity alternative to that of the world. Gilbert Bond writes, "Anabaptists have been historically suspicious of the worldly *Gesellschaft* [society or nation], not only because they were themselves persecuted by macro-institutions of the church and the world, but also because they contended that certain institutional structures were

---

52. Dodson and Townsend Gilkes, "There's Nothing Like Church Food," 535. Direct quote originally spoken by Father Divine November 16, 1931, quoted in Watts, *God, Harlem U.S.A.*, 49.

53. Dodson and Townsend Gilkes, "'There's Nothing Like Church Food,'" 535.

54. Ibid., 536.

incapable of manifesting or mediating the Kingdom of God."[55] Anabaptists practice the Love Feast as an enactment of living alternatively toward a holy *Gemeinschaft* [family or community].

At first glance, it may appear that an Anabaptist Love Feast is exclusive and inhospitable because it exhibits a boundary between the community and its relationships with the outside world. Here, it is important to unpack the identity-shaping nature of the activity and the role of boundaries as they relate to a community's identity and its hospitality practice. Outsiders are permitted to be present during the Love Feast, however, only members of the community are allowed to partake in the three movements of the Feast: foot washing, agape meal, and bread and cup.[56] The work of reconciling within the community to prepare for a Love Feast is central because the feast is to reflect the manifested Christ already in the community. It may take many months and years of preparation, while the Love Feast is postponed until all relationships within the community are made right. The feast day begins with a full worship service in preparation, until the foot washing begins. Men and women are divided into two groups, and each person in each group carefully washes one another's feet. After exchanges washing, two participants stand, embrace, and confess their brotherly and sisterly love for one another. The progression is slow and deliberate as the purpose is building community. An agape meal follows, accompanied by prayer and Scripture reading. The tone is solemn, as the passages narrating Jesus' last acts before his crucifixion are read. The third and final movement follows with sharing the bread and cup. This is the only time "communion" is celebrated because only in "reconciled community" are the bread and cup truly celebrated.[57] Contrary to other traditions, the bread and cup do not make community. Rather, bread and cup signify the community's covenantal bond while also setting apart the community from the world. Though Anabaptists do not expect outsiders to participate in these rituals with them, their relationships with those outside the community do not end with this boundary. Through the Love Feast practices they are called out and sent into the world as suffering servants.[58]

There is an important role for boundaries within community, yet they also produce tensions in hospitality practice. Boundaries often more

---

55. Bond, "Liturgy, Ministry, and the Stranger," 144.

56. Ibid., 145.

57. Ibid., 146.

58. Ibid.

poignantly disclose a community's identity as *distinct from* the world; at the same time they serve in identity formation, as was illustrated in both African American and Anabaptist congregations and contexts. Vanier's reflections are helpful as he describes both the necessity and the tension of boundaries in community-building: "A community has to be apart from society and open to it at the same time. To the extent that its values are different from those of society, it must necessarily be apart from it."[59] Situated within culture, the ecclesial community walks a fine line between relating to broader society and remaining distinct from it. Both tensions are necessary, particularly in the practice of hospitality. Vanier cautions against communities throwing off their traditions and the sense of their beginnings too quickly because when a community loses identity, it also loses its community.[60]

Yet, ecclesial boundaries must also be porous and remain open to the mystery of encountering God's providence in others. Vanier continues, "One of the risks that God will always ask of a community is that it welcomes visitors, especially the poorest people, the ones who disturb us."[61] Being disturbed and disrupted is important for growth in a community; after all, a community can easily slip into complacency and isolation, assuming an insular status quo, even (and perhaps especially) while it remains distinct from the world. The tensions that boundaries bring to a community are necessary for identity formation, continued growth, and relationship with others.

Drawing upon the Chicago First Church of the Brethren's experience with federally-supported food services in the 1980s, Bond illustrates the challenge of identity-forming boundaries. The church opened its doors throughout the week to be a food distribution center to help those in need in their surrounding community. The congregation received a food subsidy of cheese and powdered milk for distribution, yet this subsidy also required the Church of the Brethren to "prove" that the recipients of the cheese were poor. Bond points to the irony of this requirement, "when one reflected upon who else would wait in the Chicago winter outside a church for several hours to receive a five-pound brick of processed cheese if they could afford to buy it or a better grade of cheese in a grocery store."[62] As

59. Vanier, *Community and Growth*, 61.

60. Ibid.

61. Ibid., 99.

62. Bond, "Liturgy, Ministry, and the Stranger," 142.

the community enacted the condition for federal funding, soon resentment began to fester among the recipients and eventually a feud broke out. The violence in their community forced the congregation to face the tension: on the one hand, the government-supported food distribution ministry to the community was reflective of Anabaptist commitment to sacrificial servanthood; on the other, the community could not sacrifice its commitment to peaceful resistance to violence that Anabaptists have maintained for centuries. After painful discernment the community shut down the food distribution ministry deciding that the requirements of the program conflicted with the community's Anabaptist identity. In negotiating the tension between such requirements and boundaries, the congregation reclaimed part of its identity and also decided to re-shape its hospitality ministry to be reflective of this identity. This reformed hospitality would still involve the sharing of food. A pastor in this congregation, Bond reflects:

> That violent Saturday called us to ourselves. We eventually . . . contacted some of the people who used to line up outside the church for cheese and powdered milk and invited them to a meal, a meal that members of the church prepared. And with some fear and trembling, we sat and ate with people who were very much not like us, people who knew little about being Anabaptist or Brethren; but in eating together, we discovered we were very much like each other.[63]

Eventually these meals blossomed into deeper, long-standing relationships. Though this congregation would continue to maintain the boundaries of the Love Feast outlined above, its own Anabaptist identity led the community to discern how to share in a different love feast with others. Despite the pain the community experienced as the boundaries of its community were stretched, its understanding of itself and perception of others grew.[64] Negotiating identity within boundaries was a necessary part of restoring integrity within the community's practice of hospitality.

Challenges of "Place" in Hospitality Practice

In addition to the Anabaptist Covenant congregation, Bond also highlights welcome and hospitality practice in the Afro-Baptist congregation,

---

63. Ibid., 147.
64. Ibid.

Immanuel Missionary Baptist Church in New Haven, Connecticut. His specific focus is to uncover and wrestle with the differences in gestures of welcome offered to persons entering the sanctuary for Sunday-morning worship and the welcome offered to others through the congregation's shelter for homeless men at another location. Bond illuminates the challenges surrounding the "place" where welcome occurs, such as church, home, social service agency, etc., as well as the guest/host roles and relational dynamics. Each of these dynamics also provides insight into a community's intentions of shaping hospitality practice and the tensions that may arise as a community comes to understand and continues to shape its identity.

The church as the place of refuge and gathering together is of particular importance in the black church because of how slavery severely dismembered the African American family. Familial and conjugal bonds were continually broken, as slaves and their children were sold and resold, to populate an ever-expanding slave market. Drawing upon the work of Cheryl Sanders, Bond notes that after the Civil War,

> the church became the place wherein displaced and dislocated slaves could seek out lost or missing relatives in an effort to reunite families. Rituals of hospitality and welcome were therefore integral to the condition of their lives and the character of the church community. Hospitality as an African American Christian practice thus addressed an array of overwhelmingly urgent social and historical conditions.[65]

Keeping this painful yet important history and motivation in mind, Bond explores how the Immanuel Baptist Church enacts hospitality in the sanctuary and in the shelter through particular bodily gestures of "the gloved hand," which symbolize a relationship to both the personal and the collective body of the church.[66] Bond describes the elaborate and well-received gestures and physical touch of the ushers, each with hands gloved in white, who invited him into the sanctuary on his Sunday-morning visit, greeted him with a hand shake, and guided him forward to each step of welcome process with soft touch.[67] Continuing this tactile theme, Bond notes how

65. Ibid., 149. Bond draws from Sanders, *Saints in Exile*.

66. Ibid. Here, Bond is following Vergote's argument that "the ritual gesture reveals and unfolds the intentions of the body as lived. It inserts itself into the space of the humanized world, concretely links the subject to the human community, and attaches it to the Other who is source and ultimate meaning of its existence." Vergote, "Symbolic Gestures and Actions in Liturgy," 46.

67. Bond, "Liturgy, Ministry, and the Stranger," 151.

the sermon carried such gestures to a crescendo as the pastor concluded his sermon: "none are strangers; but all are children of the Most High."[68]

Later that day, Bond visited the shelter for homeless men in another building. Here he was met with different tactile rituals of greeting. Though he himself had been warmly received, he later watched as men began to enter the shelter. Contrary to that morning, the greeting was cold and sterile, and touch was now turned around to be alienating and isolating. The hosts (employees working at the shelter) wore yellow latex gloves and examined each man who was required to spread his legs and raise his arms. Suddenly the sterile distance evoked in this sort of touch was made real. Bond writes: "The movement across the boundary from outside to inside made each man an inside alien, as each received the confirming touch that marked his presence as a potential source of contamination, so dangerous that his hosts were required to don protective equipment."[69] As one might imagine, the alienation and social isolation triggered by this distant and cold touch upon entering the shelter did not end here. The shelter evidenced a different kind of welcome—one severely limited by the surroundings and place of welcome, one which would necessitate large barriers and boundaries for safety, one mechanized by the routine of welcoming so many men each night, one of institutionalized social service.

Certainly, many different dynamics play out here due to the boundaries, the place, and the intentions of such a service of hospitality. In light of his experience of hospitable gesture and touch, Bond laments that fact that something is seriously lost between the gloved hands attached to worship in the sanctuary on a Sunday morning and the gloved hands of the shelter. He ends questioning: "What could help heal the rupture between the ritual of hospitality that invites communion and community within the sanctuary and the ritual of contagion enacted at the shelter?"[70] Bond's comparison illustrates how Christian practices are ambiguous and messy. On the one hand, the purposes of the practice may waver and are not determinate, yet the strength of practices lies in their capacity to be transformed.[71] Perhaps the fluid nature of such practices is due to the fact that they involve human community, human bodies, and how they live and react in an array of contexts. Practices do not exist in isolation. Bond notes, "We all struggle

68 Ibid.

69. Ibid., 153.

70. Ibid., 155.

71. Ibid., 156.

with the tension between self-preservation and the inherent risks we face as human beings and as Christians."[72] Boundaries are necessary, yet so is the need to live at the point of tension such boundaries create within community. The boundary between identity and openness to change must always remain fluid, in order to maintain a community and to preserve its capacity to be transformed.

Further questions remain to be asked and explored in light of the tensions inherent in hospitality practice and ecclesial identity. Here, I have begun to address issues of boundaries and identity formation within communities that practice hospitality. Additionally, I have introduced how sharing food and meals, as well as the "place" of hospitality and welcome, play important roles in this practice. More remains to be explored in each of these areas and further investigation is yet to be done regarding the challenges of guest/host roles and relationships in contemporary manifestations of hospitality in Christian communities. For now, I turn to discuss the relationships between ecclesial identity and hospitality practice when it is specifically oriented toward the "margins" of society.

ECCLESIAL IDENTITY AND HOSPITALITY PRACTICE

On the Margins

Pohl devotes a chapter of her book *Making Room* to "Hospitality from the Margins," adding important insights with regard to the identity and positioning of Christians as guests and hosts. She notes, "we offer hospitality within the context of knowing Jesus as both our greater host and our potential guest."[73] Those who Christians have historically welcomed often bear a status "on the margins" of society. This is certainly reflected in key passages in the Gospel of Matthew, such as chapters 5:1–11 and 25:31–46. The degree to which the host bears a marginal identity, however, is somewhat different and changes over time. She notes how the biblical narrative makes clear that marginality for the People of God is normative. For example, "alien status for the early Christians suggested a basis for a different way of life and loyalties to a different order, which in turn challenged conventional boundaries and relationships."[74] Additionally, the alien status of Christians

72. Ibid.

73. Pohl, *Making Room*, 105.

74. Ibid., 105.

afforded them the vantage point to see the importance of taking root in a home and nurturing hospitality for others, but this perspective also altered their understanding of "home." In fact, because of the journeying existence of early Christians as resident aliens, home was always provisional. It is precisely because home is always provisional for Christians who trust in the abundant provision and welcoming grace of God, that they are called to lavishly extend hospitality to others, and particularly to those who fall between the cracks of society.

Pohl draws upon Victor Turner's notion of liminality to describe the particular identity and place associated with hospitality practice in the church. Christians historically welcomed persons who were the poor, marginalized, and outcast by virtue of the ecclesial community's own marginalization and alien status. Liminal persons and communities, claims Turner, "slip through the network of classifications that normally locate states and positions in cultural space. Liminal entities are neither here nor there; they are betwixt and between the positions assigned and arrayed by law, custom."[75] Pohl notes certain figures in Christian history who sought to deliberately create and sustain a liminal identity, such as Chrysostom, Olympias, John Wesley and the early Methodists, etc. Liminality becomes an important characteristic of Christian identity and how Christians historically resided in the world—that is, *on the margins.* Turner's notion of liminality—in the sense of slipping through the network of classifications—will have more bearing as this study continues to explore the relationship between ecclesial identity and place in reference to issues of migration, borderlands, and empire.

Hospitality on the margins, however, did not last long in Christian history. The lavish care and welcome of the poor and marginalized in the name of Christ often waned in Christian history as wealth, power, and influence grew in the Christian community.[76] The other spheres to which hospitality was relegated also changed. Pohl writes,

> Christians moved their expressions of hospitality into places like hospitals, hospices, and orphanages, the "hosts" were assigned specific roles and were often paid for their work. As a result, they

---

75. Turner, *The Ritual Process*, 95, quoted in Pohl, *Making Room,* 106.

76. Pohl, *Making Room,* 113. Pohl adds, "As Christians became more established in positions of influence and wealth, their marginal status was diminished and their hospitality was more likely to reflect and reinforce social distinctions than to undermine them."

experienced little encouragement to develop normal relationships or to find things in common with the "guests." Specialized institutions tend to flatten social relations to one dimension—that of caregiver and recipient, or professional and client. These roles are not interchangeable, and the bonds among people are narrowly defined.[77]

The flattening of the guest/host relationship to a patient/client dichotomy, severely limits relational dynamics to the single dimension of care and service. In fact, this flattening was of great concern to Vanier and one of his motivations for beginning his L'Arche houses where deeper relationships could be established. He specifically encouraged assistants, and all human beings, to discover their own human weakness and need in and through their relationships. Additionally, Pohl notes that as the relationship between society and Christians continued to change, hospitality also came to be associated with smaller, private households, separate from the church. For example, as property and ownership became more common, hospitality became less and less associated with Christians' identity as aliens, pilgrims, and sojourners. Such changes in place and performance, not to mention ties between Christian identity and hospitality practice, altered how hospitality would be carried into future centuries of the church. This also would have a profound effect on the relationship between hospitality and power. Pohl cites Anthony Gittens's caution on the subject:

> Unless the person who sometimes *extends* hospitality is also able to sometimes be a gracious recipient, and unless the one who receives *the other* as stranger is also able to *become* the stranger received by another, then, far from "relationships," we are merely creating unidirectional lines of power flow, however unintended this may be. And that is quite antithetical to mission in the spirit of Jesus.[78]

Because of the dangers of a one-way or one-directional flow of hospitality and how this shapes power dynamics between guest and host, hospitality bears the inherent risk of reinforcing social distinctions while offering the illusion of relationship. The guest/host relationship can domesticate the guest and perpetuate the guest's indebtedness to the host, while the host is always in a position of power and control as benefactor.[79] These dangers still

77. Ibid., 114.

78. Gittens, "Beyond Hospitality?," 399, cited in Pohl, *Making Room,* 119–20.

79. See Pohl, *Making Room,* 120.

are present in a hospitality in which the host takes on voluntary poverty, as Dorothy Day herself feared. One cannot neglect to see the differences in the guest and host—the status of the host may be a chosen identity, while the guest's marginal identity in society is no choice of her or his own.

Pohl's work *Making Room* serves as a comprehensive resource for hospitality practice within congregations and she points out challenges communities must bear in mind. She specifically draws attention to a Christian counter-cultural identity that nurtures a distinct way of life for Christians.[80] In all cases, hospitality practice is never a static enterprise. The relationships between Christian identity and performance always require discernment, evaluation, and negotiation. These communal processes are a necessary part of residing "on the margins." At the same time, Pohl's analysis stops short of adequately questioning hospitality's boundaries, identifying its margins, and unpacking what is at stake in this practice for both the guest and host. She makes mention of power dynamics in guest/host relationships and indebtedness in hospitality practice, but does not address what some have deemed as the impossibility of equality or mutuality within hospitality. While Pohl addresses these issues from an observational standpoint, more is needed to reach beyond the surface and critically analyze hospitality practice and its relationship to Christian identity and ecclesiology. Further work remains to be done to address tensions and objections within hospitality practice, specifically as ecclesial communities engage varying contexts in their hospitality practice.

Ecclesiological Challenges in Hospitality

As the church is always called to look forward and live into God's coming reign, it is continually being shaped toward God's purposes as it seeks to live out the good news in particular times and places. The next chapter will introduce the context of transnational migration, and specifically U.S. Latino/a migration in the context of the United States. Subsequent chapters will further articulate challenges posed to ecclesial communities seeking to live out hospitality amidst the difficult reality of displacement and mobility for migrating persons. Specifically drawing from U.S. Latino/a and postcolonial theologies, I return in later chapters to investigate and question the dimensions of hospitality and ecclesiology—place, gestures of welcome,

80. See ibid., 124. Pohl specifically mentions this in reference to Hauerwas and Willimon, *Resident Aliens*.

gift and exchange, borders and boundaries, and journey or pilgrimage—as they relate to transnational and Latino/a migration. This deeper investigation demands new imagination in how hospitality and ecclesiology must be retooled in response to contemporary patterns of migration.

3

Understanding the Complexities of Migration

Contextual Considerations in Hospitality

FACTORS CONTRIBUTING TO THE growing phenomenon of global migration are complex and multilayered, while also deeply intertwined with globalization in the twenty-first century. At the same time, there is an increasing prevalence of transnational migration in societal life. Global migration affects the lives of persons, families, nations, cultures, as well as Christian faith practice and communal gathering across the world. To examine this context critically and with depth, I draw from the fields of anthropology, cultural studies, postcolonial theory, theology, and ethics. Additionally, in order to concretely address the complexities surrounding migration, I turn to the particularities of the U.S. Latino/a immigration context. The insights and challenges of U.S. Latino/a theologians and ethicists, which specifically speak into the experience of migration and its effects on the life of the church in the United States, point me toward deeper theological analysis of ecclesial practice. Juxtaposing their important, contextual theological work with hospitality practice, I unearth the potentially problematic conceptions and expressions of hospitality in light of persons displaced and on the move as migrants, refugees, or itinerants.

PART I:
THE COMPLEXITIES OF TRANSNATIONAL MIGRATION

The capitalism of the late twentieth century and the increasing globaliza-tion and geopolitical market construction have proliferated peoples on the move. While migration, exile, diaspora, and pilgrimage are phenomena vis-ible throughout all of history, the reality and urgency of coerced migration in a globalized world is complex and alarming. This section will identify the multifaceted factors contributing to transnational migration, while also beginning to introduce how questions of identity, home, and borders/boundaries are challenged and stretched as they relate to global migration.

Avtar Brah suggests that the twenty-first century question for trans-national migration is not simply *who* travels, but *when*, *how* and under what socio-economic, political, and cultural circumstances. Asking such questions is necessary in order to understand the complex forces that drive migration. The intersectionality of power relations and the confluence of economic, political, cultural, and psychic processes are central to contem-porary explorations of migration.[1] While such forces overlap, they are not all the same. Brah specifically calls attention to how present-day migration inhabits not only those who have migrated and their descendants, but also those who are represented as indigenous, or possessing citizenship in host countries. In turn, all persons might consider the reality of migration and their participation in it. The phenomenon of transnational migration en-compasses citizens and permanent residents in "host" countries, as well as those persons perpetually moving and crossing borders. The interconnect-edness of the globalized twenty-first century landscape allows no person or nation-state to consider itself exempt from acknowledging and participat-ing in this reality.

Transnational migration, particularly for persons forced to migrate, confronts traditional notions of home and familial community and also draws notions of belonging and national identity-construction to new com-plexity. In the 1990s, both the fields of cultural studies and anthropology began to turn focused attention toward the global phenomenon of migra-tion. Nina Glick Schiller, Linda Basch, and Cristina Szanton Blanc explore the various definitions of transnational migration. "Transmigrants," they

---

1. Brah, *Cartographies of Diaspora*, 178–210. Brah understands diaspora not as a transcendental consciousness, but develops it as a conceptual category that signals the processes of muti-locationality across geographical, cultural, and psychic boundaries. In her work, diaspora is a space for theoretical crossovers and intersections.

note, "are immigrants whose daily lives depend on multiple and constant interconnections across international borders and whose public identities are configured in relationships to more than one nation-state."[2] Interestingly, transnational migrants both reflect continual movement and settle in multiple locations. The move between "home" and "host" is not so easily defined. The authors further explain this complexity:

> [Transnational migrants] are not sojourners because they settle and become incorporated in the economy and political institutions, localities, and patterns of daily life in the country in which they reside. However, at the very same time, they are engaged elsewhere in the sense that they maintain connections, build institutions, conduct transactions, and influence local and national events in the countries from which they emigrated.[3]

Naturally, the reality of transmigration alters understandings of who is the immigrant. Often the immigrant is conceived of as a person who uproots from a home and country, and seeks to incorporate herself or himself into a new society and culture.[4] Likewise, it is assumed that the immigrant will "assimilate" into the new society's presumed way of life, language, cultural customs, etc. In contrast to this widely held perception in society, cultural theorists point out that transnational migrants maintain complex relationships and remain embedded in more than one society.[5]

Additionally, Luis Eduardo Guarnizo and Michael Peter Smith note the scale and scope of multivalent cause and effect factors surrounding increased transnationalism:

- the globalization of capitalism with its destabilizing effects on less industrialized countries;
- the technological revolution in the means of transportation and communication;
- global political transformations such as decolonization and the universalization of human rights; and

2. Schiller, et al., "From Immigrant to Transmigrant," 48.
3. Ibid.
4. Ibid.
5. Ibid.

- the expansion of social networks that facilitate the reproduction of transnational migration, economic organization, and politics.[6]

In light of the number of intersecting factors contributing to transnational migration, these scholars point out the disconnect between the host country's nation-building processes and transnational migrants' own identity-construction that encompasses two or more countries/nation-states. Migrants' positioning is termed "multi-local" to signify that they actually have multiple "homes" or nation-state localities to which they are responsible. These migrants are not necessarily recognized by home or host nation-states.

Brah's observations above pose the necessity of investigating the circumstances from which persons migrate. It is equally important to explore how transnational migration relates to the global economy as well as other intersecting factors noted by Guarnizo and Smith. Economics, politics, technology, and social networks all naturally feed into the lives and economic practices of church members. Transnationalism, of which transnational migration arises, is a phenomenon of global interconnections necessary for and sustained by a capitalist system of production.[7] Interestingly, the forces of the global economy draw twenty-first century transnational migrants to uproot to global centers, while also maintaining ties to home countries:

> Three conjoining potent forces in the current global economy lead present day immigrants to settle in countries that are centers of global capitalism but to live transnational lives: (1) a global restructuring of capital based on changing forms of capital accumulation has lead to deteriorating social and economic conditions in both labor sending and labor receiving countries with no location a secure terrain of settlement; (2) racism in both the U.S. and Europe contributes to the economic and political insecurity of the newcomers and their descendants; and (3) the nation building projects of both home and host society build political loyalties among immigrants in each nation-state in which they maintain social ties.[8]

6. Guarnizo and Smith, "The Locations of Transnationalism," 4.

7. Schiller, et al., "From Immigrant to Transmigrant," 50.

8. Ibid. The authors continue: "Faced with wide-spread deterioration in their standards of living, professionals, skilled workers, unskilled workers, merchants, and agricultural producers all have fled to global cities or to countries such as the U.S. that still

While Brah's observations point out the effects of global economic policies in contributing to migration, they also draw attention to how negative perceptions in the United States and Europe further perpetuate risks for transnational migrants. Racism and questions of national identity contribute to migrants gathering in ethnic enclaves in receiving countries and provide further impetus for migrants to maintain strong ties to sending countries. In turn, both voluntary and involuntary "ghettoization" contribute to what majority populations in receiving countries may perceive as resistance to assimilate into a new culture, triggering misunderstanding, angst, and often anger. Transnational migration is contested space—both the factors that contribute to it and the perception of migrants in host countries have unique social consequences for how migrants reside in host countries and simultaneously continue to understand themselves as residents of sending countries.

On top of the challenges of multi-local identity construction, migrants are further confronted by U.S. identity construction. Guarnizo and Smith also critically analyze U.S. nation-building processes in light of migration. They argue these processes reflect hegemonic tendencies both in the perpetuation of transnational migration as well as in policies toward transnational immigrants who criss-cross U.S. borders. Guarnizo's and Smith's observations, though made in 1995, are still applicable to the transnational migration situation today:

> Concepts of "America, the white" are reinforced. Yet at the same time, documented immigrants are being drawn into the debate on the side of enforcement, validating their right to belong but differentiating themselves from other migrants. There is a dialectic between inclusion and exclusion that disciplines transnational migrants by focusing public attention on the degree to which they belong in the U.S. The current debate on immigrants in U.S. will lead not to the effective policing of national borders but to the re-inscription of boundaries. It serves to counter transnational identities and loyalties and creates a terrain in which immigrants are drawn into defending whatever they have achieved or obtained by defending it against the undocumented. They are therefore

---

play central roles in capital accumulation. However, once in these countries, immigrants confront a deepening economic crisis that often limits the economic possibilities and security many are able to obtain. Moreover, those sectors of the current immigrant population who find themselves racialized as 'Hispanic,' 'Asian,' or 'Black' find that even if they obtain a secure position, they face daily discrimination in the pursuit of their life dreams." Ibid.

drawn into a discourse of identity that links them to the U.S. nation state as a bounded structure of laws and institutions as well
as a defended territory. Yet none of the nation-building processes
encompasses fully the complexity and multiple identities which
constitute the lives of transmigrants.[9]

If nothing else, their observations illustrate the lack of attention to the
complexities migrants face in understanding U.S. nation-building. Persons
who emigrate from other nations are themselves drawn into the U.S. immigration debate and encouraged to turn against one another for their own
survival. Guarnizo's and Smith's observations also point to other factors
that must be considered—specifically the question of both physical and
psychosocial boundaries and borders in identity discourse.[10]

Ecclesial communities across the United States are largely divided
on the immigration debate, yet most agree that the system is broken and
needs to be fixed. Varying perspectives in the U.S. government have their
own interests to defend in this debate, and Christians follow suit in "taking sides." As a result, the Christian positions are polarized and divided in
accordance with partisan politics. The debate over immigration summons
Christian scholars from various traditions to examine and investigate the
role of the church in assisting and welcoming migrants. The next section
will explore various theological perspectives that advocate on behalf of migrants, specifically for their rights, safety, and well-being. The purpose of
this study is not to outline in full the various sides of this national debate.
Rather, I seek to address how U.S.-based ecclesial communities might adapt
and appropriate Christian hospitality practice differently as they begin to
understand and become affected by the complex situations migrants face as
they journey to and reside within the U.S. borders.

U.S LATINO/A MIGRATION AND
THE ROLE OF ECCLESIAL COMMUNITIES

The historical particularities, complex identities, and multi-local influences
encapsulated in transnational migration pose new challenges when placed
alongside Christian faith communities' identity formation and hospitality
practice. While my overall investigation will focus on these factors, it is
also important to briefly note the larger role faith communities may play

9. Ibid., 59.

10. Guarnizo and Smith, "The Locations of Transnationalism," 6.

in the various stages of the migration process. Jacqueline Hagan and Helen Rose Ebaugh detail this process through their research of a transnational Mayan community with members in the western highlands of Guatemala and Houston, Texas. Their study traces the role of religion and the influence of faith communities in each step of a migrant's journey. Specifically, they highlight the role of religion and faith communities in: 1) the decision to migrate; 2) preparing for the trip; 3) the journey; 4) the arrival; 5) the role of the ethnic church in immigrant settlement; and 6) the development of transnational linkages.[11] While their observations do not necessarily evaluate the role of these faith communities and their role in shaping migrants' own understanding of their journey, I draw attention to them here in order to reveal the layered importance of migrants' relationships with the faith communities they leave, the faith communities from which they continue to seek guidance, the new faith communities they encounter along the way, and any faith communities they may join as they reside in another country. In this sense, the practices of hospitality and accompaniment may take on various forms as ecclesial communities encounter migrants along the stages of their journey.

In *Trails of Hope and Terror: Testimonies on Immigration*, Miguel A. De La Torre details a typical migrant's journey from Mexico, across the U.S.-Mexico border, and into the United States. His description is worth quoting at length:

> Their journey may start in Altar, Mexico, where they first have to avoid becoming prey to government officials, *coyotes* (smugglers), and criminals trying to take advantage of their desperation. Women and children face the additional hazard of becoming victims of physical or sexual abuse. And they need money to live on the Mexican side of the border while they wait to cross—for many this is an event that must be repeated.
>
> If they make it to the border, they must spend several days walking through mountains and deserts. Men, women, and children follow trails where at any turn they can be robbed, beaten, raped, or murdered by drug-smuggling gangs, U.S. anti-immigrant vigilante groups stationed on the border, racist ranchers, and rogue Border Patrol or Mexican law enforcement agents. A foot blister or a sprained angle can be a death sentence because those who cannot keep up are left behind. Unless they receive help, they die of exposure. Thousands have already died this way. Those who

11. Hagan and Ebaugh, "Calling Upon the Sacred," 1145.

elude the border vigilantes or the official Border Patrol and make it to a major city quickly try to blend into the community's fabric. But they still live with the daily terror of being detected, arrested, and deported, being forced to leave behind parents, spouses, and children.[12]

Even if one makes it safely across the U.S.-Mexico border and into the United States, the threats, risks, and dangers of deportation abound. Life is not easy for migrants north of the border—there is little to no job security and protection against exploitation in the workplace, not to mention discrimination, distrust, and many unknowns. The threat of being deported always looms as a present and future possibility.

In *Border of Death, Valley of Life: An Immigrant Journey of Heart and Spirit,* Daniel Groody uncovers the suffering endured by migrants along their journeys northward through Mexico and across the U.S.-Mexico border. Many migrants leave their families behind and travel the dangerous journey alone to the United States for economic reasons. They face all the emotional and practical challenges of leaving behind everything that is familiar to them. Upon arriving in the United States, the insecurity continues as the immigrant faces alienation and marginalization (political-cultural, socio-economic, psycho-spiritual).[13] The migrant is quite literally "a stranger in a foreign land." In addition to isolation from family, culture, language, and communities of faith, in the United States "many immigrants live in isolated and rural areas. Because their experience of the institutional Church is often limited, some see priests infrequently, so they have little contact with the sacramental life of the Church. They often have a negative or neutral understanding of God and the institutional Church."[14]

Groody explores the spirituality migrants bring from their families, culture, and faith communities in home or sending countries and the challenges that test their spirituality in the journey northward. He examines the spirituality that may be lost along the way as well as that which remains as sojourners come to reside in the United States. He then investigates possibilities for spiritual transformation through *Encuentro Misionero* retreats offered as a part of the Valley Missionary Program, which the Congregation of the Holy Cross in Southern California's Coachella Valley began in 1973. The Coachella Valley, located about 60 miles north of the U.S.-Mexican

---

12. De La Torre, *Trails of Hope and Terror*, 2.

13. Groody, *Border of Death*, 31. Also see pp. 20–33.

14. Ibid., 29.

border, is a prime area for agricultural development. The valley offers many possibilities for finding seasonal agricultural labor and has been a chief destination for many Mexican migrants seeking employment. Adapted from the Roman Catholic *Cursillo de Cristianidad* (short course of Christianity) retreat focusing on how God's love touches each person in a unique way, the *Encuentro* is contextualized by Mexican immigrants for fellow immigrants. Through the retreat, Groody explores the process of conversion of the heart and revitalization of faith when one's spirituality becomes deeply intertwined with the social circumstances surrounding migration. A central aspect of the retreat is the continued support and community cultivated through the Valley Missionary Program as migrants are invited to intentionally share life together through ecclesial base communities in the Coachella Valley.[15] These communities and their activities are specific to the Mexican immigrant experience, spiritual journey, and struggle. I will revisit Groody's insights regarding how hospitality is contextualized in light of immigrants' experiences in later chapters. For now I draw attention to how the migrants' spiritual journeys, which include the traumas of migration, reflect what Graham Ward terms "the fierce spirituality of being a migrant, that body which is marked by a wandering."[16] U.S. Latino/a immigration is often understood as an increasingly transnational phenomenon; persons crisscross the U.S.-Mexico border without documentation, undergoing an extremely dangerous journey multiple times.[17] Border crossing(s) require a costly rite of passage signified by both "uprootedness" (of culture, family, and identity) and a life-threatening journey.

15. Badillo in *Latinos and the New Immigrant Church* describes this program as an offshoot of Latin American Liberation Theology, which took shape through small ecclesial gatherings of lay people in what has been called "ecclesial based communities." Though such communities are often considered a south-of-the-border phenomenon, the experiences of migrants bring them into the U.S. ecclesial landscape.

16. Ward, "Hospitality and Justice toward 'Strangers,'" 1.

17. See Passel and Cohn, "A Portrait of Unauthorized Immigrants in the United States," 2. Their research illustrates this "border passage" phenomenon. They write, "Patterns of migration between the U.S. and Mexico are varied. Many immigrants come from Mexico to settle permanently, but large numbers also move both ways across the U.S.-Mexico border throughout the year, sometimes staying for only a few months, a pattern known as circular migration. Mexican-U.S. migration also tends to be seasonal, with larger northbound flows in the spring and summer and larger southbound flows in the fall and winter."

Understanding the Causes of Migration
and the Residual Effects of NAFTA

The risks that migrants face to make the journey northward are great. Many seek to understand and describe the strong motivation that outweighs the risks and continues to drive many to leave their homes and families south of the U.S. border to attempt the journey. The reasons for embarking on this difficult journey are multifaceted. Aviva Chomsky seeks to clarify the root causes of migration and debunk common myths by pointing out the incredible complexity of the variety of factors that contribute to transnational migration.[18] Each immigrant has particular motivations for migrating, but patterns of immigration also have structural and historical causes.[19]

The forces providing an impetus to migrate are commonly—though perhaps too simplistically—referred to as push- and pull-factors. Push-factors include poverty, lack of opportunity, and danger or threat, which push persons to leave. Pull-factors, then, may be new situations that offer opportunity, jobs, education, and safety.[20] Push- and pull-factors, however, only describe the surface reasons for migration and do not address the complexities and root causes of migrants' situations. Chomsky writes, "They fail to explain just why some places seem to be characterized by poverty, lack of opportunity, and danger while others offer opportunity, jobs, education, and safety. They also don't explain why long-standing inequalities among regions or countries lead only sometimes to flows of migration."[21] De La Torre echoes that, contrary to popular opinion, the goal for immigrants is not merely to find a "better life" and live off the social services provided in the United States. In fact, many would rather stay with their families and friends and their culture, traditions, and birth places. Rather, migrants "attempt the hazardous crossing because our foreign policy has created an economic situation in their home countries in which they are unable to feed their families."[22] Complex economic factors that include the economic trade policies of the United States with other countries are important considerations in U.S. Latino/a migration.

18. Chomsky, *They Take Our Jobs!*

19. Ibid., 121–22.

20. Ibid., 122.

21. Ibid.

22. De La Torre, *Trails of Hope and Terror*, 16.

The 1994 establishment of the North American Free Trade Agreement (NAFTA) is a large motivating factor for northward migration across the U.S.-Mexico border. De La Torre presents how NAFTA directly relates to U.S. economic expansion, in which, "free trade came to be defined as moving goods freely across borders—free from tariffs or taxes."[23] Free trade, however, also signifies a limited freedom. This agreement is only "free" for the movement of certain goods and free for only some persons, as it turns out. De La Torre details the effects of NAFTA on people living south of the border:

> while workers looking for better jobs were *not* intended themselves to cross borders freely, the products of their cheap labor did, as goods were produced and exported. While people were expected to stay in place, factories moved across borders in order to maintain their high profit margins by paying the lowest possible wages. The quest for low wages meant that many industries relocated south of the 1,833-mile border between the United States and Mexico.[24]

The U.S. perspective often overlooks the consequences of NAFTA upon the Mexican economy. While it appears that the agreement would benefit Mexican economic export, it simultaneously allowed U.S. industry to cross the border and generate production in the south taking advantage of a relative lack of restrictions and cheaper working conditions. As companies migrate southward, Mexican economy, businesses, and laborers bear many costs. De La Torre outlines the spiraling, negative effects of NAFTA on the Mexico side of the agreement, particularly for the workers:

> Although large numbers of U.S. jobs moved to Mexico, in general Mexicans did not experience a windfall. While numerous factories, known as *maquiladores,* opened along the border after the implementation of the North American Free Trade Agreement (NAFTA) in 1994, Mexicans sank deeper into poverty. Many Mexican farmers were forced to abandon their lands because they were unable to compete with U.S.-subsidized imported agricultural goods. At first they saw salvation in the *maquiladoras,* but this proved to be an illusion.[25]

23. Ibid., 13.

24. Ibid.

25. Ibid., 13–14. De La Torre cites the following authors as contributing to this statement: "It is estimated that in the first ten years after the implementation of NAFTA, approximately 780,000 jobs in textile and apparel manufacturing in the United States

Maquiladoras proved unhelpful because they were poorly regulated, did not pay a living wage, and undermined the vitality of the agricultural sector.

A 2014 Pew Hispanic Center reports that 11.2 million unauthorized immigrants live in the United States and 8.1 million are in the U.S. labor force.[26] The center estimates that undocumented migrants make up roughly 3.5 percent of the nation's population and account for 5.1 percent of its workforce.[27] The summary report continues that just over half (52 percent) of all unauthorized immigrants are from Mexico.[28] Douglas Massey sheds light on further historical and structural factors behind NAFTA that contribute to persons migrating northward:

> That Mexico is by far the largest source of U.S. immigrants is hardly surprising. In addition to sharing a land border with the United States, it was twice invaded by U.S. troops in the 20th century (in 1914 and 1917), it has been the target of two U.S.-sponsored labor recruitment efforts (during 1917–18 and 1942–64), and since 1986, at U.S. insistence, it has undertaken a radical transformation of its political economy and entered the global market. Moreover, since 1994 it has been linked to the United States by NAFTA, a comprehensive economic treaty that presently generates $250 billion per year in binational trade.
>
> Under these circumstances, immigration between the two countries is inevitable, even though Mexico is wealthy by Third World standards. With a per capita gross domestic product of $9,000, it is one of the richest countries in Latin America. It is in the interest of the United States, therefore, to build on this economic base by accepting Mexican immigration as a reality and working to manage it in a way that minimizes the costs and maximizes the benefits for both nations.[29]

The U.S–Mexico association is just one example of how global economic exchanges intensify transnational migration all throughout the

---

were lost." Public Citizen Product ID 9013, *Another America is Possible*, 5. Also see De La Torre, "For Immigrants," 73–84.

26. See Krogstad and Passell's November 2014 Pew Research Center article: "Five Facts about Illegal Immigration in the United States," http://www.pewresearch.org/fact-tank/2014/11/18/5-facts-about-illegal-immigration-in-the-u-s/.

27. Ibid. Interestingly, the 2014 estimated totals are down significantly from 2012 (at 5.9 million Mexican unauthorized immigrants) and even further from its peak in 2009, with 6.9 million Mexican unauthorized immigrants.

28. Ibid.

29. Massey, "Closed-Door Policy." Also see, Chomsky, 131.

world. Chomsky also seeks to place migration in a larger historical context, as part of a larger global system.[30] She writes, "Citizen workers who have lost their jobs to global restructuring and migrants who have come to the United States to fill the new secondary labor market are part of a system that is much larger than themselves."[31] In this sense, contrary to popular opinion in the United States that migration is a *cause* of global economic exchanges, Chomsky makes a case for how migration is a result or product of such changes.[32]

Additional policies, as well as a politics of fear toward the immigrant in the United States, complicate the situation and further the risks for many migrants. One such example is U.S. Homeland Security's "Operation Gatekeeper," a program that strove to reduce undocumented migration in the San Diego area, thus forcing migrants eastward into more dangerous mountainous and desert terrain. It was thought that the possibility of death would hopefully deter further migration attempts. Operation Gatekeeper has not resulted, however, in any substantial decrease in border crossing attempts, despite the increased risks. Rather, as De La Torre notes, there has been a 20 percent increase in known deaths associated with unauthorized border crossing, and this has resulted in a conservative estimate of nearly thirty-six hundred bodies recovered on the U.S. side of the border between 1995–2005.[33] The increase in deaths can be attributed to the harsh terrain and conditions of the desert east of Tijuana/San Diego through which Hispanics are funneled. Nearly 60 percent of these deaths can be attributed to exposure to the extreme temperatures of the desert and attempts to cross water passages.[34]

30. Chomsky, 132.

31. Ibid.

32. Ibid.

33. De La Torre, 14–15.

34. De La Torre writes, "The unforgiving and harsh terrain toward which Hispanics are presently funneled can have daytime temperatures in excess of 115 degrees Fahrenheit, higher during summer months, and frigid nighttime temperatures that pose the risk of hypothermia. The majority of deaths, almost 60 percent, are caused by exposure to the elements, specifically hyperthermia, hypothermia, and drowning. Most who perish are in the prime of their lives; around one-third are between the ages of eighteen and twenty-nine, and almost 20 percent are thirty to thirty-nine. Even if death does not claim the life of a border crosser, many still suffer permanent kidney damage caused by dehydration. Women are nearly three times more likely to die of exposure than men, and those women who do not succumb to the cruelty of the desert face the cruelty of sexual assault. It is now common practice for women preparing to make the crossing to use a

The populations surrounding the U.S.-Mexico borderlands are large. It is estimated that about 12 million people live along the 1,833-mile U.S.-Mexico border, with about 6.3 million living on the U.S. side of the border and 5.5 million living on the Mexican side.[35] While it may appear that the division, as well as the risks, are most concentrated at the geopolitical borderlands of the southwestern United States, the suffering endured as migrants cross the U.S.-Mexico border remain scars imprinted on minds, hearts, and lives no matter where migrants may settle or find work. De La Torre raises the point that geopolitical borders are also an existential reality of Latino/a alienation that extends far beyond being located in geographical proximity of the border.[36] Borders are also encountered "in every state, country, city, and town that separates Hispanics from Euroamerican-designated spaces. The invisible walls are as real in Kansas City, San Francisco, and Chicago as are the visible walls in Chula Vista, California; Douglas, Arizona, or El Paso, Texas."[37] *La Frontera* (the Border) is a multifaceted symbol of danger, fear, and trauma for many migrants who have survived it. Likewise, it represents a bleak memory for the many people who have lost love ones to it. *La Frontera* also is a symbol of racial/ethnic and class division, separating Mexico from the United States. *La Frontera* has become an identifying marker of persons who came from "south of the border" as foreign, unwelcome, other, and assumed to be lesser and not eligible for human rights. For many migrants, *La Frontera* symbolizes the imminent reality of the many walls that they face and will continue to face as long as they reside north of the border, with or without documentation. In fact, "to be Latina/o living anywhere in the United States is to face constantly a border that separates him or her from the benefits that society has to offer . . . evident in the continuing segregation existing in housing, public schools, and employment."[38] In summary, the U.S.-Mexico border is much more than a geopolitical boundary marker. It reflects a social imaginary perpetuated by U.S. dominant culture that marks inclusion and exclusion based on class, ethnicity, and race.

---

method of birth control prior to their journey as they are more than likely to be sexually assaulted." Ibid., 15.

35. As reported in De La Torre's 2009 figures; see ibid., 115.

36. Ibid.

37. Ibid.

38. Ibid.

PART II:
THEOLOGICAL REFLECTION ON MIGRATION

The poetic image of Francisco Alarcón reflects the realities of transmigratory existence—"mis raices las cargo siempre conmigo enrolladas me sirven de almohada (I carry my roots with me all the time rolled up I use them as my pillow)."[39] Perpetual migration does not afford a migrant the luxury of home, rootedness, family, comfort, or safety. In fact, the complex realities of twenty-first century migration contest space, place, and home because one is made to be perpetually "on the move." A one-time border crossing or the mixing of two races or ethnicities no longer characterizes migration. Rather, the complexities of transnational migration insinuate bodies marked by wandering and the mixing of socio-cultural, political-economic, and spiritual-religious aspects of one's identity. These aspects point to the need for new constructions of mobility as well as hybrid identity that will better direct the church toward embodying faithfulness in new spaces and coming alongside persons who are marginalized and "othered" in its surrounding community. The remainder of this chapter will reveal how realities of migration contest and disrupt traditional notions of the ecclesial community and the geographical space and the places of power and privilege it occupies within larger communities.

Borders and Identity

Cuban American theologian Fernando Segovia reflects not only how a migrant's state of existence is perpetually on the move, but also how the migrant is permanently refused welcome and denied a home or place in which to settle. Segovia's description of the migrant experience as "two places and no place on which to stand," reflects the reality of bicultural identity but also the experience of being a perpetual outsider within a society.[40] He writes,

> We are a people living in two worlds: away from our traditional home, creating and establishing a new home; firmly tied to a rich cultural past, yet ready and struggling to take on yet another dimension of cultural miscegenation; accustomed to intolerable

39. This line of Francisco Alarcón's poetry is cited in Nanko-Fernández, *Theologizing in Espanglish*, 110.

40. Segovia, "Two Places," 33, 35–36.

> levels of political oppression and instability, searching for a mea-
> sure of political peace and freedom; rejected and denigrated, poor
> and ignored in our new home, culture, and country—in the very
> midst of the land of promise and plenty. We are thus a bicultural
> people at home in neither world—the permanent "others."[41]

Segovia reveals how many U.S. Latino/a peoples are made to be "other" indefinitely in the United States—no matter where they were born or how long they reside in a country or among a group of people. They are "oth-ered" because of language, because of the color of their skin, because of class, because they are deemed other than the "norm."

Borders divide nation-states geographically, yet they can also come to symbolize one's "otherness" socially. Borders may be cultural, economic, linguistic, and political, dividing ways of life and people groups in hidden but exploitative ways.[42] Borders and boundaries are also religious and may divide civilizations, such as the "Islamic World" or "Hindu Civilization."[43] Likewise they can be bodily, as in differing ableness or sexual orientation.[44] Nation-state borders both perpetuate and also come to symbolize bicul-tural "placelessness." *La Frontera,* for example, embodies dividing lines of exclusion by documentation, employment, gender, language, poverty level, and/or skin color.

The prevalence of peoples "on the move" in twenty-first century mi-gration challenges how ecclesial communities embody their identity in Jesus Christ within the place in which they reside. Ecclesial identity and place must be reconsidered when the space ecclesial communities occupy is contested in light of geopolitical borders, motives for assimilation, and desperate circumstances inherent in forced migration. The complexities of global migration challenge ecclesial communities to self-reflect on their own relationship to power and how this may be reflected toward Others they welcome through hospitality practice.

41. Ibid., 33.

42. Kwok, "A Theology of Border Passage," 104. Kwok talks about these borders in reference to Anzaldúa's *Borderlands/La Frontera: The New Mestiza.*

43. Ibid. 104.

44. Ibid. In reference to ableness, see Eiesland, *The Disabled God*; Betcher, *Spirit and the Politics of Disablement;* and Yong, *Theology and Down Syndrome: Reimagining Dis-ability in Late Modernity* and *The Bible, Disability, and the Church: A New Vision of the People of God.*

Mestizaje/Mulatez and Hybrid Identity

U.S. Latino/a theology arises from theologians' own experience of immigration into and marginalization within the United States. Mayra Rivera notes that the main focus of U.S. Hispanic theology is "not those physically outside the geopolitical centers of power but those marginalized subjects within it" because it is a theology, by definition, "of Others *within* the territory of hegemonic power."[45] U.S. Latino/a theologians' concrete embodiments of living on the margins as a bicultural or multicultural people offer new ways to consider identity as hybrid.

Latino/a concepts of *mestizaje* and *mulatez*, as well as the broader notion of "hybridity," point toward the reality of a "politics of identity" within both national and ecclesial identity.[46] De La Torre details the multilayered heritage of Latino/a identity and *mestizaje*: "Latino/as are heirs of several different cultures, including Amerindian or indigenous peoples (the Taíno, Mayan, Aztec, and Zapotec), remnants of medieval Catholic Spain (influenced by Muslims and Jews), and Africa (primarily the Caribbean and Brazil), Asia, and due to their continuous presence within the United States, various European groups."[47] While some Euroamericans may look upon such mixture with disdain, U.S. Latino/a theologians point out there is no such thing as a "pure" Hispanic or American. While a whiter-skinned majority may prefer to overlook their own cultural, racial, and ethnic mixture, there is no "pure" U.S. citizen. Disrupting the myth of racial purity, U.S. Latino/a theologians embrace *mestizaje* as the reality of identity, in which many cultural and racial influences are united into one. It is for this reason that many U.S. Hispanic theologians characterize their own identity by mixture, *mestizaje,* and borderland.[48]

Ada María Isasi-Díaz further elaborates upon *mestizaje/mulatez* as signifying a new people, a new ethnic group, with cultural as well as biological characteristics.[49] Isasi-Díaz thus expands *mestizaje/mulatez*

45. Rivera, *The Touch of Transcendence*, 78–79.

46. Traditionally, these terms in the Spanish language signify new racial/ethnic constructions indicative of the mixing of lighter-skinned Spanish colonizers with indigenous women (*mestizaje*) and black women (*mulatez*). Yet, these terms also signify underlying notions of racial privilege that generate a "politics of identity" within society.

47. De La Torre, *Trails of Hope and Terror*, 114.

48. M. A. Gonzalez, "Who Is American/o?" 67. More will be discussed on this more complicated symbol of identity in the next chapter.

49. Isasi-Díaz, "The New *Mestizaje/Mulatez*," 207.

from a mixing of race and ethnicity to the interweaving of culture, history, religious practice, and experience within identity.[50] Isasi-Díaz observes that the Spanish language, popular religion, social-cultural-psychological survival, economic oppression, and a vision of the future draw together the *mestizo/a* community residing in the United States.[51] Thus *mestizaje/ mulatez* embodies the mixing and bringing together of many elements of difference, including but not limited to race or ethnicity, to form deep community. Isasi-Díaz suggests strategies for developing relationships amidst difference in community, rather than allowing differences to divide and exclude or force assimilation.[52] Because of the hypermobility of today's world, she calls this "travelling between worlds," which signifies "entering the world of other people in such a way that not only do we learn how they see us but also we come to understand better how they construct themselves in their own world and the role we play in that construction."[53] Such traveling demands recognition that the worlds of difference are always under construction, relative, and fluid.[54] In turn, coalition-building among marginalized groups and redefining difference through relationships are paramount for survival and thriving.[55] This way of being and relating in the world is always a continual praxis "to situate oneself in time and space, to exercise one's creative potential, and to assume one's responsibilities" in order to form authentic community.[56] Recognition of differences in relationships requires a deeper critical awareness of one's own identity and intentional fostering of dialogue with others.

Embracing the Complexity of Hybrid

Yet, while the mixing of *mestizaje/mulatez* is challenging and complex, it is also contested. *Mestizaje* involves an ambiguous mixing of human identity that reflects how power—especially colonial influences—shape identity

50. See Isasi-Díaz, *En la Lucha.*

51. See Isasi-Díaz "The New *Mestizaje/Mulatez*," 216. Also see Isasi-Díaz, *En la Lucha,* chapters 1–2.

52. Isasi-Díaz, "The New *Mestizaje/Mulatez*," 203.

53. Ibid., 213.

54. Ibid.

55. Ibid., 214.

56. Ibid. See Gutierrez, *A Theology of Liberation,* 92. For more on concientization see Freire, *Pedagogy of the Oppressed,* 3.

construction. Michelle Gonzalez cautions against a glorification of *mes-tizaje/mulatez* because it covers over the violent colonial history behind the mixing of races. This difficult history is more complicated than earlier U.S. Latino/a theologians acknowledge as they have turned to embrace the categories of *mestizaje/mulatez*. The mixing of lighter-skinned Spanish coloniz-ers with indigenous women and black women is an oppressive and violent history. Thus, from a critical race perspective, it is important not to gloss over the fact that "claiming a *mestizo/a* or *mulato/a* identity is a manner of 'whitening' one's racial identity, gaining privilege over black and indig-enous peoples."[57] While this history is contested, Gonzalez also presents *mestizaje/mulatez* as important categories, which point to the realities of mixture and ambiguity that characterize Latino/a peoples. Gonzalez prob-lematizes identity, exposing the privilege of a "whitened" identity, in order to question *who* is Americano/a at all. The complexities of Latin American identity and Latino/a peoples challenge the oversimplified categories and typologies of race and ethnicity that dominate U.S. discourse.[58]

In like fashion, one of the major tasks of postcolonial theology is to disrupt and destabilize the Western production and implementation of bi-nary identity construction. Such binaries include: center/margin, civilized/savage, same/other, white/black, male/female, First/Third worlds, West/East, North/South, etc. Postcolonial theorists particularly seek to uncover the hidden power dynamics that create and perpetuate the first term of the binary as primary, while the second term is unthinkingly dominated or de-fined as a lack of the first. Postcolonial theologians challenge the boundar-ies and borders created by binary identity constructions and point toward a more fluid hybrid identity in which all are mixed. Additionally, they seek to disrupt the myth of a "pure" identity—not only a racially or ethnically "pure" identity—but socially, economically, politically, or religiously "pure" identities as well. Rather, the myriad of experiences and differences woven into each human life contributes to a hybrid or mixed identity.

To illustrate a crisscrossing of multiple sociocultural boundaries, post-colonial theologian Kwok Pui-lan explains how, from the beginning, the cultural forms of theologies in Asia reflect a hybridity of Christian ideas,

57. Gonzalez, "Who Is American/o?" 67.

58. See ibid., 59–60, where she adds, "Far from accepting the unified subject of West-ern European philosophy and theology, the anthropology underlying Latin American and Latino/a communities is mixed, hybrid, and contentious. At the historical root of this subjectivity is the birth of an 'American' colonial subject that resulted from the vio-lent meeting of African, indigenous, and European cultures within the Americas."

symbols, and thought forms that were appropriated by non-indigenous languages, cultural forms, and thought patterns.[59] Christian theologians from within the sociopolitical and religious contexts of Asia specifically seek to liberate the gospel from the colonization and homogenization imposed by the West. Today, Kwok argues, a process of liberation from the West must embark upon encountering newer narratives. She draws upon R. S. Sugirtharajah's development of "hermeneutics in transit," which reflects the diasporic border passages undergone by Asian intellectuals. Seeking to recover one's authentic "roots" in a narrative history or return "home" to one's theological origin is an impossible task in the diversity of a globalized world.[60] Fluidity, however, creates the problem of how to understand theological identity that is always elusive and hard to grasp.

The mixing of identity is often an extremely difficult and painful task. Asian theological reflection also evokes the experience of dislocation, displacement, and coping with the reality of living "in-between" two or more worlds. Japanese American theologian Fumitaka Matsuoka writes:

> A liminal world is the "place of in-betweenness." It is at once the world of isolation and intimacy, dislocation and creativity. A person in a liminal world is poised in uncertainty and ambiguity between two or more social constructs, reflecting in the soul the discords and harmonies, repulsions and attractions. One of the constructs is likely to be dominant, whether cultural or linguistic. Within such a dominant construct one strives to belong and yet finds oneself to be a peripheral member, forced to remain in the world of inbetweenness."[61]

The reality of liminality suggests that theologians do theology *on the border*. Doing theology from the in-between space, one faces the difficult tensions of isolation and intimacy, dislocation and creativity. It is not possible to "solve" this conflicted existence or attempt to alleviate the complexities of identity. Rather, identity arises from within the painful experience of racial or cultural prejudice. In turn, the possibility for creative resistance to cultural hegemony is expressed in more honest representations of the in-betweenness of identity, evidenced in *mestizaje/mulatez* or hybridity. In turn, *borderland* spaces and the presence of borders and boundaries represent this reality of conflicted and in-between existence.

59. Kwok, "A Theology of Border Passage," 104–5.

60. Ibid., 109.

61. Matsuoka, *Out of Silence*, 54.

Postcolonial theologians uncover how Christians stand in varying positions with regard to hegemonic power. Recognizing that one cannot completely escape colonial influence, to seek the "post-colonial" is to disrupt imperial control and look for ethical alternatives. The spatial imagery of borderlands, interstices, or in-between places of society though painful sites of exclusion, become important in order to escape the full grasp of empire. While the margins are the spaces relegated to "those" deemed "Other" by empire, such spaces also afford new opportunity beyond the control of empire by virtue of their marginality. Borderland or interstitial spaces can become sites for identifying and embodying alternatives to empire. In revealing the church's complicity in power, such spaces become important for prophetically calling the church to challenge empire. Thus, while the border may be a social imaginary of division and exclusion as was demonstrated above, it also is a contested space where empire can be evaded and new possibilities may arise. Let us now turn to teasing out new symbols and spaces.

Spatial Imagery: Communities of Border Passage

Border crossings conceived compositely include national, racial, social, and cultural characteristics. Reflecting mixed and complex social symbolism, borders can include or exclude, reflect fixity and fluidity, and open up an in-between alternative space that generates distinct meaning. The state of being forced into perpetual migration for economic survival is more than a one time "border crossing." In turn, the reality of transnational migration and bodies marked by wandering is better reflected by what Kwok identifies as "border passage."[62] Though a relatively recent phenomenon, the "border passage" many persons (or family members) continually undergo has become necessary for economic survival. Migration characterized by "border passage existence" signifies persons who are continually journeying; they may not necessarily be in search of one home, or perhaps they have multiple homes. This existence not only calls the very possibility of a home into question, but challenges how persons who can afford stability define home.

The notion of border passage is tied to a diasporic imagination.[63] Though traditionally diaspora has its roots in the Jewish tradition, it has in-

62. Kwok, "A Theology of Border Passage," 104.

63. Kwok, *Postcolonial Imagination and Feminist Theology*, 45. Kwok defines diaspora as follows: "Since the 1960s, the term 'diaspora' has been more generalized to apply

creasingly become a global phenomenon related to cultural and economic grouping after decolonization. It speaks to forced and voluntary migration, as well as transnational migration related to globalization.[64] Kwok writes, "Today, the term 'diaspora' shares a broader semantic domain that includes words like immigrant, expatriate, refugee, migrant worker, exile community, and ethnic and racial minorities."[65] As the term has broadened, so have the characteristics of diaspora so that memory of, longing for, and continual identification with one's homeland may no longer be the ideal. Returning to Alarcon's image, today we might more realistically associate diaspora with the migrant who perpetually carries one's roots in one's pillow. The very notion of *transition,* "destabilizes a fixed time and space, and resists pinning down by preconceived identities or satisfaction with ready-made answers."[66] Thus, diasporic discourse continually disrupts the construction of the center and periphery, borders and boundaries. It encompasses the negotiation of multiple loyalties and identities, the relationship between "home" and the "world," and the political and theoretical implications of dislocation and border crossing.[67]

The realities of border passage existence raise important ecclesiological and theological questions regarding the *place* that the church occupies in the world. As new realities of home, journey, pilgrimage, and space and time represent the unique experiences of migration in the twenty-first century context, they challenge how ecclesial communities relate with persons who are migrating in their midst. For example, though safety and a place of refuge may be immediate needs for some migrants, others' experiences are continually shifting. Access to a phone or the Internet to notify family, a ride to the bus station, and/or connections to employment or legal services may be needed, for example. Diasporic actuality problematizes how ecclesial communities come to understand both Christian identity in the world and the places of power they may occupy. Thus, twenty-first century migration realities demand critical reflection in light of changing circumstances and contexts and summon the church to search for alternative

to many contexts besides the classic cases of Jewish, Greek, and Armenian diasporas. Such a development is the result of the migration of formerly colonized peoples to the metropolitan West, the weakening of the nation-state, and the displacement of people because of the massive transnational flows of capital and labor in late capitalism." Ibid.

64. Ibid., 44.

65. Ibid., 45.

66. Ibid., 43–44.

67. Ibid., 46.

spatial imagination. In turn, the mode of being *en route*—holding together "traveling-in-dwelling" with "dwelling-in-traveling"—may afford new possibilities for the church as it journeys with persons whose lives are marked by wandering, while it seeks to live faithfully to the ways of Jesus and disentangle itself from the push and pull of empire.[68]

The Borderlands of Empire

According to Joerg Rieger, "empire" signifies the massive concentration of power that cannot be controlled by any one actor alone.[69] Yet, this power seeks to infiltrate all aspects of life—political, economic, geographic, as well as cultural, intellectual, religious, and spiritual—giving the illusion of control.[70] Imperial power is predicated on the illusion that there are no alternatives. Empire is complex, always morphing, and difficult to identify. At the turn of the twenty-first century, empire might have been seen as synonymous with the United States as a global superpower. Given continued transnational market expansion and the boom of Internet technology, however, empire is no longer affiliated with a single nation-state alone. Rather, empires are complex, multi-headed, and decentered—akin to what Rui de Souza Josgrilberg refers to as a "global machine."[71] Comprised of massive conglomerations of power that direct macroeconomics, as well as the innermost desires of the individual, empires are social and political imaginaries.[72] Charles Taylor develops the notion of "social imaginary," to refer to an "ensemble of imaginings that enable our practices by making sense of them."[73] As we think of ways of gathering communities, delegating human efforts, organizing the work force, and dictating purchasing choices and habits, empire administrates a complex set of "social habits, relations, patterns that habituate us (often unconsciously) into ways of living and acting that come to be understood as not only possible but natural and right."[74]

68. Ibid., 43–44.

69. Rieger, *Christ and Empire*, 2–3, 11.

70. Ibid.

71. De Souza Josgrilberg, "Wesley e a experiência cristã," 41, quoted in Stone, "The Missional Church and the Missional Empire," 2.

72. See Rieger, *Christ and Empire*, vii. Also, see Stone, "The Missional Church and the Missional Empire."

73. Charles Taylor, *Modern Social Imaginaries*, 165.

74. Stone, "Wesleyan Ecclesiology," 10.

In light of the pervasive control of empire that morphs and moves and cannot be tamed or grasped, postcolonial theologians employ the continual task of disrupting the perceived control of empire. One such example of a political and economic illusion of control is U.S. Homeland Security's heavy policing of the southern geopolitical borders of the United States. Though this border represents where the U.S. nation-state begins and ends, the U.S.-Mexico border as *La Frontera* has come to symbolize economic, political, and psycho-social exclusion for undocumented persons who travel or have traveled northward. Yet even the existence of this border demonstrates that unilateral control is impossible. Even as the social imaginary of the U.S.-Mexico border has perpetuated "us" vs. "them," it also has become a space through which people pass back and forth regularly and by which new livelihoods have been created. Indeed, the in-between space of the borderlands becomes a site of transaction, of passage, of underground economic survival. This contested space of political and economic imperial control demonstrates that borders permit a passage that can never be fully controlled; undocumented migrants still find ways through the border. Geopolitical borders give the semblance of control, but something can always slip through.

The myth of imperial hegemony comes into view by identifying spaces where the containment of unilateral power leaks. The borderland and border passage cannot be fully controlled by nation-state boundaries or global market economies. In turn, both the border and passage of it represent the potential for existence outside the grip of empire. Borderlands become a site that resists imperial grasp because it is deemed "no man's land." It is the space in which people are expected to pass through rather than take up residence. Additionally, as Kwok notes: "In our globalized world in which time and space have shrunk, many have argued that traditional borders do not hold anymore because the market economy and the information highway have linked so many people together in unprecedented ways."[75] In fact, for many who are perpetually "othered" and do not find a space in society in which to "fit," residing on the figurative borderlands "between worlds" is a way of life. As marginalized persons provisionally reside in the borderlands, this territory becomes "in-between space," a "third space," and perhaps even an "imaginary homeland" in which new possibilities for survival and human thriving may arise.

---

75. Kwok, "A Theology of Border Passage," 104.

The space of borderlands becomes an important location in which the church might dwell both literally and figuratively. The church, by virtue of the fact that it is a community of people located in a particular space and time, is always negotiating identity amidst any number of influences in the context in which it finds itself. In order to escape the grasp of imperial forces, postcolonial theologians argue, Christian identity must remain "slippery"—always on the move. Borderland spaces present possibilities for the mixing of identities that weaves together many experiences, influences, and narratives within ecclesial communities. Postcolonial and U.S. Latino/a theologians attest to a Christian identity that is never pure or free from cultural influence, but always emerges from hybrid identity construction that is furthered by engagement with the Other. Hybridity also illuminates a complex tension within the church. That is, ecclesial identities always encompass a history shaped by colonialism and empire. Yet at the same time, they also embody possibilities of resistance to how personhood is determined by empire and hopeful glimpses of God's plans of restoration for humanity.

Postcolonial theologians insist that the church critically examine its surroundings, the powers driving social and political influences, and its complicity within them. Yet, postcolonial imagination also invites a continual searching for where the church is happening on the borderlands and enacting concrete alternatives, though they may be but small glimpses of resistance and hope amidst ever-present hegemonic social imaginaries. The complex tension in which postcolonial theologians dwell, however, does not necessarily provide a constructive path forward for the church's hospitality practice in light of twenty-first century transnational migration. More work remains to be done to help point communities in intentional directions as they continue to practice self-reflection and resist the pulls of empire. These strategic directions will be explored further in the final two chapters.

CONCLUSION

The factors contributing to forced transnational migration and U.S. Latino/a migration I have presented here challenge U.S.-based ecclesial communities to reconsider how they offer hospitality from the position of power as "host," while also being part of the "host nation." Power dynamics at play in hospitality open it to important objections that question whether hospitality is possible at all. The powerful positioning of the host certainly should raise suspicion about what sort of formation is enacted in this practice. If hospitality in the church is possible—and I argue that it is—what steps are necessary to construct an alternative hospitality? How will hospitality counter-act negative perceptions of migration imprinted in U.S. national consciousness and sterile national policies implemented to deter or prevent migrants from crossing and residing north of the U.S.-Mexico border? Can and does the church embody alternative understanding and action toward persons on the move? A new sense of belonging in Christ that contests *borders* of control and *places* of privilege may allow for the possibility of a new *us*. The development of ecclesiology as the people of God journeying together toward the new creation *beyond all borders* in Christ Jesus offers a radically new way to be human that confronts the classism, ethnocentrism, and racism that divide persons from one another.

The complexities and questions surrounding migration placed alongside the mission of the church reveal that much work remains to be done with regard to the practice of hospitality. This process is far from simple. In discerning and negotiating hospitality practice, ecclesial communities must take into account: 1) concealed economic and political factors within migration; 2) barriers and borders that perpetuate racism, marginalization, and exploitation of migrants who come to reside (however provisionally) in the United States; and 3) the effects of power dynamics and boundaries on national and ecclesial identity formation. From a theological standpoint, the next chapter will critically analyze how the migration-related complexities introduced here evidence themselves in the life of the church in order to further imagine how hospitality might be retooled differently. Any steps an ecclesial community takes forward in affirming the possibility of hospitality will involve a difficult journey of awareness, reflection, and change indicative of the deepening of human interaction and relationships. Certainly, the above treatment of twenty-first century transnational migration and, more specifically, U.S. Latino/a migration into the United States, demand an urgency that presses the church to reflect on how its witness is manifested and made visible through the practice of hospitality. The next chapter delves into the difficult questions U.S. Latino/a and postcolonial theologians pose to ecclesial communities regarding economy, race, and power.

4

Objections to Hospitality and Possibilities for New Ecclesial Imagination

RECONSIDERING HOSPITALITY IN CHURCH ON AND OF THE BORDERLANDS

"HOSPITALITY IS NOT ENOUGH!" exclaims U.S. Latino/a theologian Carmen Nanko-Fernández.[1] What is not enough about hospitality is the hidden power disparity when the Other is "invited" into assimilation because entrance into the community requires the stranger to be "like us." The problem with hospitality, Nanko-Fernández adds, is that it assumes one is welcoming the newcomer—the migrant—but does not also turn to see that the inhabitant also is encountered by the sojourner.[2] Such hospitality prevents a two-way exchange, raising suspicion that the community is not truly open to the contribution of Others, but rather assumes assimilation to the majority. In such cases, true hospitality is not practiced.[3] True hospitality, in contrast, involves the double recognition that both host and guest are receiving one another as strangers. Critical evaluation is necessary so that the host, who may be in a position of power or privilege within society, does not cover over or exploit the guest.

1. Nanko-Fernández, *Theologizing in Espanglish*, 119.
2. Ibid.
3. Ibid.

The last chapter's investigation of how twenty-first century migration realities problematize identity construction and reveal power dynamics that pervade theology and the church better positions us to address the complexities within ecclesial communities' hospitality practice. Can critical examination of one's place and identity overcome tendencies toward homogenization in the church? Both postcolonial and U.S. Hispanic theologians draw attention to how difference and diversity are understood and covered over in building relationships in the church. Though the church claims unity in Jesus Christ, this unity often manifests itself as uniformity achieved at the expense of marginalizing certain perspectives and social locations in the community. In order to move forward to critically examine both hospitality and ecclesiology, an understanding of unity that is distinct from uniformity must be developed.

The postcolonial perspective casts a critical gaze toward Christian hospitality's historical abuse as a force for assimilation into a particular homogeneous way of life that neglects to value the contributions of the stranger, outsider, or Other, and often inflicts harm upon them. Postcolonial critics of hospitality argue that the alterity of the Other will always be covered over or seized in some sense by the host. Because of this inescapable power differential, they claim true hospitality is impossible. Others may remain critical of the practice, however, they do not believe it should be abandoned altogether. I walk this fine line and seek to uncover how true hospitality is indeed possible, though perhaps more accurately reflected on as an "impossible possibility."[4]

Jewish philosopher Emmanuel Lévinas and French phenomenologist Jacques Derrida develop some of the most important challenges to hospitality in the twentieth and twenty-first centuries. Their work centers on the absolute differences between persons who encounter one another in a guest/host relationship. Lévinas articulates how hospitality must always be marked by the alterity, exteriority, and infinity of the Other, so much so that the guest is always the one who makes a demand on the host, and the host is prisoner to the demands of the guest. In fact, difference is so upheld that relationship can never be achieved for Lévinas. Building upon this

---

4. Letty Russell presents the "impossible possibility" of unity in hospitality in *Just Hospitality*, 68. I agree with her assessment that the impossibility of hospitality/unity is made possible because the church has hope in God's promise to "mend the creation that has been so torn apart." Hospitality must be re-imagined in light of context and reformed because of its abuses in the church. This is made possible in God as the church responds to the call to live into, albeit always inadequately, God's restoration.

impossibility of true hospitality, Derrida articulates an absolute hospitality by which the host gives the guest the keys to his or her house, thus deeming himself or herself hostage of the guest. Thus, hospitality must involve the voluntary reversal of power differentials, so that the host becomes willfully in bondage to the guest. Such reversal of power must be addressed with respect to hospitality in the twenty-first century.

Challenges in Guest/Host Relations

Amos Yong plays out the consequences of Lévinas's and Derrida's exchange on hospitality and points to the necessity of rooting Christian hospitality in God's abundance rather than scarcity in order to provide an ontological home for the "impossible possibility" of hospitality. Because the guest/host dynamic is complex and risks re-inscribing colonial tendencies and unbalanced power dynamics, Yong relies on Derrida's notion of "hospitality as a set of not merely interpersonal affairs but of political relations."[5] Hospitality in the twenty-first century must address the contemporary challenges of economic and political exchanges and social constructions of gift and debt. Derrida and Lévinas illuminate the dangers of violence subscribed within hospitality and gift-giving. For Lévinas hospitality necessitates the host's infinite obligation to the guest. Thus, hospitality becomes ethical responsibility in the face of the Other. The host who is infinitely obligated to the guest must divest her/himself of her or his own concerns so as to be made "hostage" to the guest. Lévinas's responsibility to the Other is such that "the face of the Other 'orders' and 'ordains' me, placing me under (even infinite) obligation."[6] For Derrida, the impossibility of hospitality lies in the original violence of hospitality in which the stranger has to ask for hospitality from another, often in a language that is not her or his own. A secondary violence arises when the stranger is then made to receive hospitality, creating an obligation or debt to repay the host. Derrida struggles in the impossibility of hospitality, because "what is owed or obligated cannot be freely given."[7]

In an economy of exchange, hospitality perpetuates an endless cycle of indebtedness.[8] Yet, Yong draws attention to how Derrida suggests a

---

5. Yong, *Hospitality and the Other*, 119. Yong draws from Derrida's discussion of hospitality in chapter five of *Politics of Friendship*.

6. Ibid., 119. Here Yong draws from Lévinas, *Totality and Infinity*.

7. Ibid.

8. Ibid., 120.

possibility around the never-ending obligation of the guest. Distinguishing from the "conditional hospitality" of reciprocity that perpetuates the violence of indebtedness, Derrida identifies an "absolute hospitality" that is unconditional.[9] "Absolute hospitality" reverses the guest/host obligation because the host can intentionally take on a voluntary indebtedness. The host always must remain "unprepared, or prepared to be unprepared, for the unexpected arrival of *any* other."[10] In reception of another, then, the guest is permitted to assume control, as the host displaces her or his power. In this sense, the guest holds the keys to the house.[11] What is more, for Derrida the guest then comes as liberator, freeing the host who was hostage in his own house.[12]

From a theological perspective, Yong argues that Derrida's absolute hospitality assumes a Trinitarian logic of abundance.[13] While the impossibility of hospitality and the impossibility of gift, lie within the logic of exchange, reciprocity, and scarcity, Christian hospitality can enact an alternative.[14] The economics and politics of Christian hospitality arise out of God's abundance, which affords the possibility of hospitality. It is out of the ecclesial experience and understanding of God's abundance that the host can continually give herself away without losing herself.[15] As one gives oneself to another, one also encounters the possibility of love. Such giving and receiving is reflective of the mutual self-giving love enacted in the Trinity. The movement of hospitality reflects how in and through our encounter and welcome of the Other we come to see God. Karl Barth's words are ap-

9. Ibid.

10. Ibid., 120–21.

11. Ibid. Yong draws from Derrida, *Acts of Religion*, 362.

12. Ibid., 120. Yong describes the Derridean reversal as "the host is hostage even as the guest now hosts the host/age's salvation, redemption, and liberation." Ibid., 121. To make this point, Yong draws from Derrida and Dufourmantelle, *Of Hospitality*, 124.

13. Ibid.

14. Ibid.

15. Yong, *Hospitality and the Other*, 128. Yong continues, "When set in a pneumatological perspective, such a theology of hospitality points to the dynamic rather than static aspect of our witness such that we can never be too comfortable in any one role. Rather, we are participants in the redemptive hospitality of God, even while we are conduits of this hospitality to the world, albeit from its margins as aliens and strangers. Hence, we find ourselves in a paradoxical state of being guests in a strange land on the one hand, even as we embody the divine hospitality on the other. But in either case, we are caught up in the excessive hospitality of God that has been revealed in his Son and poured out through his Spirit upon us and even upon all flesh."

ropos, "my neighbor acquires for me a sacramental significance."[16] It is the neighbor or stranger who reveals the redemptive hospitality of God to us.

Yong continues to draw from Derrida as he unpacks the conditions and boundaries of guest and host relationships within hospitality. In recognizing the Other as stranger, one must recognize that the Other is "not me." Boundaries are necessary for understanding difference, rather than assuming sameness and thus assimilation. There is no hospitality, no invitation, without boundaries. Yong asserts: "Hospitality needs to preserve the alterity of the other in at least two senses: in recognizing the distinctiveness with which the other represents the image of God and in rejecting the attempts of the unholy other to overwhelm and destroy the self."[17] In this sense, Yong's development of guest/host relations also must preserve the boundary between the two individuals. The boundary allows for difference and distinctiveness that cannot be turned into "sameness."

Yet, hospitality as it relates to Christian identity also turns certain conceptions of borders and boundaries on its head. Christian hospitality practice is such that it demands the Christian to be both guest *and* host and the guest/host relationship takes place on the margins of society. Yong notes that "the Christian condition of being aliens and strangers in this world means both that we are perpetually guests, first of God and then of other, and that we should adopt postures appropriate to receiving hospitality even when we find ourselves as hosts."[18] In turn, the practice of hospitality must directly shape and form Christian identity as it relates to being a perpetual "guest" in the world. The unique place of the church in the world, then, is most aptly situated on the margins.

16. Cited in Yong, *Hospitality and the Other*, 151. For further detail on how this sacramental encounter fits within Yong's overall project, also see p. 153. He writes, "I propose that Barth's notion of our meeting with, loving, and being loved by strangers being sacramental moments of encountering God is a thoroughly pneumatological idea. If the love of God is poured out into our hearts through the Holy Spirit (Rom. 5:5), then not only is our loving our neighbors the means through which the love of God is given to them, but our being loved by our neighbors, including those of other faiths, is also the means through which the love of God is given to us. In this way, I suggest, the practices of hospitality—of being hosts as well as guests—become the concrete modalities through which the gifts of the Holy Spirit are poured out on all flesh."

17. Ibid., 123.

18. Ibid., 124–25.

Irreducible Otherness in Community

In *The Touch of Transcendence: A Postcolonial Theology of God*, Mayra Rivera builds upon and challenges Lévinas's important insights regarding hospitality. Her analysis helps to thicken ecclesial communities' encounters with the Other and move communities toward a more complex inter-human transcendence by which the differences encountered in the Other are delicately received and preserved. Rivera nuances Lévinas's totality of difference and the necessity of spatial exteriority between persons by understanding difference and otherness analogically from a relational anthropology.[19] Similar to divine transcendence in historical Christian thought, the Other is always inexhaustible and, therefore, can only be understood by analogy. Though the Other is never fully understood, communication and relationship are possible.[20] Rather than emphasize "*absolutely* Other," as in the philosophy of Lévinas, Rivera qualifies otherness as "*irreducibly* Other."[21] The differences of the Other are inexhaustible and cannot be reduced to "sameness," though they are not binding or absolute.[22] This signifies that the differences between persons do not alienate them from one another, making it impossible to truly encounter another. Rather, differences must be preserved as irreducible in order for true relationships to be possible. Modifying Lévinas's definition, Rivera proposes the following: "*Transcendence designates a relation with a reality irreducibly different from my own reality, without this difference destroying this relation and without the relation destroying this difference.*"[23]

Rivera challenges Lévinas's exteriority in hospitality so as to emphasize the possibility of true community in which differences are not covered over.[24] U.S. Latino/a theological anthropology, which emphasizes connectedness in community across generations, helps her arrive at this. She writes,

19. Rivera, *The Touch of Transcendence*, 79. See the entirety of Rivera's fourth chapter, "Transcendence in the Face of the Other." Also see Enrique Dussel, *Invention of the Americas*.

20. Ibid., 73.

21. Ibid., 79. Also see chapter 4 "Transcendence in the Face of the Other."

22. Rivera, *The Touch of Transcendence*, 79.

23. Ibid., 82; italics in original.

24. Here, Rivera adds, "A theology of interhuman transcendence incorporates Lévinas's insight to define subjectivity in terms of 'welcoming the other, as hospitality,' but does not follow him in defining a subject as 'a *separated being* fixed in its identity, the same, the I.' Instead subjectivity is described as constituted in relation, always unfinished:

> Mestizaje/mulatez in contemporary Latina/o discourses not only embraces the complex and ambiguous product of a colonial past, but attempts to redeploy it as a critical tool for rethinking identity in/as mixture. Choosing mestizaje/mulatez as privileged metaphors for the articulations of identity implies that the singularity of an individual person becomes unthinkable outside a network of relations—sociopolitical as much as familial—that extends spatially through the continents and temporally through generations.[25]

Rivera's rich relational anthropology awakens a new spatio-temporal imagination so that community is formed over time into a complex mixture of differences, rather than a uniform sameness. Uncovering the rich, yet painful history embodied within the complex *mestizaje/mulatez* identity mixture over centuries, as well as how this identity is still being shaped today, are central to her theological anthropology. She suggests *mestizaje/mulatez* identity as a model that links the subject to "the history of encounters from which it emerges."[26]

Our responsibility in hospitality is not reduced to a single event because through our encounters we are opened to those who have come before. "The encounter with the poor, the stranger, the migrant, or the Latina/o is not represented as a self-contained event," Rivera notes, "but as one that reopens past encounters and future possibilities."[27] All our encounters are connected so that we build upon them, but we are not reduced to them. Drawing from Sara Ahmed in *Strange Encounters,* Rivera writes,

> "What is required is a hospitality that *remembers* the encounters that are already implicated in such names (including the name of the 'the stranger'), and how they affect the movement and 'arrival'

---

produced in relation to the transcendence of the Other." Ibid., 82.

25. Ibid., 80.

26. Rivera has developed this theme as a part of her larger argument in which she challenges Emmanuel Lévinas's encounter with the Other, claiming that his "failure to elucidate the sociopolitical specificities that mark a person as the excluded Other may lead to the interpretations of otherness as a characteristic of that person rather than as the historical product of modes of encounter." Rather than 'totality' or 'exteriority,' one is always connected to others by the history of exclusion that has produced power dynamics that have organized today's world. She notes how "a model of identity that takes mestizaje/mulatez as its main metaphor links the subject, and thus the self-Other encounter, to the history of encounters from which it emerges." Rivera, *The Touch of Transcendence,* 80.

27. Ibid.

of others, in a way which opens out the possibility of these names being moved *from*." As it opens itself up to the multiple ramifications—past, present, and future—this model of encounter recognizes that it is in the particularity of a single encounter that we are called to respond.[28]

Thus, on the one hand, social analysis and self-reflection must accompany our present hospitality connecting it to past encounters and seeking to understand how and why a person has been deemed a "stranger" or "Other" in our perception and within society. On the other hand, Rivera reminds that the presence of another before us simply demands hospitable response. Connecting the two moves, "it is in the particularity of a single encounter that we are called to respond" and it is because of our past encounters that we do respond. Rivera's attention to *irreducibility* in encounter with the Other—that self-critically connects past, present, and future encounter—confronts where previous expressions of hospitality may have neglected power dynamics of guest and host roles and manifested themselves as initiations into the sameness of the dominant majority.

NEW SPATIAL AND RELATIONAL IMAGINATION IN THE CHURCH

In order to challenge the impetus toward assimilation and homogenization, one must challenge the false premise in the church that unity is built upon uniformity. To do so, I return to the site of *borderlands* as the place where the church can construct new spatial imagination for hospitality practice and ecclesiology. The borderlands create an expectation for identity to be continually explored and discovered anew. In fact, the provisional and contested space in geopolitical boundaries is exactly where the church must journey to rediscover unity amidst irreducible otherness and difference. Borderlands are spaces that represent the encounter and coming together of differences, they are spaces in which differences can never be collapsed into sameness. In a sense, borderlands also are spaces in which everyone is encountered as a stranger. I reflect upon borderlands both in terms of new spatio-temporal imagination for the church, but also in terms of how they affect relationships and community.

---

28. Rivera, *Touch of Transcendence*, 80.

From a Christian perspective, borderlands are most appropriately understood through a Judeo-Christian theology of exile—traditionally conceived as making a home in a strange land and journeying toward a homeland. Yet, when a theology of exile is placed alongside contemporary postcolonial intimations that there may not be a "home" to which one can return, it demands a re-appropriation of ecclesial space and Christian identity. There is something important about the church's identity remaining on the margins and characterized by diaspora that preserves distance from the world's status quo. Christian heritage draws from Israel's nomadic, national, and exilic experiences that shaped Israel's identity as the People of God—always sojourners in the eyes of God—and their obedience to God's continual reminder to care for the alien and stranger. Identity as a sojourning people continues in the Christian diaspora, in that "they were pilgrims on a journey, called to follow after Jesus their great high priest while living at peace with everyone."[29] Thus, the people of God continue to be a journeying people, on a pilgrimage, following Christ toward God's heavenly reign. Paralleling the fierce spirituality of the migrant with Abraham's own migratory existence and God's calling of the pilgrim people, Ward writes,

> because we are stretched out towards a future hope in faith. And anyone who knows what such a stretching out means, anyone who knows what it is to live in that condition, given over to the grace of God in a radical dependency, will understand why I call it a 'fierce spirituality.' To live for a promise that is not received, to confess you are a stranger and a pilgrim on the earth, to set out not knowing where you will end up, for a place which will be received only retrospectively: that is not easy. But I suggest nevertheless that is our human condition as God has graciously fashioned it.[30]

The postures learned in journeying are not saved for the eschatological reign to come. Rather, through being a journeying people—learning how to live as aliens within a strange land—has everything to do with how we encounter others now.[31] A theology of exile is not limited to the fact that we are journeying, or even that we are journeying somewhere in God's name. Rather, it includes the fact that in our journeying together we are afforded

---

29. Yong, *Hospitality and the Other*, 115. Yong draws from Hebrews 12:14 to build this image.

30. Ward, "Hospitality and Justice toward 'Strangers,'" 1–2.

31. See Yong, *Hospitality and the Other*, 125. Also see Yoder, "See How They Set Their Face to the Sun."

an alternative vantage point. Our experience of relationships and understanding of what it means to be human are shaped by different patterns, postures, and practices.

Still relying upon theology of exile, I turn toward new spatial conceptions of ecclesial gathering through themes of temporary residence and journeying patterns on the borders. Where the church locates itself and in whose company it resides have much to do with its grappling with its own identity as *strange* and as a community of *strangers* in the world. Postcolonial theologians reveal how the prevalence of borders and margins that divide and exclude have negatively shaped ecclesial identity by excluding minority voices. In turn, borders and margins must also be reinterpreted and recovered as the spaces where the ecclesial community provisionally resides, and thus, how the community continually negotiates identity and learns new postures for receiving Others and constructing community differently.

Emphasizing the building of partnerships and community amidst difference, Isasi-Díaz's words are instructive for the church:

> The goal here is not to replace our perspective with that of another but rather to embrace the partiality of all human perspectives and to admit the point of view of others as a corrective lens to our own. We see that the present understanding of difference depends on a comparison between people with reference to a human-made norm that need not remain the way it is. It is a norm that must be challenged.[32]

Particularly when societal boundaries are based on categories of difference that perpetuate social misunderstanding and prejudice, critical reflection and communal re-envisioning of difference are necessary. It is only within relationship that one can be encountered by another and challenged to look inwardly in self-analysis as well as outwardly toward all that the Other brings and offers. When these relationships are mutually receptive, persons' encounters with one another challenge them each toward change. In turn, they are together shaped into a new community. I propose, however, that this new community may not look the same as Christians today think about "gathering" or "being gathered" as the body of Christ.

Borderlands as spaces that encompass and represent many differences also are spaces in which new community is potentially born and reformed.

---

32. Isasi-Díaz, "A New Mestizaje/Mulatez," 212. Also see Minow, *Making All the Difference*, 9–10.

Kathryn Tanner puts forth that Christian identity is not determined by sharp cultural boundaries of inclusion and exclusion. Rather, borders and boundaries shape Christian identity, but they must be permeable and fluid. She writes, "The distinctiveness of a Christian way of life is not so much formed *by* the boundary as *at* it; Christian distinctiveness is something that emerges in the very cultural processes occurring at the boundary, processes that construct a distinctive identity for Christian social practices through the distinctive use of cultural materials shared with others."[33] As Tanner displays, boundaries, margins, and borders are the spatial locations where Christian identity is continually worked out. Thus, "gathering" and "being gathered" as the body of Christ is not comfortable, natural, or easy.

At the same time, recognizing the unavoidable threat of borders and boundaries in continuing to divide and exclude what has been united in the church, Tanner challenges the congregations of today to recognize the hard work it takes to build community that respects differences and resists uniformity. She instructs ecclesial communities to return to the spirit of the early church—"to become *a genuine community of argument*, one marked by mutual hearing and criticism among those who disagree, by a common commitment to mutual correction and uplift, in keeping with the shared hope of good discipleship, proper faithfulness, and purity of witness."[34] Becoming genuine communities of argument requires deep relationships and recognition of differences that strengthen the commitment of the church community rather than dividing it or seeking to make it all the same. Argument is not for the purposes of dividing, but for the purposes of genuinely seeking to understand differences and negotiate a way forward together. For precisely these reasons, both feminist and postcolonial theologians emphasize that churches are communities of faith *and* struggle. They caution against the church turning too hastily toward unity, because such unity can too easily eclipse difference. Uniformity neglects the voices of margin and voices of opposition in community, which are necessary for a community of faith and struggle. At the same time, however, Tanner's imagery of communities of argument may go too far and imply a more combative tone than I would like to display.

33. Tanner, *Theories of Culture,* 115; italics original.
34. Ibid., 123–24.

Challenges of Unity and Difference

Letty Russell similarly focuses on hospitality as an activity that must be done *at the boundaries* and as a distinctive way of forming identity that tends boundaries uniquely. It is when the body of Christ fails to adjust and negotiate its identity on the margins that it compromises its mission in the world. Drawing upon Botswana theologian and New Testament scholar, Musa Dube, Russell exposes the domination of the West in setting universal standards in education, culture, politics, etc. which are imposed upon non-Western groups. She uncovers a perpetuation of Western "sameness" in education rather than the recognition and value of differences between cultures.[35] Before working toward what she terms "just hospitality," Russell calls for an examination of how ecclesial identity is predicated on covering over the voices and participation of members who embody differences that threaten the status quo.[36] Difference, Russell explains, is often misused as a tool to silence, exclude, or oppress the Other because she or he does not match the universal norm carried by the dominating group. Critical examination of how a Western worldview has dominated knowledge production is needed in order to determine where Western cultures are inadvertently reinforced as "better" or more "advanced." This calls for further examination of how globalization has shaped the multilayered and intersecting oppressions of racism, classism, and imperialism, etc.

Through exposing various layers of oppression, Russell develops a framework for a hermeneutic of hospitality. First, members of the church must uncover the various levels of power and access one has based on his or her social location.[37] Second, Russell insists that priority be given to the perspective of the outsider and marginalized, which will in turn be given privilege in influencing the "center" of the church. Lastly, the church must understand the work of hospitality as directed toward the larger purposes of God's unfolding promise in mending creation.[38]

35. Russell draws from Dube, *Postcolonial Feminist Interpretation of the Bible*, "Postcoloniality, Feminist Spaces, and Religion," and "Go Therefore and Make Disciples of All Nations." Russell also relies upon Young, *Justice and the Politics of Difference*.

36. Russell, *Just Hospitality*, 31. Here, she also explains the theme "emancipatory difference," which will be discussed in later chapters.

37. Ibid., 49.

38. Ibid. Russell writes, "Today, God's hospitality as a partnership with humankind in the 'repair of the world' becomes the mandate as we look for ways to work with one another to transform the world." Ibid., 50.

Understanding unity and difference in the church requires self-examination and intentionality so as to not reinforce binaries—"either/or," "right/wrong," "win/lose"—or seek to create unity through uniformity.[39] In turn, a just hospitality models communion and the sharing of many gifts. She explains:

> There are numerous options for ways to faithfully express our unity in Christ and unity among religions and nations. Hospitality in community is a sharing of the openness of Christ to all as he welcomed them into God's kin-dom. Because this unity in Christ has as its purpose the sharing of God's hospitality with the stranger, the one who is "other," it assumes that unity and difference belong together. When they are not together, and unity is achieved through exclusion or domination of those who are different, this is no longer unity in Christ.[40]

The test for such unity is a community's ability to break down barriers, seek the marginalized, and welcome the outsider.

Russell develops hospitality as *partnership* with the "Other." This sort of partnership is nurtured in the community of Christ in which the source of unity is Christ's presence calling for openness to one another.[41] Russell cautions against welcoming the Other in ways that continue to suppress and the gifts that the Other brings and may even seek to conform the Other to be "like us." She recalls Henri Nouwen's observation that "Hospitality is not a subtle invitation to adopt the lifestyle of the host, but the gift of a chance to the [guests] to find [their] own."[42] The ecclesial community does not welcome in order to "convert" its guests to *one* way of doing things but as a catalyst for creating partnerships in the gospel.[43] Russell challenges the church to welcome with an openness that allows for a safe and welcoming space where each can find a sense of humanity and worth.[44]

Hospitality as partnership in the gospel is reflective of God making possible communication "across differences of language, culture, and social location (Gen 11:1–9; Acts 2:1–12)."[45] Unity, difference, hospitality, and

39. See ibid., 63–66.
40. Ibid., 65–66.
41. Ibid., 69.
42. Russell, *Church in the Round*, 173.
43. Ibid., 173.
44. See ibid., 173–75, 180–81, 192.
45. Russell *Just Hospitality,* 71–72.

overcoming what Russell terms the "impossible possibility" of differences are reflective of Christ's presence on earth, a presence that constitutes the church through the power of the Holy Spirit.[46] The "impossible possibility" is discovered in recognizing the church's grave failures to truly welcome difference today and throughout history, while also finding hope and trust that God will one day fulfill this unity of the church and mend creation. God's hospitality to humanity in Christ is the cornerstone of such good news. The church is continually transformed to see its neighbor with new eyes, to welcome and receive them as Christ, and to learn of God's welcome through the neighbor as the body of believers continues to nurture the practice of hospitality. For Russell, just hospitality opens the church toward continuing God's mission of justice concerned with ending oppression and restoring creation.[47] The ongoing work required of hospitality is the "impossible possibility" that gives the church reason to hope.

Working through challenges of unity and difference in hospitality practice may lend itself toward new ecclesial spatial imagination. In fact, perhaps Russell's most groundbreaking contribution to theology is found in her development of "church in the round" symbolized in the community gathered to the round table.[48] She cultivates the notion of a table principle that challenges the church body toward back-and-forth movement and continual discernment between margin and center. Russell calls for ecclesial communities to reread tradition and Scripture for new insight and in

46. Ibid., 68–69. Russell adds, "It is a *community of Christ* because Christ's presence, through the power of the Sprit, constitutes people as a community gathered in Christ's name (Matt 18:20; 1 Cor 12:4–6)." Ibid.

47. Russell, *Church in the Round*, 115.

48. See Russell, *Church in the Round*. Russell arrives at "church in the round" based on the notion that all are welcome *in the reign or household of God*. Ibid., 23. The ecclesial image of a round table comes from C.S. Song's description of Chinese culture and hospitality that has influenced Chinese paintings of Jesus and the disciples sharing a "last supper at the round table." Ibid., 12. In this sense, based on the celebration of the eucharist and the church gathered together around the Lord's Table, Russell notes that "the round table is a sign of the coming unity of humanity." Ibid., 17. She continues, "If the table is spread by God and hosted by Christ, it must be a table with many connections. The primary connection for people gathered around is the connection to Christ. The church is the community of faith in Jesus Christ . . . Because Christ is present in the world, especially among those who are neglected, oppressed, both church and society, always welcoming the stranger to the feast to sharing the feast where the 'others' gather. Christ's presence also connects us to one another as we share in a partnership of service. . .The round table itself emphasizes this connection, for when we gather around we are connected, in an association or relationship with one another." Ibid., 18.

order to "talk back" to the tradition using the critical lens of marginality and power relationships.[49] Russell's understanding of hospitality within a "church in the round" builds upon what she terms "kitchen table solidarity," which reflects living with and among Others and being drawn into a partnership of sharing and reflection amidst the "sweaty" tasks of daily living.[50] Her imagery is important because it highlights the fact that community, relationships, and partnerships are born in difficult and often mundane tasks. Ecclesial communities continue to be shaped as all members perform life together in "the ordinary" and not necessarily in a worship environment that may separate out the chaos and difficulty of our lives.

For Russell, hospitality practice embodies the difficult and multilayered task of the church to live as a dynamic community of faith, compassion, and justice in the world.[51] Hospitality practice is imbued with the complex human interaction of developing partnership and working together toward the common goal, of extending the welcome of God's household to all people.[52] The church must address and overcome its sins of prejudice, racism, and complicity in the status quo that neglect and cover over the voices communicating difference in the Christian community. Russell challenges the church to become an antiracist community of faith by developing awareness of contradictions between how white persons (or persons of privilege) may understand reality and how reality is keenly experienced by persons of color in social, economic, and ecclesial ways.[53] She continues, "From the

49. Russell, *Church in the Round*, 24–29.

50. Ibid., 75.

51. Russell writes, "The self understanding of the church as one body, united in one faith in Jesus Christ, would be interpreted in terms of the purpose of that unity in mission. The church is a community called to share in the passion and compassion for humankind shown by God in Jesus Christ. It is called as Christ's partner to live as a community of faith, compassion, and justice." Ibid., 173.

52. Ibid., 161, 173. "Hospitality is an expression of unity without uniformity, because unity in Christ has as its purpose the sharing of God's hospitality with the stranger, the one who is 'other.'" Ibid., 173. Also see Ogletree, *Hospitality to the Stranger*, 1–2.

53. Ibid., 156–57. Russell's ecclesiology and her turning to hospitality practice are crucial to the church's awareness of repentance of "White racism." She defines this as "a social system of domination and subordination that assigns persons of color to subordinate roles and ensures that, all other things being equal, those persons of color will always come out in the subordinate position. Along with other structures of oppression that support a hierarchy of domination and subordination on the basis of gender, sexual orientation, class, nationality, age, or physical ability, racism forms a web of oppression that operates to crush those caught in the web. The social structures that support this web include unfair distribution of political power, inadequate access to financial and material

point of view of those of us who have benefited from unearned advantage and conferred dominance, imaginative and constructive repentance includes seeing the contradictions in our ways of life and taking steps for change."[54]

Hospitality becomes the practice that infiltrates beyond a simple encounter, but rather calls persons of faith toward deeper awareness, confession, and repentance of sins of exclusion and dominance of Others in the body of Christ. In this way, even as hospitality arises from ecclesiology, hospitality practice also challenges and informs ecclesiology, transforming congregations toward deeper faithfulness in light of the persons they encounter. Nicolas Healy's earlier cited definition of the ecclesial task is instructive but not only because the concrete church performs its task of witness within ever-shifting contexts, but specifically because *"its performance is shaped by them* [italics mine]."[55] There is a careful balance between the church's faithfulness to God's call and how it discerns and appropriates this call in a specific context. The church is always provisional and always in need of critical reflection and renewal.[56] Thus, one of the central tasks of ecclesiology is: "Critical theological analysis of those contexts, and the present shape and activity of the church within them."[57] Hospitality is one

resources, inability to set cultural standards of behavior, and lack of power to name reality and define truth." Ibid. Additionally, she speaks out against forms of structural sin in which "dominant groups perpetuate structural sin because they have control of the political, economic, cultural, and educational forces that define the standard of life for the entire society and justify the status quo of that society to their own benefit." Ibid.

54. Ibid., 161–62.

55. Healy, *Church, World, and the Christian Life*, 39. Full definition reads: "The concrete church, living in and for the world, performs its task of witness and discipleship within particular, ever-shifting contexts, and its performance is shaped by them."

56. Russell, *Church in the Round*, 161–62. Also see pp. 13–14: Russell notes that the church is "always provisional and is in constant need of renewal in order to make an authentic witness to God's love and justice in the changing historical, political, economic, and social contexts."

57. Healy, *Church, World, and the Christian Life*, 39. Healy notes that the church is not simply a repository of truth, but argues that the church is better conceived by theodramatic performance in context: "A theodramatic horizon or metanarrative is particularly appropriate for reconfiguring ecclesiology as a practical prophetic discipline. This is because it can hold together in tension a number of elements that otherwise may be confused or separated or treated one-sidedly. These tensive elements include the following: the church's identity is *fully* constituted by *both* divine and human agency, permitting *theological* reflection upon the *concrete* church; the church's role includes the *formation* of the individual disciple's *distinctive* identity; the church's orientation renders it *superior* to others, yet it is *dependent* upon others and is always more or less *sinful;* the church

of the practices that most poignantly demands that the church to see itself through the eyes of another. The church's acknowledgement of sin and failure as well as dependence upon the challenges of voices both inside and outside of the church are central to its authentic witness to God's love and justice.

CONCLUSION: TOWARD A JOURNEYING HOSPITALITY AND A JOURNEYING CHURCH

Mark Griffin and Theron Walker paint the church as both "an inn for weary travelers of the borderlands/frontiers, and an *outpost of hope* for exiles bound for the city of God."[58] The juxtaposition of these images illustrates the ecclesiological tension between theology of place and theology of pilgrimage embodied within a faith community living in the midst of global migration. Holding these two images together challenges a community of faith to ask: *What is the place we embody for persons on the move? How do those we encounter and with whom we build relationships challenge and change us? How do we as a church provisionally reside and journey in the world?* The answers to these questions are rooted in the nature and mission of the church in the world and arise out of ecclesial communities' appropriation of their vision in ever-shifting contexts. The place the church offers, I argue, is intimately tied to its provisional residing and journeying in the world. In turn, the church's hospitality practice is intimately tied to its ecclesiology—as a journeying people pointing to the "already/not yet" Reign of God, ecclesial communities offer glimpses of this reign even as they continue to journey toward it.

The realities of twenty-first century migration, and specifically U.S. Latino/a migration in the United States, expose how hospitality perpetuates assimilation and occlusion of differences as well as uniformity and homogenization. U.S. Hispanic and postcolonial theologians challenge the church to recognize and embrace differences as gifts within the church body that uniquely shape the community in unity and diversity. This chapter has

---

claims to be orientated to *ultimate* truth, yet it must acknowledge that our view of that truth is *limited* by our location within the ongoing drama." Ibid., 22. Healy seeks to hold together the church's orientation toward ultimate truth in God, on the one hand, and the church's acknowledgement of sin and failure as well as dependence upon the challenges of voices outside of the church, on the Other.

58. Griffin and Walker, *Living on the Borders*, 182.

wrestled with U.S. Latino/a and postcolonial theologians' critical analysis and questions of whether hospitality is possible in light of the church's complicity in promoting homogeneity in identity, the impulse toward unity as uniformity achieved by covering over of differences, and the seemingly insurmountable power dynamics within guest and host relations. At the same time, I have tried to show that these theologians' insights also provide tools by which new discoveries in ecclesiology are possible. The church resides in the tension between its cultural manifestation and God's perpetual invitation toward something more. While this "something more" often is clouded and unidentifiable this side of the eschaton, it can only be discovered in small encounters with Others and glimpses of hope manifested *on the way.*

The following chapter begins the final section, which will center on strategic practical suggestions in response to the challenges posed to the church and hospitality in light of the context of U.S. Latino/a migration in the United States. I bring to light not merely suggestions but several current manifestations of hospitality practice that embody concrete, creative expressions with and among migrants. These lived examples are further proof that despite the insufficiency of traditional models, true hospitality is possible. The contemporary hospitality expressions I highlight uniquely arise from within ecclesial liturgy and performance, simple ecclesial practices, and communal partnerships. They exhibit the fostering of deeper relationships and the cultivating of friendships in community. Through critical theological analysis of these lived examples, I propose new conceptions of hospitality in light of how the journeying church in exile on the borders of empire continually crafts provisional places for refuge and replenishment. Becoming a church *on the way* is central for shaping the church's hospitality practice toward a radical accompaniment and *journeying with* persons who are migrating.

5

Re-Imagining Hospitality and Ecclesiology

Practical Theological Embodiments

INTRODUCTION

Reciting the poem taught to him by his father, a Cuban exile, Roberto Goizueta describes the migrant's existence through the words of Antonio Machado: "'*Caminante, no hay camino, se hace camino al andar.*' (Traveler, there is no path, the path is forged as one walks.)"[1] Much insecurity, many unknowns, and many risks mark migration journeys. As a migrant lives between two places with no firm place to stand, forging the path as one walks becomes a necessary route of survival.[2] Goizueta places the insecure and unknown journeys of migrants parallel to the ecclesiological invitation, "'*Caminemos con Jesús*' (Let us walk with Jesus)," words from a Holy Thursday liturgical procession performed by the Mexican-American parishioners of San Fernando Cathedral in San Antonio, Texas.[3] Goizueta describes his own life as living between these two statements: "*No hay camino*" and "*caminemos con Jesús*."[4] These are the cries of the exile who resides in

1. In Goizueta, *Caminemos con Jesús*, 1.

2. Segovia, "Two Places," 35.

3. Goizueta, *Caminemos Con Jesús*, 1. For further information on the San Fernando parish and its activities, see Elizondo and Matovina, *San Fernando Cathedral*.

4. Goizueta, *Caminemos con Jesús*, 1.

the "solitude and loneliness of an alien country."[5] Yet, as Goizueta notes, the inviting words, "*caminemos con Jesús*," arise from one who has discovered a new home in the midst of exile. While this home may not be a stable and secure physical place of welcome and refuge, the parishioners fashion these words into an ecclesiological invitation for dwelling-in-community and journeying together as a community of faith. They embody a new belonging and a new kind of home as "a community of persons, who as exiles themselves, are together 'walking with Jesus.'"[6]

The mobile "dwelling" of the Holy Thursday liturgical processional incorporates the journey and performance of faith together in community. The liturgy mirrors the experience of journeying as it is re-formed into a procession down the streets of San Antonio and incorporates language that speaks into the daily, lived experience of migrants. Here, accompaniment in the San Fernando parish means that the parishioners exit the comforts of their sanctuary building to enter the streets and walk with and among those marked by wandering. The language of the liturgy and the bodily movement of the procession interweave themes of exile as a stranger in a foreign land with the performative welcome of Jesus walking amongst the body of Christ.

In order to examine the integration between practices of hospitality and the life of the church more deeply, I turn to several contemporary embodiments of hospitality practice in ecclesial communities that specifically focus on welcoming Latino/a undocumented migrants. These contemporary embodiments portray new imagination and expressions of ecclesiology and hospitality that are: (1) performative, (2) reflective of early Christian communities, and (3) collective and cooperative. Each of these expressions challenges ecclesial communities' hospitality practice toward more robust and complex welcoming gestures and behaviors in relation to giving and receiving in community. At the same time, they challenge contemporary ecclesial communities toward deeper faithfulness in their embodiment of place and pilgrimage in light of twenty-first century context. The following section continues to address performative dimensions of hospitality within ecclesial liturgies and rituals.

5. Ibid.
6. Ibid.

PERFORMATIVE DIMENSIONS OF
HOSPITALITY AND ECCLESIOLOGY

Ecclesial communities' liturgical performance shapes their understanding and embodiment of faithfulness by invoking Scripture and tradition within new ecclesial contexts.[7] Eastern Orthodox theologian Alexander Schmemann notes how the original sense of *leitourgia* was "an action by which a group of people become something corporately which they had not been as a mere collection of individuals."[8] Corporate formation in *leitourgia* happens as a community gathers in particular times and places so that their life together is fashioned toward the way of the kingdom. In fact, Schmemann goes on to say that the performance of liturgy shapes the community into church: "The Church itself is a Christian *leitourgia*, a ministry, a calling to act in this world after the fashion of Christ, to bear testimony to Him and His kingdom [*sic*]."[9] Through liturgy God transforms the community, and the Spirit also guides the community's own creative and contextual witness as each gathers and follows in a specific time and place.[10] Schmemann continues,

> The journey begins when Christians leave their homes and beds. They leave, indeed, their life in this present and concrete world, and whether they have to drive fifteen miles or walk a few blocks, a sacramental act is already taking place, an act which is the very condition of everything else that is to happen. For they are now on their way to *constitute the Church*, or to be more exact, to be transformed into the Church of God. They have been individuals, some white, some black, some poor, some rich, they have been the "natural" world and a natural community. And now they have been called to "come together in one place," to bring their lives,

7. MacIntyre's work is important here for understanding traditions; He defines a living tradition as "an historically extended, socially embodied argument precisely in part about the goods which constitute that tradition. Within a tradition the pursuit of goods extends through generations, sometimes through many generations." *After Virtue: A Study in Moral Theology*, 22.

8. Schmemann, *For the Life of the World*, 25.

9. Ibid., 26. For Schmemann, the eucharist is the sacrament and *leitourgia* by which the church becomes what it is. He describes the eucharist as a journey or procession into the way of the kingdom. I will devote more attention to the centrality of eucharistic liturgy as it relates to performance and journey in the next chapter.

10. See Healy, *Church, World, and the Christian Life*, 22.

their very "world" with them and to be more than what they were: a *new* community with a new life.[11]

The community is transformed into God's new life from within the particularity of a specific context. Herein lies the good news breaking into the world in a time and place.[12] This process of transformation into the new life is ongoing. The church is continually made new, and the church's vocation is always adapting and journeying.

Liturgical and ritual performances highlight the journeying movement of the church, which in turn inspires and informs ecclesial communities' hospitality practice in new ways. Goizueta's recounting of the Holy Thursday procession demonstrates how individual bodies can be incorporated into a new pattern of journeying as the body of Christ. Though bodies marked border passage may continually be journeying and migrating for various reasons, at a moment in time they are gathered together in a particular place in the name of Christ. As they journey together through the liturgical procession, they find themselves enacting a new way of understanding human existence and how it is shaped toward God's working in the world. The journey of this new people no longer has to be forged in isolation. On Holy Thursday, good news arises as the community now journeys *together*, accompanied by Jesus. It is the embodiment of "*caminemos con Jesús.*" Persons without proper documentation are often criminalized and dehumanized, stripped of their dignity. The trials and terrors migrating persons endure in their journeys may continue to fill them with pain and shame. The invitation to worship and walk with Jesus in the liturgy is a calling to restoration and a new journey of life. It is a calling to be human in relationship with God and in relationship with others.[13] For those living in continual fear of rejection and deportation, a new way of life in the welcoming community of Christ may be good news indeed. In performing the liturgy, the San Fernando parish embodies a journeying hospitality that bears witness to God's good news in Christ.

11. Schmemann, *For the Life of the World*, 27.

12. See Lohfink, *Does God Need the Church?* Lohfink here notes, "God's new society, its arrival is not something that happens at just any time and everywhere; it is bound to a concrete place and time: to the people of the twelve tribes and its history." Ibid., 26.

13. Smith, *Desiring the Kingdom*, 167.

Las Posadas

Often celebrated in Spanish-speaking Roman Catholic parish communities, *Las Posadas* rituals originated as a specific performance of Scripture: a communal reenactment of the Luke 2:1–9 account of Joseph and Mary looking for shelter. The Spanish word *posada* means "shelter" or what has been interpreted as an "inn." Traditionally, the performance takes shape as a faith community journeys together for nine nights during Advent to reenact the difficult and inhospitable journey of Joseph and Mary searching for a place where Jesus could be born.[14] The community of *peregrinos* (or pilgrims) travel from home to home singing hymns and prayers that speak toward following the Way of Jesus as they engage in an interactive pilgrimage song that narrates Joseph and Mary's journey of rejection and refusal by the households or sites they encounter. After the *peregrinos* have been rejected at a number of homes, one site finally welcomes them in and extends gracious hospitality.

The *Posada* tradition of communal drama, street theatre, and public liturgy has been celebrated as a house-to-house procession for years in Latin America. In recent years, it has also taken on new forms in the U.S. Hispanic context, often uniting one or many faith communities within cities, towns, and neighborhood communities. Persons may travel between specific public sites of significance such as monuments, government offices, or civic and ecclesial buildings. These rituals may also be celebrated within an intimate community that travels between the homes of their neighbors. Virgilio Elizondo and Timothy Matovina describe how *Posada* performances in a U.S. Hispanic context enact two gospel themes that coincide with the experience of being an immigrant in the United States: "the *rejection* of the poor, nameless couple from the 'inferior' region of Galilee and the *joy* that comes to those who open the door of their home and heart to shelter and welcome the rejects, because they recognize them for what they truly are, God's chosen ones."[15]

In similar fashion, additional liturgies are performed during Holy Week outside of church buildings, on streets, and in public spaces. Good Friday processions, for example, involve enacting the last seven words of Christ, or the Way of the Cross, in and around a city or town. Often such rituals are specifically appropriated to the U.S. Hispanic context and relate

---

14. For more on *Posadas* see: Pineda, "Hospitality," 29–42.

15. Elizondo and Matovina, *Mestizo Worship*, 11.

to the difficult experience of migration for many followers of Christ. Rituals may re-enact Scripture by relating harsh realities of migration to Israel's exile experience, the wandering of Jesus and his followers, or persecution in the early church. Such performative liturgies offer the possibility for faith communities to embody and engage Scripture in a visible way that is meaningful to their context. Elizondo and Matovina describe the necessity for the church to enculturate the gospel so that it may be understood and lived by peoples of diverse cultures.[16] The process of helping the good news become "a natural substratum of a people's life" involves deliberate mixing with culture so the gospel becomes implanted and a truly local church begins to emerge.[17] In this sense, rituals and liturgies, as contextual embodiments of Scripture and enactments of the gospel, also become formative in shaping Christian communities into the body of Christ. In the case of *Posadas*, for example, enacting the liturgy also habituates the ecclesial community toward being a hospitable people.

As the community embodies the narrative of Scripture within its experience and context, such ritual and liturgical performance take on identity-forming and identity-renewing characteristics. The performance of Scripture inwardly nurtures a way of life within the faith community and, at the same time, continually calls the church toward incarnating the gospel outwardly for Others. The enactment of Luke's Gospel account breaks forth the good news in a new time and space. In *Posadas*, the performance of good news among migrants offers comfort and accompaniment to a community that knows rejection and what it means to be marked by wandering. Themes of rejection and joy in the ritual conjure up collective memory of lived experience. Yet, as the performance is fashioned and re-appropriated in present contexts, it also re-orients the community toward the good news they have received in Christ. They are continually reminded to greet new immigrants with the joy of Christ rather than rejection.[18] The ritual renews ecclesial identity—in ways that embrace the communities'

---

16. Ibid., 20.

17. Ibid., 12.

18. Louis Marie Chauvet draws upon Biblical scholar P. Béguerie, "The Bible is born out of the 'liturgical activity of the cultic centers where the Israelite tribes were able to fashion and reappropriate their collective memories and to identify the single eponymous ancestor, the 'Wandering Aramean' (Deut 26:5)—from whom they inherited their confession of faith in Yahweh, the one God, who was responsible for their unity.'" Chauvet, *Symbol and Sacrament*, 191.

unique contextual experiences—and prophetically calls toward further faithfulness in Christ.

Place, Performance, and Prophetic Call

As the ecclesial community performs the liturgy and appropriates according to the injustice and suffering migrants experience, an interesting relationship develops between the "place," or physical location, and the participating "bodies" (both individually and corporately). Particularly when *Posada* rituals or liturgies are brought out from ecclesial space designated for the community of faith and proceed down streets or past municipal buildings, the faith community enacts a specific ethic or scriptural way that displays prophetic outward witness in the larger community. Christians in San Diego, for example, have celebrated a citywide *Posada* procession for nearly 20 years called, *La Posada Sin Fronteras* (The Inn Without Borders).[19] This ritual highlights the plight of migrants (or pilgrims/*peregrinos*) who have died crossing the U.S.-Mexico border. Christians in Boston also celebrate several citywide *Posada* processions, one of which also calls attention to immigrant rights within the United States. The ritual takes place as an immigrant tradition and is enacted in and around a centralized public park, known as the Boston Common. The group travels through the park, to the State House and to a neighboring chapel, in each place engaging in a litany that calls these public places to justice, peace, and love particularly in their treatment and relationship to persons who have migrated to the United

19. Gates, "Communion at Friendship Park," 2–3. Gates describes: "*La Posada sin Fronteras* is a gathering of Christians on both sides of the Mexico/US border where the border meets the ocean, a breathtaking site named "Friendship Park" on the US side in 1971 by then First Lady Thelma 'Pat' Nixon. *Tijuanecos* refer to this area as *Playa de Tijuana* (Tijuana Beach). For generations residents of San Diego/Tijuana have come together at Friendship Park to be with friends and families at the one spot where they could see one another, talk to one another, and even touch one another. *La Posada Sin Fronteras* is an open air liturgical drama of lament for those who have died crossing the Mexico-US border. Conducted in both Spanish and English, celebrants sing migrant songs and Christmas carols, are often treated to a skit by local Catholic high school actors on the dangers of border crossings, receive a prophetic sermon from local clergy, declare '*presente*' as the names of the fallen are read out loud, and end the evening by lighting candles in *luminarias* artfully and lovingly decorated the night before in memory of those who have died on this border. Primarily a celebration of the hospitality, unity, and hope found in Christ and Christian fellowship, it is also a not-so-subtle critique of nationalism, border politics, and the theology/anthropology of the modern nation-state." Ibid., 1–2.

States. The performance speaks prophetically against rejection of immigrants by both state and church and calls for hospitality. The community of travelers ends their journey at an immigrant-rights non-profit organization that welcomes the travelers for a meal and celebration.

In public spaces, the ecclesial enactment becomes heightened (or hyper-visible) so that the *place* becomes symbolic to the faith community's prophetic call for change in society. The community's performance may claim the space as a sacred place in which the church resides, collapsing the divide between sacred and mundane, private and public. The community may call the power a specific place represents to greater accountability. In Boston, for example, the *Posada* pilgrims visit the State House to visibly call the state to address comprehensive immigration reform. In this case, the *Posada* ritual involves parallel purposes of witnessing to Christ, advocating on behalf of migrants, and prophetically addressing the agents of power and wealth within society.

When the community's performance assumes a more prophetic role with regard to society, however, there is an inherit risk involved. The ritual may be performed as a platform or spectacle. When other narratives and ideologies are incorporated alongside the gospel narrative the potential of conflicting allegiances may arise. It is possible that other agendas subsume the gospel for another purpose. For example, the ritual may become a spectacle that promotes a particular partisan agenda in U.S. politics and compromises the integrity of the Christian practice. Christian liturgical performance is always an iconic encounter that points to God and, therefore, directs the Christian community toward faithfulness in its witness. Performances directed toward alternative agendas risk becoming static mirrors, turned in on themselves, rather than encounters reflective of the Word of God and the way of Christ found therein. Therefore, the ecclesial community must continue to question whether it is performing another narrative or ideology (i.e. using Scripture for a certain agenda or end) or whether the witness of Christ in the liturgy, in fact, patterns the church *into* the Christian narrative.[20]

20. One cannot deny that a community's embodiment of Scripture is always interpretive—seen through the present context and circumstances of the bodies involved. Yet, the church's performance traces the narrative movement of Scripture in an active remembrance of the story of God that also calls the church forward in the faithfulness. The church's liturgical performance of Scripture remains an iconic encounter "stretched between the past it recounts and the future it announces. It continually calls the church into existence." Chauvet, *Symbol and Sacrament*, 219.

Liturgical performance cannot be reduced to a product of human effort. The community always receives liturgy as a gift. The gift of God encountered in Scripture renews the church to become a gift for the world, a sacrament of God's reign. That is to say, the church's response to the gift of God encountered in the Word is to be made a gift for the world. The church's movement in the world is always in a spirit of God's hospitality, wherein we all move together in compassion and love. This posture is derived from God's own self-giving—a giving that arises out of Trinitarian abundance and plentitude. It is from this that the church is made to always be facing outward to the world, offering God's love with open arms.

Returning to *Posada* rituals, such performances present an opportunity to encounter the spirit of Christian hospitality through the central Christian ethic of giving and receiving. Such performances habituate Christian bodies (individual and communal) to both rejection and welcome as the community and its members take on the roles of both guest and host and practice the postures of both giving and receiving. Ana María Pineda's description is fitting: "[ecclesial communities] ritually participate in being rejected and being welcomed, in slamming the door on the needy and opening it wide. They are in this way renewed in the Christian practice of hospitality, the practicing of providing a space where the stranger is taken in and known as one who bears gifts."[21] Just as participants encounter the Word of God anew in their performance, so they must also encounter the stranger as a gift. The rhythm of giving and receiving shapes bodies as they enact Scripture in unfamiliar and familiar places, and these actions form the Christian community into a new way of being.

Unpacking Place within Pilgrim Existence

In seeking to understand "place" and residence alongside the movement of journey, migration, and pilgrimage, a dialectic ensues that forms the identity and life of the church and shapes its hospitality practice. Followers of Jesus Christ are called to reside in the tension between place and pilgrimage reflected in Scripture as well as in Christian history and tradition. Both place and pilgrimage, however, have come to be understood quite differently in the contemporary context of globalization.

---

21. Pineda, "Hospitality," 31.

French philosopher Michel de Certeau notes how contemporary spatial imagery arises out of a modern framework of maps.[22] Certeau argues that from a flattened grid of a map one can view the entirety of space at once, allowing for operations and decisions to be made from a universalized center. Those who voluntarily travel for tourism may reference such maps before making a decision about where to travel. Of course, the "30,000-foot" vantage point of maps is intensified with the Internet and GPS mapping capabilities (e.g. Google Earth) through which we are made to believe we have the whole world at our fingertips. These technologies often distort our sense of place and distance. In contrast, pre-modern spatial representation of travel was understood through the notion of "itineraries" reflective of the many destinations and meeting points along a pilgrim's journey. Rather than seeing the whole all at once, pre-modern pilgrim itineraries traced paths of movement from destination to destination, and often from home to home, where the pilgrim was continually received as guest. Point to point spatial construction accentuates the points of connection—unknown persons to be encountered, hospitality to be extended and received, relationships to be built, gifts and stories to be exchanged, and meaning and identity to be constructed in key places along the journey. The understanding of pre-modern itineraries echoes back to the Judeo-Christian tradition of pilgrimage, as journey following a holy itinerary in sacred geography.[23] Christian *Posada* rituals in which communities travel from home to home similarly mirror the itinerary-based construction of pilgrim identity. Itinerary travel helps one not lose sight the importance of homes and places along the journey.

While we cannot avoid the technological advances available to us in mapping and freely recognize the great value of such tools, attention to itinerary construction lays bare the interconnectedness of distance traveled, encounters with others, and places that have shaped our lives. Itineraries provide a different vantage point than maps, offering the potential to generate new awareness of how our bodies are shaped through journeying. Similarly, because of their embodied and communal nature, contextually appropriated liturgies and rituals can help foster deeper theological discernment of place and pilgrimage in Christian identity and ecclesial formation.

22. De Certeau, *The Practice of Everyday* Life, 18–122. I draw upon William T. Cavanaugh's insights regarding Certeau's unpacking of maps presented in his essay: "The Myth of Globalization as Catholicity," in *Theopolitical Imagination*, 97–122.

23. See Inge, *A Christian Theology of Place*, 91.

Place and pilgrimage are not mutually exclusive, but are held together in Christian hospitality. I now turn to address the value of place within early Christian acts of welcome that help sustain a pilgrim on his or her journey.

EARLY CHRISTIAN PRACTICES OF HOSPITALITY

Hospitality as depicted in the Scripture is generally seen as simple gestures of welcome, such as offering a place of rest and refuge for the weary and sharing of meals and resources with wanderers. Despite the complexities of twenty-first century global migration and U.S. Latino/a immigration into the United States, one cannot neglect the necessity and impact of simple acts of welcome on behalf of persons migrating. Home, places of rest and refuge, provision, and care are often the most essential and immediate needs for many undocumented migrants as they enter the United States. Place, however temporary and difficult to find, can offer the most gracious welcome for those tired and in need of rest and refuge. Though I have challenged the static notions of place as a shortcoming in contemporary hospitality practice and ecclesiology, one cannot neglect the value of place. In fact, the movement of pilgrimage does not dismiss, but rather relies upon the needs of home and house, places of refugee, rest, and safety at various points along the journey.

Uniting place and pilgrimage, John Inge develops the notion of "storied place" out of the historical meaning, identity, and memory found in place in the Judeo-Christian tradition.[24] Inge notes, "A place, as it is coupled with past, present, and future memories, identity, and hope is a *storied* place."[25] The construction of storied place captures the perpetual movement of pilgrims or migrants through narratives in *places*, therefore not neglecting the value of place even as there may be many places experienced. While the centrality of place for Israel—seen in the symbols of holy land, temple, etc.—fades somewhat in the Christian scriptures, Inge observes how the incarnation offers a new understanding of place. God coming in the flesh established a new category of human and spiritual experience in which "the

---

24. Inge, *Christian Theology of Place*, 57. Inge draws from Brueggemann's description of the Promised Land in the Hebrew scriptures in order to expand the biblical understanding of place. For example, in Genesis two paradigms of place are quickly established: in Genesis 1:11 with expulsion from place—the Garden—and in Genesis 12:50 when Yahweh promises possession of place to Abraham. In the latter example, God's promise of dwelling overcomes the original expulsion from place. See Brueggemann, *The Land*.

25. Inge, *Christian Theology of Place*, 36.

seat of relations or the place of meeting and activity is in the interaction between God and the world."[26] Here, the church becomes a primary place between the tension of particular place and (universal) placeless character of the church at large.

It is clear in Scripture that "God relates *to* people *in* places."[27] Inge further asserts salvation as not *from* places, but *in* and *through* places.[28] Through storied place, Inge extends the notion of sacrament to encompass "sacramental encounters" within particular places and how these places come to be designated as holy. Even the final promise of salvation and restoration is expressed in terms of place—the New Jerusalem. Thus, we can understand the eschatological place of the New Jerusalem as a sacramental encounter, the abundance of God breaking into our lived experience, through people in places. The recovery of place helps the Christian community itself be a sacramental sign to the world. Places in which ecclesial communities may reside and welcome Others are precisely where a new way of life—which is their salvation—may be experienced and encountered.

The concept of storied place is not only valuable for reflecting ecclesiologically, but for uncovering the role of hospitality in continually opening a community to sacramental encounter. Sacramental encounters through place reflect the teachings and ministry of Jesus and the primitive growth of the early church. It is through simple acts of sharing that take place in ordinary *places* that Jesus extends the feast of the kingdom.[29] Koenig writes, "For Jesus, the kingdom is not so much the reigning activity of God itself as [it is] 'a community, a house, an area where the goods of salvation are available and received.'"[30] The kingdom comes and salvation is offered through the most basic elements of hospitality—sharing food, drink, and home.[31] At the same time, the value of place is not necessarily associated with it being fixed or permanent. The feast is movable and shared among

---

26. Ibid., 52.

27. Ibid., 58.

28. Ibid., 92.

29. See Koenig's chapter 2, "Sharing the Feast of the Kingdom," in *New Testament Hospitality*, 15–51.

30. Ibid., 43. Also see Sverre Aalen, "'Reign' and 'House' in the Kingdom of God in the Gospels," 223.

31. Koenig, *New Testament Hospitality*, 43–44.

neighbors.[32] Place and home are important images of God's reign, and the actions that take place within them are dynamic and multi-faceted.

The Catholic Worker Contextualized: Casa Juan Diego

The mission of the Catholic Worker—and, specifically, Casa Juan Diego in Houston, Texas—arises out of simple acts of sharing in ordinary places indicative of scriptural images of God's reign in Jesus Christ. Casa Juan Diego, by virtue of its location in Texas, fulfills its particular mission by extending hospitality to migrants and refugees. The encounter with the poor migrant and refugee takes place in sharing meals and offering a place of rest and refuge. According to Casa Juan Diego's founders Mark and Louis Zwick, since its foundation in 1980:

> more than seventy thousand refugees and migrants have passed through Casa Juan Diego, staying at least a night. Often some 150 guests have stayed the night in our Houses of Hospitality at a single time. It has not been unusual for 50 to 100 new homeless people to arrive each week. At the time we write, 500,000 meals are provided each year.[33]

Just as the Catholic Worker movement is founded on the works of mercy and mission of Matthew 25:31–46, Casa Juan Diego highlights coming to know Christ—and the kingdom—in the encounter with the poor migrant.[34] In the pattern set by Day and Maurin, hospitality and voluntary poverty are held together in the household community. Locating these moral obligations in Scripture, particularly in Matthew's account of Jesus' Sermon on the Mount, the Zwicks write:

> It is easier to do this work without compensation if we remember what Peter Maurin called the shock maxims of the Gospel: Going the extra mile, giving your extra shirt to the one who asks, loving your enemy, forgiving in the face of criticism and persecution,

---

32. Ibid., 43–44.

33. Zwick and Zwick, *Mercy Without Borders,* 39.

34. The Zwicks write, "We try to keep the perspective that, as the Gospel of St. Matthew tells us in chapter 25, Jesus himself comes to us in the guise of the poor, who today are often refugees and immigrants, and it is by how we respond to him in that guise that we shall be judged. In that Bible passage, Jesus tell[s] us what it will be like when he comes again, how he will separate us into the sheep and the goals—sheep on the right and goats on the left." Ibid., 34.

turning the other cheek, seeking first the Kingdom of God. The life of the Catholic Worker, of Casa Juan Diego, is a reversal of values seen in society. In the Kingdom, the greatest are not the most powerful, not the richest, not the strongest, not the smartest. The Lord tells us that he is present in the poor and weak.[35]

Naturally, these values are difficult to live by, especially given the tiring work of hospitality. The Zwicks note difficulties they have endured over the years since the start of Casa Juan Diego in 1980—from fires, to safety issues, to the continual need for resources, to withstanding the demands in their human bodies.[36] Despite the chaos of day-to-day challenges at Casa Juan Diego, their commitment to hospitality is primitive and sacrificial in direct response to the words of Jesus in the Gospels.

The waves of migrants and refugees they have welcomed over the years have changed over time—from Central American refugees of war to undocumented immigrants and refugees of global economic crises from Central America and Mexico.[37] Casa Juan Diego has learned to adapt its hospitality and continue to address the immediate needs of many traveling over the borders into the United States. The needs are complex and diverse—whether the house welcomes a woman who was raped during the journey and is now pregnant, a young man in his twenties who lost a limb on the train northward, or a migrant who is trying to find a brother in another U.S. city and simply needs a phone, a meal, and shelter for the night. Houses of primitive welcome like Casa Juan Diego remain the "first responders" for migrants treading what De La Torre calls "trails of hope and terror."

The Zwicks note how some people comment on the radical nature of their work, but they see it as very ordinary, though there is always much work to do.[38] The community of Casa Juan Diego responds every day to the needs of those they encounter through continual response to the complex needs of the stranger, the migrant, the refugee, and the homeless. This, in turn, shapes the lives and service of volunteers by orienting them toward the Other and toward the way of Christ in the most primitive and profound

35. Ibid., 40.

36. For further detail on these challenges, see ibid., chapter 5 "Casa Juan Diego Rises from the Ashes," 78–99, and chapter 6 "Oh, Freedom!," 100–117.

37. Additionally, the socio-economic makeup of the community surrounding Casa Juan Diego has changed over the course of 30 years. The Zwicks narrate the changes to Casa Juan Diego over time in *Mercy Without Borders*.

38. Zwick and Zwick, *Mercy without Borders*, 45.

ways. Some of the most rudimentary ecclesial practices, such as sharing food and meals together, gave birth to the early church and continue to shape people's care for one another and economic practices within ecclesial communities today.

Yet, the formation of strangers into a community of friends—and not food, drink, and homes in and of themselves—is the most fundamental element of Christian hospitality and ecclesiology. The way of life nurtured in community, which may take place in a home or on the road, deeply shapes Christians in discipleship and in relationship with one another so as to offer the love of God to the world. God continually is shaping God's people "on the way" in this journey. Through relationships nurtured in *koinonia*, the church always is becoming and being made new. The simple elements of hospitality reflective of early Christian communities remain important because these are the ingredients that have comprised the church; yet, these elements also can be re-appropriated and juxtaposed with new features that contribute to fresh embodiments of church today.

COLLECTIVE PARTNERSHIP IN HOSPITALITY

Hospitality expands to new, complex, and unique territories as ecclesial communities develop communal and corporate partnerships in the context of twenty-first century migration. The wide array of needs and life challenges that migrants experience may outweigh the services and support one community can offer. Hospitality in today's context can be more expansively offered when Christian and non-Christian communities collaborate in assisting migrants. An ecclesial community's knowledge of other service agencies for migrants in a geographical community may allow it to provide a more holistic welcome to migrants. Additionally, as communities build relationships with one another, the spirit of partnership between them grows. In fact, this partnership, as it exhibits relationship building, can become an exercise in hospitality itself.

In *This Bridge Called My Back*, activist and author Gloria Anzaldúa plays with Antonio Machado's poetic words: "'*Caminante, no hay camino, se hace camino al andar.*' (Traveler, there is no path, the path is forged as one walks.)"[39]. She writes, "*Caminante no hay puente, se hace puente al andar.*"[40] (Traveler, there is no bridge, the bridge is made as one walks.) Replacing

39. In Goizueta, *Caminemos Con Jesús*, 1.

40. Anzaldúa, foreword to the 2nd ed. of *This Bridge Called My Back*, iv.

"way" with "bridge," Anzaldúa insinuates how life is sustained and survival made possible in the borderlands. While borders and boundaries may be set up to divide, they are also points of crossing. Such crossing is made possible (and made safely passable) when bridges are constructed. Anzaldúa's work encourages and challenges women in the hope and courage necessary for building bridges; she writes: "Mujeres, a no dejar que el peligro del viaje y la inmensidad del territorio nos asuste—a mirar hace adelante y a abrir paso en el monte (*Women, let's not let the danger of the journey and the vastness of the territory scare us—let's look forward and open paths in these woods).*"[41] Many U.S. Latino/a and postcolonial theologians discuss bridge-building as a strategy for survival and human flourishing on borders and in the borderlands for both individuals and communities.[42] For Goizueta, the words *"caminemos con Jesús"* creates a bridge that unites people in a new way of relating and coming together in the world through the Way of Christ. As a community builds bridges, it transcends borders that divide and transforms them into border passages. Bridges do not erase differences, but they permit crossing so difference can be encountered and joined in relationship. Bridge-building also proves an important image for exploring ecumenical, interfaith, and intercultural partnerships that cross the "divides" within faith and society. Below, I explore bridge-building activities in reference to hospitality and migration in the borderland town of El Paso, Texas.

Building Bridges in El Paso

"El Paso" which literally means "the pass" or "passage" in Spanish, is located along the U.S.-Mexico border in West Texas. The international Bridge of the Americas that spans the Rio Grande (or Río Bravo) links El Paso to its southern neighbor, Ciudad Juárez, Mexico. An estimated two million persons live in the El Paso/Juárez metropolitan area, with two thirds estimated to be located in Juárez.[43] In El Paso, one can quickly encounter a network

---

41. Ibid.

42. See authors featured in edited volume Moraga and Anzaldúa, eds., *This Bridge Called My Back*; and Russell, et al., *Inheriting Our Mothers' Gardens*.

43 See http://www.elpasotexas.gov/demo.asp. See link to PDF "Fact Sheet El Paso/ Ciudad Juárez," which describes the challenges of identifying an accurate population for Ciudad Juarez. Also see PDF, "Historical Population of El Paso/Ciudad Juárez," for a combined population figure from 2006.

of Christian communities and of non-profit organizations with no faith affiliation, each addressing aspects of undocumented immigrants rights, welcome, and care. Although working with undocumented migrants is risky business, various organizations and houses of hospitality intentionally focus their work toward accompanying migrants in the various situations they encounter in the United States.[44] Undocumented migrants, persons in need of immediate medical attention, victims of abuse, single men and women, families, etc. each require different sorts of immediate assistance. Partnership is crucial to ensure immediate needs are met as quickly as possible.

El Paso is home to several Christian hospitality houses whose mission and work is similar to those of Casa Juan Diego in Houston. Annunciation House is one such Christian hospitality house that opened its doors in 1978 "in a Gospel spirit of service and solidarity."[45] The house specifically services undocumented persons who often are not eligible to receive social services available to the poor because of lack of *papeles* (papers or documentation of citizenship or visa). Annunciation House commits to, "accompany the migrant, homeless, and economically vulnerable peoples of the border region through hospitality, advocacy, and education."[46] The community seeks to place itself "among these poor so as to live our faith and transform our understanding of what constitutes more just relationships between peoples, countries, and economies."[47] Annunciation House offers food, shelter, and connections to the community where persons mi-

44. For example, the Annunciation House, which will be referenced below, describes the risk they undergo as follows: "Specifically, volunteers understand that their decision to live and work among these poorest of the poor—to offer hospitality to the undocumented stranger among us—carries with it a certain amount of risk. While the nature and consequence of that risk is not quantifiable, we recognize that efforts have been underway in the United States to make life unbearable for the undocumented and to penalize those of us who serve them. For example, legislation proposed in 2005 (HR 4437) threatened to criminalize groups and individuals who provide humanitarian assistance to the undocumented. In this punitive environment that generates such inhumane legislation, we at Annunciation House remain committed to serving our immigrant sisters and brothers regardless of their immigration status. Our decision to serve and to bear witness to their reality remains a choice of conscience. As Cardinal Roger Mahony, Archbishop of the Diocese of Los Angeles, poignantly reminded us, 'Denying aid to a fellow human being violates a law with a higher authority than Congress—the law of God.'" http://annunciationhouse.org/about-2/who-we-serve/.

45. See http://annunciationhouse.org/mission/.

46. Ibid.

47. Ibid.

grating may be able to find assistance. Over the span of more than 30 years, Annunciation House has hosted close to 90,000 refugees, immigrants, and undocumented persons from over 40 countries.[48]

Located just 10 blocks from the U.S.-Mexico border, the house may be the first stop for a person who just crossed the border. A person migrating may have heard about Annunciation House on the journey or stayed at the house during prior arrivals to the United States. Interestingly, at times, he or she may have been directed to Annunciation House by border patrol or Immigration and Customs Enforcement (ICE). When the house is full or it is not advisable for families or single women to be housed there, the staff may recommend other services in the community. This network of service agencies and ecclesial communities works together to help vulnerable migrants survive and build connections. The Opportunity Center homeless shelter a few blocks north may provide temporary shelter for single men, and families may arrange temporary refuge through a Roman Catholic parish. Additionally, women and men who have connections to work on farms in Texas and New Mexico may find shelter, food, and transportation assistance at *Centro de Trabajadores Agrícolas Fronterizados* (Center for Border Farmworkers), located close to the border bridge and situated across the street from the Department of Homeland Security (DHS).[49] Others may find spiritual counseling at Sacred Heart Church[50] or undocumented single mothers may join a cooperative at *Mujer Obrera* (Woman Worker)[51] to get training and secure work to support their families. These organizations and the services they provide illustrate bridges built out of a common vision to walk alongside persons migrating in and through El Paso. Amidst the work of hospitality, the "workers" or "hosts" themselves may discover friendships and support in their unique alliances with strangers and partners.[52]

Koenig challenges Christians toward new frontiers of hospitality by forming partnerships and alliances with strangers today. In order to

48. See http://annunciationhouse.org/voice-of-the-voiceless/.

49. See the Centro de Trabajadores Agrícolas Fronterizados Website: http://www.farmworkers.org/centresp.html.

50. See the Sacred Heart parish Website: http://www.sacredheartelpaso.org/. "Our church is located 3 blocks from the Mexican border where El Paso (population 750,000) meets her twin city Juárez (population 3,000,000). Our neighborhood, known as the "Segundo Barrio" or "Second Ward," is one of the poorest neighborhoods in the US with a host of problems and social challenges."

51. See http://www.mujerobrera.org/mission.html.

52. See Koenig, *New Testament Hospitality*, 124.

accomplish this, Christians must move "through the ordinary events of our days with a readiness for partnership."[53] One of the most challenging aspects of this readiness is the courage to begin and the open oneself to, what Koenig terms, a "ministry of introduction." The organizations and ecclesial communities listed above demonstrate the value of partnership with strangers, daring to build a bridge even where the political climate for assisting undocumented persons is unfriendly at best. Koenig notes that "in the risky business of bringing alienated people together, introducers must see through the stereotypes and fears that prevent mutual welcoming so as to claim ground for the powerful exchange of gifts which happens when partnerships between strangers are actually forged."[54] Bridge-building partnerships in El Paso illustrate how the fears of introductions and the challenges of forging new relationships are overcome. Hospitality practice on behalf of migrants is strengthened through the matrix of communities welcoming and walking alongside individuals and families, and forging relationships with other communities who do the same. The spirit of collaboration overcomes the fears and risks that pervade the borderlands, not to mention the competition for scarce resources.

Partnership in Advocacy, Awareness, and Education

A ministry of introduction and the development of partnership between the above communities begin by meeting the needs of migrants. They then extend into advocacy, awareness, and education regarding the challenges migrants face. Many congregations, ecclesial groups, and non-profit groups in El Paso generate funding and support by hosting border experience trips in El Paso/Juarez. These trips may include college students, professors or professionals, church groups, or other parties interested in learning about the complex issues that affect life in the border areas and the persons that pass between them. The Annunciation House began offering a Border Awareness Experience in 1990.[55] The intention behind these trips is to facilitate face-to-face encounters between participants and both persons and groups residing in the border region in hopes of raising participants' consciousness about issues of immigration, economic development, human

53. Ibid., 125.
54. Ibid., 128.
55. See http://annunciationhouse.org/baexperience.

rights, and social justice.[56] As part of the border immersion experiences, the groups practice partnership by arranging visits to organizations on the U.S. side of the border so that participants can learn about the justice and hospitality work that each organization offers.

Partnership in advocacy, awareness, and education is valuable for assessing how an ecclesial community's hospitality practice can be dynamically shaped toward *journeying with* persons who are migrating. Hospitality does not always end with the provision of a single night's shelter or a meal, but can also include addressing the daily challenges migrants face for survival. Because communities of hospitality may not journey with migrants in every aspect, communal partnerships help fill in the gaps. I offer two snapshots of integral partnerships drawing from the work of non-profit organizations in the El Paso area—La Mujer Obrera and Centro de los Trabajadores Agrícolas Fronterizados. These two organizations exemplify advocacy and accompaniment alongside migrants seeking to establish economic livelihoods north of the border. More specifically, they demonstrate advocacy through grassroots mobilization and community organizing. They address the ongoing economic needs of migrants not only as they enter the United States, but also as they seek a living on that side of the border. Though these organizations are not faith-based, they have become invaluable partners for many ecclesial communities. They have taught these communities the economic realities migrants face and how to walk with and among persons migrating in and through El Paso.

Community Organizing: La Mujer Obrera and Sin Fronteras

La Mujer Obrera began in 1981 in response to this question: "In the midst of globalization, how do we, as women and as workers, defend our rights and build sustainable communities rooted in justice and human dignity?"[57] The

56. Ibid.

57. The Mujer Obrera Website describes three focus areas: "Women's Empowerment: Secure the right and the capacity to develop as women, in community, and for our families, as a people with a history and a rich cultural heritage to affirm and share; Economic Development: Generate women's economic empowerment through social enterprises, small business support, and bilingual workforce development; and Community Development: Build community, while sustaining our roots through neighborhood revitalization, job creation, housing development, and educational projects that celebrate Mexican cultural heritage, as Mexican immigrant women workers." http://www.mujerobrera.org/mission.html.

organization focuses on empowerment, economic development, and community development specifically for women who are Mexican immigrant workers. Of the many programs offered at Mujer Obrera, *El Puente* (The Bridge) specifically focuses on the economic and labor needs of women following the changes that ensued as a result of the 1997 North American Free Trade Agreement (NAFTA). Mujer Obrera recognizes the displacement, trauma, and impact on women and workers that NAFTA caused, specifically for those women living and working in the South Central *barrio* (community), the former Garment District of El Paso.[58] In chapter 2, De La Torre's insights helped me to unravel NAFTA's negative consequences for vulnerable populations living south of the border. Yet, El Paso's Garment District and the agriculture industry of the Southwest United States also were deeply affected by NAFTA. After 1997, the majority of the garment district factories moved to *maquiladores* south of the U.S.-Mexico border. As a result, 3,000 women in El Paso lost their jobs. In light of this tragedy, Mujer Obrera's El Puente program seeks to generate economic opportunity for women by offering training in job creation, micro-enterprise development, social enterprises, and small business support. To strengthen community members' skills and knowledge, El Puente offers entrepreneurial and workforce training, basic skills education, and access to technology. El Puente seeks to build community capacity while sustaining cultural roots through house and neighborhood revitalization, cultural enrichment and arts programs, and urban agriculture and healthy living initiatives.[59]

The Centro de los Trabajadores Agrícolas Fronterizos, located in an 8,000 square foot facility just over the U.S.-Mexico border on the Border Highway, is part of the *Sin Fronteras* (Without Borders) Organizing Project.[60] The organization exists to meet the immediate needs of agricultural

58. See http://www.mujerobrera.org/elpuente.html.

59. "With these programs, in conjunction with its parent La Mujer Obrera, El Puente has achieved outstanding results and recognition for women's empowerment and community economic development including the conversion of four dilapidated buildings into a hub for dynamic neighborhood revitalization and seven social purpose businesses: Rayito del Sol Daycare, Café Mayapan, Uxmal Apartments, Lummetik Trading Company, Mercado Mayapan Festival Marketplace, CDBES, and PLAN MAYACHEN." http://www.mujerobrera.org/elpuente.html.

60. The Sin Fronteras Organizing Project: http://www.farmworkers.org/sinfreng.html is a non-profit organization in Texas that began in 1993 as part of a growing labor movement on the U.S.-Mexico border. The organizing and educational work of Sin Fronteras (meaning without borders) takes place in the border region that links Southern New Mexico, far West Texas, and Northern Chihuahua where 14,000 farm laborers live

workers and their families and to organize workers to challenge and change the (public and private) agricultural system's perpetuation of exploitation and poverty.[61] The center offers services to farmworkers and low-income residents in the El Paso-Juárez area, which include English classes, arts and recreation for children and adults, a cafeteria, and a modest clinic. It operates 24 hours a day—as a refuge for agricultural laborers needing safety and shelter in the evening and as a place of service to the general public during regular business hours.

It is estimated that 12,000 agricultural workers live or work in the New Mexico and Texas region, and 5,000 of them are *chile*-pickers.[62] The Center draws attention to how these workers "suffer the most inhumane recruitment practices and the worst working conditions existing in the Southwest."[63] *Chile*-pickers are the lowest paid agricultural laborers. Many lack a place to live. Few have access to medical services and educational opportunities. Additionally, women who work in the fields—many of whom are single mothers and heads of household—often earn less than men while suffering abuse and sexual harassment.[64] The typical workday of a *chile*-picker involves long hours, backbreaking labor, and little job security and protection against abuse. The workers often wait for two hours at the recruitment site and spend four hours total traveling to and from the fields; then they work six to eight hours picking *chiles* and wait one to two hours more to get paid.[65] When their potentially 16-hour workday is complete, the farmworkers may earn about $30 USD each.[66] To accommodate the

and work.

61. The history of migrant agricultural workers between Mexico and the United States runs deep, and one of the roles of the Centro and Sin Fronteras is to raise awareness about this history. For more information on this history and that of the Braceros program see: http://www.farmworkers.org/bracerop.html; http://www.farmworkers.org/immigrat.html; http://www.farmworkers.org/usneedbp.html; http://www.farmworkers.org/bpaccord.html.

62. http://www.farmworkers.org/bawpdesc.html. Also see http://www.farmworkers.org/chileeng.html for a description of the *chile* industry. *Chiles* are used in many products the most famous of which is "picante" sauce. The website adds: "New Mexico produces two-thirds of all the chile peppers consumed in this country."

63. Ibid.

64. Ibid.

65. http://www.farmworkers.org/bawpdesc.html.

66. See http://www.farmworkers.org/chileeng.html: "Chile pickers get paid by "piece" rate for what they each produce. For example, for each bucket of "California" without stem, the chile picker receives one plastic chip. Each chip is worth 60 cents. In order for a

needs of agricultural laborers Centro de los Trabajadores Agrícolas Fronterizos offers food and shelter for the farmworkers who have to meet the bus transportation to the fields at 2:00 am each morning. Each night, the center's multi-use room is converted into lodging at 9:00 pm. The floor is lined with wall-to-wall mats and farmworkers trying to get a few hours of sleep before the 16-hour day begins again.[67]

Sin Fronteras and the Center collaborate on the Border Agricultural Workers Project, which seeks to improve the lives of the poor agricultural workers and their families. Specifically, the project promotes and protects the civil and human rights of both documented and undocumented agricultural workers. The project organizes the farmworker community into committees to raise consciousness among workers and to put collective pressure on employers with the goal of improving the working conditions and increasing services offered for farmworkers.[68] The Sin Fronteras project reveals how "the combination of poverty, lack of education, inability to speak English and fear of losing their jobs makes farmworkers vulnerable to unjust practices, low wages and hazardous working and living conditions."[69] For these reasons, the advocacy role the Centro plays is crucial to many migrants' survival and well-being.

The New Sanctuary Movement

Many faith based organizations throughout the United States also inspire ecumenical and interfaith partnership as they advocate in Congress for immigrants' rights and more comprehensive services for immigrants, including food, shelter, legal services, medical attention, etc. This type of advocacy

picker to make at least the Minimum Wage they have to fill eight buckets, which contain about 40 pounds of product, then carry it to a trailer to be unloaded every single hour."

67. There are two murals in the center; the multi-use room houses one. The second is located on the first floor level multi-use room. The mural "tells the story of a farm worker's day, but contains an overlaying tone of life and hope that farm workers experience as basic human beings. The story begins as a night-time scheme representing how the workers rise at 2 a.m. to wait for the buses that will take them to the fields. The moon and stars gradually turn to daylight showing a mountain range serving as a background for three children dancing around a tree. A blue river runs through the mural originating at the moon in the nighttime scheme and represents a river of dreams. This river passes through the head of one of the children representing the dreams we embrace as children." http://www.farmworkers.org/centreng.html.

68. http://www.farmworkers.org/bawpdesc.html.

69. Ibid.

is distinct from grassroots mobilization and often is led by persons who have U.S. citizenship and use their voice and vote to represent migrants.[70] One such partnership network is the New Sanctuary Movement, which has chapters throughout the United States to facilitate collaboration and partnership among faith communities, particularly in major metropolitan areas such as Los Angeles, Chicago, and New York. The Sanctuary Movement, predecessor to the New Sanctuary Movement, began in the early 1980s as a result of the influx of Central American refugees fleeing the human rights violations of their governments and entering the United States. Many were denied refugee or asylum status because of the relationships the U.S. has with their countries of origin. In response, Roman Catholic, Protestant, and Jewish communities offered advocacy support, sanctuary, and social services to these migrants. The network also actively sought to change federal immigration policy. Beginning in 2005, religious leaders and faith communities united to form the New Sanctuary Movement, which specifically devoted attention to accompanying and protecting undocumented immigrant families at risk for discrimination, unjust working conditions, and deportation.[71]

The efforts of ecclesial communities in immigration advocacy, awareness, and education have the potential to influence large groups of people to better understand the realities that cause persons to migrate to overcome the misunderstanding perpetuated within the United States and even many Christian congregations. Simple actions toward promoting awareness can be instrumental in re-shaping ecclesial communities' understanding and practice of hospitality with and among persons migrating.[72] The New Sanc-

70. Words like "advocate" and "represent" raise immediate postcolonial objections because migrants' voices are being interpreted by others and not heard in their own right. For this reason, there is an inherent danger is advocacy organizations and networks like the New Sanctuary Movement. Nonetheless, their work can still be extremely valuable. To overcome these dangers I argue that migrants must be instrumental in the gathering and actions set forth by these groups, even when they are unable to cast a vote or speak publically because they are undocumented.

71. See http://www.sanctuarymovement.org.

72. For example, see 2006 Pew Hispanic Center study, "Attitudes Toward Immigration: In the Pulpit and the Pew," by Gregory A. Smith http://pewresearch.org/pubs/20/attitudes-toward-immigration-in-the-pulpit-and-the-pew. The study surveyed views of white evangelical Protestants, white mainline Protestants and white non-Hispanic Catholics (who together account for nearly 60% of the population)—as well as on the views of secular Americans, who comprise 11% of the public regarding the relationship between religion and attitudes on immigration. The study concludes: "Regardless of their religious background, Americans have serious concerns about immigration and favor a

tuary Movement advocates on behalf of immigrants and continually challenges congregations and denominations to consider the broader context of migration and what is at stake for the most vulnerable populations.

Partnership networks, such as Sin Fronteras and the New Sanctuary Movement, offer a multilayered response to issues surrounding immigration and new possibilities for shaping hospitality practice partnership. Parker Palmer names partnership in advocacy and awareness as one of the major vocations of the church.[73] This vocation involves "host[ing] dialogues between groups in the community who are, or may be, in conflict . . . [i.e.] such groups as teachers and school boards, teenagers and police, blacks and whites in 'changing neighborhoods,' labor and management, 'gays' and 'straights.'"[74] The vocation of fostering dialogue proves particularly important in reference to immigration because it is a politically heated issue in the United States. Much misunderstanding and a lack of knowledge surrounding why persons migrate, their life in the United States, and their effect on the nation pervade the U.S. national consciousness, including the church.[75] Christian congregations, denominations, and para-church organizations are divided in their understandings of immigration.[76] In fact, immigration

---

cautious approach to immigration policy. This is true even of Catholics and mainline Protestants, whose leaders have been quite outspoken in support of immigrants and a more hospitable immigration policy. But within each of the three largest religious groups in the U.S., the most religiously committed Americans tend to hold views that are more favorable toward immigrants. While church shepherds may not be getting through to all of their flock, they may be having better luck reaching their most attentive parishioners." Ibid., 4. A companion piece focuses on the views of African Americans on the subject of immigration.

73. See Koenig, *New Testament Hospitality*, 128.

74. Palmer, *Company of Strangers*, 131, quoted in Koenig, *New Testament Hospitality*, 128.

75. See Smith, "Attitudes Toward Immigration in the Pulpit and Pew." http://pewresearch.org/pubs/20/attitudes-toward-immigration-in-the-pulpit-and-the-pew.

76. Ibid. The studies showed: "Overwhelming majorities across the religious spectrum see Hispanics in a favorable light and view immigrants from Latin America as a hard-working group with strong family values. But when asked about the impact of immigrants on American society and the U.S. economy, many more Americans (including members of each of the three largest religious groups) express negative views. Nearly half of the public, for instance, agrees with the statement that the growing number of newcomers threaten traditional American customs and values, compared with 45% who say that newcomers strengthen American society." The study continues, "White non-Hispanic Catholics and white mainline Protestants closely resemble the public as a whole on this question. White evangelicals seem to be particularly wary of the impact of newcomers, with 63% of them seeing immigrants as a threat to U.S. customs and values."

has come to be described as an "issue" rather than a concern regarding the safety and security of the persons migrating. A central component of hospitality for congregations today is facilitating awareness and education, as well as healthy conversation for Christians regarding immigration.[77]

Risks in Partnership and Hospitality

Partnerships with strangers always will come with some amount of individual and corporate risk. Risk is necessary for forging genuine partnership and friendship just as it is for extending and receiving true hospitality. An encounter with a stranger is an encounter for both parties. As a relationship forms, intentional adjustments and changes must be made in order for each person to respond to the Other. An encounter entails a revealing of oneself and a receiving of the Other, by which a careful process of making room happens between strangers. Interfaith partnerships and partnerships forged with secular organizations can often be interpreted as a risk or threat for a Christian community. Missiologist Lesslie Newbigin describes how Christians are called to dialogue and partnership with non-Christians:

> But this does not mean that the purpose of dialogue is to persuade the non-Christian partner to accept the Christianity of the Christian partner. Its purpose is not that Christianity should acquire one more recruit. On the contrary, *obedient* witness to Christ means that whenever we come with another person (Christian or not) into the presence of the cross, we are prepared to receive judgment and correction, to find that our Christianity hides within its appearance of obedience the reality of disobedience. Each meeting with a non-Christian partner in dialogue therefore puts my own Christianity at risk.[78]

The risk in this scenario is that the Stranger and the Other simultaneously invite *me* or *us* into another way. What is more, they *demand* that I see myself from a new perspective and, in showing me myself anew, they demand that I change. The stranger may confront me with my own shortcomings

---

77. Churches do need to be cautious about hosting some conversations within church buildings. It is important for congregations to ensure, as much as possible, that persons migrating feel safe and welcome within the walls of the church. Other spaces can be sought in which dialogue, education, and mutual understanding is sought between Christian communities and other groups which may oppose immigration.

78. Newbigin, *The Open Secret*, 182. Also see Stone, *Evangelism after Christendom*, 165.

and require my transformation in the spirit of repentance.[79] This relationship-building and partnership process ought to be seen in light of the accompaniment and journey required in all relationships, friendships, and partnerships. Though there may be different motivations underlying each community's welcome of migrants, each encounter with another presents an opportunity to learn from one another. Naturally, there are limits to these partnerships that must be discerned and negotiated by ecclesial communities. At times, a congregation may discern that they cannot participate in another partner's activities because the activities do not reflect what they profess in Christ. At other times, the Christian community will be brought to repentance and deeper faithfulness in light what is revealed to them through these relationships.[80]

CONCLUSION

Performative and early Christian expressions of hospitality, along with collective and cooperative partnerships, are vital expressions of both hospitality and broader ecclesial life in the twenty-first century. The contemporary manifestations I explored in this chapter emphasize the dynamic nature of the gospel as it is lived among diverse communities of people in new contexts. Performance of liturgy, as it involves an ecclesial community's

---

79. In this spirit, Healy seeks to: "Maintain the tension between claims for the church's orientation to the ultimate truth on the one hand and, on the other, acknowledgement of ecclesial sin and of the church's dependence upon the challenges and insights of those religious and non-religious bodies that are orientated primarily to other truths." Healy, *Church, World, and the Christian Life*, 19. Later he adds, "In all its forms, this practical-prophetic ecclesiology enables the church to engage self-critically with other religious and non-religious traditions of inquiry at the level of their respective concrete identities." Ibid., 22.

80. Newbigin in *The Open Secret* writes, "There is no substitute for the gift of discernment, no set of rules or institutional provisions by which we can be relieved of the responsibility for discernment. Dialogue cannot be 'made safe for all possible risks.' The Christian who enters into dialogue with people of other faiths and ideologies is accepting this risk. But to put *my* Christianity at risk is precisely the way by which I can confess Jesus Christ as Lord—Lord over all worlds and Lord over my faith. It is only as the church accepts the risk that the promise is fulfilled that the Holy Spirit will take all the treasures of Christ, scattered by the Father's bounty over all the people and cultures of mankind [*sic*], and declare them to the church as the possession of Jesus." Newbigin, 188. He adds: "The mystery of the gospel is not entrusted to the church to be buried in the ground. It is entrusted to the church to be risked in the change and interchange ofthe spiritual commerce of humanity." Ibid., 189.

bodily movement and can creatively be adapted to contexts or brought out into public spaces, reveals great potential as a practice that helps shape a journeying hospitality with and among migrants. Performance of Scripture as liturgy, evidenced in *Posadas* rituals and Holy Thursday processions, can become contextualized liturgies of the Christian community that gather it into the body of Christ while simultaneously embodying the community's own experiences, character, and creativity. Liturgical performance encompasses patterns of pilgrimage and journey, which take on new shapes and forms when appropriated in new contexts. In these performances, an ecclesial community is drawn out of the comforts of place and confronted with the challenges of pilgrimage. This frees the faith community to discover the people and places of its larger geographical community anew. As a result, ecclesial communities gain new perspectives and open themselves to new relationships as they emerge from the walls of a church building.

The many challenges migrants face journeying and seeking livelihood north of the U.S.-Mexico border motivate the church to recover the value of early Christian expressions of hospitality. Though my re-conceiving of a dynamic, *journeying* hospitality calls for further engagement and critical analysis beyond simple acts of welcome or provision of food in the context of migration, shelter, food, and care remain significant needs for vulnerable persons. The mission and services of Casa Juan Diego are simple, yet living this out is far from easy. Their actions demonstrate formation into the body of Christ, as revealed through Jesus' sacrificial service. The fact that Casa Juan Diego has opened its doors to migrants, refugees, and strangers for more than 30 years signifies that the "place" of their hospitality is of extreme importance. Their rootedness in a specific community has helped them become known as a place of refuge and welcome. At the same time, as the socio-economic status of the inhabitants in their geographical has changed, the ministry has had to adapt. Hospitality work in this place will continue to require discernment and negotiation for years to come as changes in the community present the ministry with new challenges and opportunities for service. It is clear that a community's "placedness" does not mean that it neglects to adapt, change, and adjust its welcome according to the persons who walk in the doors.

Finally, I investigated the value of communal and corporate partnerships in shaping hospitality through the relationships developed between agencies and ecclesial communities in El Paso, Texas. In order to sustain a journeying hospitality with and among migrants, it is essential to build bridges and develop partnerships between congregations, para-church organizations, non-profit social service agencies, and community organizing efforts. The partnership between the Annunciation House, Sacred Heart Roman Catholic parish, Mujer Obrera, and Centro de Trabajadores Agrícolas Fronterizado allowed them to challenge one another toward a broader scope of welcome, services, and mutual learning. One organization could not address all of the complex factors and challenges migrants face, but a network of organizations offers a much more comprehensive welcome and response. Learning opportunities provided by a network of organizations also uncover the interconnected and difficult situations migrants face that may have been previously overlooked, hidden, or neglected. The vulnerable economic state of migrants and the lack of protection for undocumented farmworkers are fertile grounds for concealed exploitation. Additionally, the interactions involved in developing communal partnerships can become expressions of hospitality themselves. Often ecclesial communities may shy away from non-Christian agencies, but partnering with nonprofits and community organizing efforts provides an opportunity to learn about unseen issues migrants face, and an opportunity to be challenged by new relationships to adapt, change, or even repent. In journeying with and among migrants, the challenge does not end with the work of hospitality, but extends to finding the courage for a ministry of introduction. New partnerships come with the risk of change. Yet, any practice of hospitality demands this risk.

Performative, simple, and cooperative expressions of hospitality and of what it means to be the church will continue to be explored in the next chapter alongside two central practices of ecclesiology—eucharist and baptism. I will examine how the practice of eucharist shapes and forms the ecclesial community toward new spatial imagination and journeying together in hospitality and ecclesiology. Eucharistic practices also continually challenge the church to be confronted anew by those it encounters. Grounding both ecclesiology and hospitality, the eucharist guides the church's discernment and action so that the community is continually directed toward the way of Jesus Christ and oriented to share God's gifts with the world. Additionally, the eucharist is central to forming the Christian community's economic ethic, which is vital to its hospitality practice in light of the economic challenges many migrants face as they reside in the United States. I also will explore how baptism—as a central practice that unites the church into a new humanity in Christ—complements eucharistic formation and deeply informs Christian hospitality practice, relationship-building, and *koinonia*. Christian identity learned in baptism is predicated upon the many different expressions of humanity being celebrated and united in Christ, rather than covered over or assimilated into the dominant majority of an ecclesial community.

6

Eucharistic Formation of a Hospitable Community

INTRODUCTION

THE PREVIOUS CHAPTER INTRODUCED several strategic, practical suggestions for the re-imagination of hospitality practice that revealed dynamics of accompaniment and journey with and among migrants. This chapter continues to build on contemporary expressions of hospitality in the United States ecclesial context in order to deepen hospitality *praxis* in light of twenty-first century migration. I focus on ways eucharistic practices manifest themselves in socio-historical contexts and help to shape Christian communal praxis in relation to transnational migration. I treat the eucharist as a sustaining sacrament, as well as an informal shared meal, that continues to form and shape the church community socially and ethically. I also briefly discuss baptism as an initiating sacrament that guides the church in its identity and calling to be a hospitable people. In the first section, I examine two contemporary expressions of hospitality arising out of ecclesial communities' eucharistic practice as they seek justice for undocumented migrants along the U.S.-Mexico border. The broader ties between hospitality practice and ecclesiology become more evident as I explore how the practice of the eucharist shapes the community to recognize the economic and political implications in their gathering, residing, journeying, and offering of hospitality with and among migrants in Jesus' name.

EUCHARIST AT THE U.S.-MEXICO BORDER

The eucharist can be practiced as an expression of hospitality, particularly when the community celebrates this meal in new spaces outside of the walls of the church. Below I explore two incidences of sharing eucharistic meals across the U.S.-Mexico border. While one reflects a high sacramental theology and the other embodies the low church tradition, they both challenge ecclesial communities toward new visions of hospitality across borders. The ecclesial images of household and table are extended into to new symbols and traveling metaphors that arise from the eucharist performed at the border. The harvest and production of the eucharist grapes and grain together with the centrality of meals and the nourishment they provide, remain central to this eucharistic formation. Additionally, the performance of the eucharist across the border makes space for new relationships and for the sharing of gifts across the cultural, geographic, linguistic, political, etc. divides symbolized by the border/*La Frontera*. Additionally, the eucharist performs the possibility of new relationships and the sharing of gifts across the many divisions that this border both symbolizes and enacts. These two expressions illustrate aspects of a journeying hospitality that foster deeper relationships and friendships, and confront ecclesial communities with the economic implications of the eucharist.

The celebration of the Lord's Supper across the U.S.-Mexico border is a formative and symbolic expression of the unity of the body of Christ across national boundaries. It reminds the church that God's household is without walls and borders and God's feast is movable, and shapes the church to reflect that reality. Additionally, the eucharistic meals provide sustenance for a church characterized by pilgrimage and journeying. Eucharistic patterns direct the church toward the Reign of God as it is gathered into a new community. I begin with the borderland of El Paso/Ciudad Juárez and will turn to San Diego/Tijuana borderland region later in the chapter.

The El Paso/Ciudad Juárez Borderland

In November 2003, bishops, priests, and lay people of the dioceses of El Paso, Ciudad Juárez, and Las Cruces, New Mexico joined to celebrate Mass across the U.S.-Mexico border. Daniel Groody describes the liturgy as follows:

We celebrated mass outside, in the open air, in the dry rugged, and sun-scorched terrain where the United States meets Mexico. This liturgy was a time not only to remember all the saints and all the souls of history, but also the thousands of Mexican immigrants who died crossing over the border in the last two years. Like other liturgies, a large crowd gathered to pray and worship together. Unlike other liturgies, however, a sixteen-foot iron fence divided this community in half, with one side in Mexico and the other side in the United States.

To give expression to our common solidarity as a people of God beyond political constructions, the two communities joined altars on both sides of the wall . . . Unable to touch my Mexican neighbor except through some small holes in the fence, I became painfully aware of the unity we celebrated but the divisions that we experienced. In the face of the wall between us, it struck me how we could experience concurrently our unity in Christ but our dividedness in our current reality, for no other reason than we were born on different sides of the fence. It brought to a new level the insight of Dr. Martin Luther King Jr. who said that "Sunday at 11:00 (is) the most segregated hour in America."[1]

The Mass united the church at the border in the presence of barriers representing geopolitical lines. The reality of the fence between them, however, remained looming. Two groups gathered and two altars stood on each side, yet a union formed as the two joined in performing the rituals of Mass together. The Mass was celebrated in both Spanish and English, with the scriptural readings and liturgies alternating languages as it was performed across the border fence. The unity became more powerful as the two groups joined in the sharing of one table, though divided into two altars. The body and blood of Jesus "re-membered," or gathered, them into one body.[2] The passing of the peace, even through the small fence openings, reminded

1. Groody, *A Promised Land*, 299–300.

2. See Cavanaugh, *Torture and Eucharist*, 229. Cavanaugh describes the eucharist as re-membering the church into Christ's body emphasizing the gathering of God's people rather than a remembering of Christ's sacrifice separated from bodies. He writes, "The Eucharist is an *anamnesis* of the past; Jesus commanded his followers, "Do this in remembrance of me" (Luke 22:19). If we understand this command properly, however, the Eucharist is much more than a ritual repetition of the past. It is rather a literal re-membering of Christ's body, a knitting together of the body of Christ by the participation of many in His sacrifice." Cavanaugh had previously argued that "Christian resistance to state oppression depends on the church being the body of Christ capable of resisting the fragmenting discipline of the state." Ibid.

each of their common humanity in God. Those who gathered at Mass under the heat of the sun sought to be transformed by Jesus Christ and to transform the borderland space into a bridge of unity rather than a symbol of division.[3]

As the culmination of the Roman Catholic Mass, the celebration of the eucharist was of particular importance for uniting the body of Christ across national lines. At the same time, the eucharist opened the possibility of a new hope amidst the harsh realities of migration many endured. Groody writes, "Like the Eucharist, the migrant journey revolves around the basic elements of life, around bread, around death, around hope, and around the longing for a promised land."[4] The eucharist is the practice that provides sustenance for the people of God who journey after God as the body of Christ. Therefore, community's celebration of the eucharist called forth God's provision for migrants on their journey. Through the liturgy and practice of the Mass, the participants sought understanding and reconciliation across the border on behalf of the migrants who have died or suffered in their journeys northward in search of economic survival. The community's celebration of the eucharist called out for God's justice for migrants. Additionally, it united God's people in standing for justice with those who have endured the injustices of the global economy and U.S. immigration policies. The eucharist celebrated at the border brought to light disunity in the body of Christ. It prompted repentance for the divisions between the dioceses and parishes of the borderlands and united them in God's spirit of reconciliation. The eucharist is an opportunity for repentance regarding the lines that divide the body—lines that the church often tragically perpetuates.[5]

Grapes and Grain: Material Elements of the Eucharist

The migration of farmworkers to find work, migrations caused by famine and drought, even the movement of food itself to U.S. grocery stores unearth the wide discrepancy between scarcity and abundance of food and between those who have access to it as means of survival and those who

3. See *One Border One Body*, DVD. The film presents the Mass in this light, and includes several persons commenting on the transformation of the border space through the Mass.

4. Groody, *A Promised Land*, 306.

5. See Los Angeles Archbishop Mahony's words in *One Border One Body*.

do not. Ecclesial formation through eucharistic ethics and journeying with and among migrants requires that ecclesial communities recognize how economic forces dictate the lives of many migrants. The agricultural industry in the United States relies largely on immigrant labor.[6] Groody notes that in many regions of the U.S., this labor has been called "a modern form of slavery."[7] The evidence of migrants' labor lies within the eucharistic elements themselves—the bread and wine are "the fruit of the vine and the work of human hands."[8] *Eucharista* simply means "thanksgiving." Thus, thankful recognition of the labor that goes into the production of grapes and grain, not to mention other foods that provide our daily sustenance, must not be neglected in our celebrations of the eucharist. Not only are Christians shaped by the eucharist toward an ethic of mutual love and sharing of socio-economic resources, but the eucharist itself celebrates God's abundant provision of good news and life that is continually offered to the world. Below, I will continue to show how the eucharist table, as a reflection of God's table, requires that the church not turn away those who are hungry nor ignore suffering in its midst.

Reflecting on the Roman Catholic Mass celebration at the U.S.-Mexico border, Groody describes the eucharist through the labor of the migrant:

> On the altar, then, we see not only the body and the blood of Christ, but we see in the bread and the wine the hands, the feet, the labor, the sweat of those who worked in the fields. We see those who tilled the land so grain could be planted under the hot sun. We see those who fumigated the vines, even while their eyes turned red, their lungs filled with pesticides, and their children were born with birth defects because of it. We see those who harvested the grapes, even for less than minimum wage, so they could send what

6. See Groody, *A Promised Land*, 310.

7. See ibid., 310. Groody draws from John Bowe's observations: "Modern Slavery exists not because today's workers are immigrants or because some of them don't have papers but because agriculture has always managed to sidestep the labor rules that are imposed upon other industries. When the federal minimum-wage was enacted, in 1938, farmworkers were excluded from its provisions, and remained so for nearly thirty years. Even today, farmworkers, unlike other hourly workers, are denied the right to overtime pay. In many states, they're excluded from workers' compensation and unemployment benefits. Farmworkers receive no medical insurance or sick leave, and are denied the right to organize . . . [T]here's no other industry in America where employers have as much power over their employees." Bowe, "Nobodies: Does Slavery Exist in America?" 122.

8. Groody, *A Promised Land*, 310.

they earned to their families in Mexico. We see those who woke up at four o'clock in the morning to bake bread or work in the wineries, those who drove trucks and finally brought the bread and wine to our doors, to our altars. In the Eucharist, we see not only bread and wine but also the footprints of the migrants.[9]

As a Roman Catholic, Groody understands the elements of the eucharist to be the actual body and blood of Christ. The elements consumed actually shape the church into his body. At the same time, Groody narrates the eucharistic liturgy as a framework through which to read the reality of immigration. He draws the parallel between, "the breaking of bread and the breaking of migrants' bodies, between the pouring out of Christ's blood for his people and the pouring out of migrants' lives for their families, between Christ's death and resurrection and the migrants' own."[10] Central to understanding these parallels is understanding migrants' suffering and the call for justice, particularly as one examines the perilous journey northward and the exploitative situations in which migrants find themselves in order to make a living once in the United States.

Though embodying a specific theology of the eucharist, the celebration of Mass at the U.S.-Mexico border between Ciudad Juárez and El Paso reveals how the practice of the eucharist breaks into the time and space of human lives to uncover the situatedness of the eucharistic elements. Groody's reflection on the eucharist celebration connects the lives of migrants to the production of the eucharist elements. The bread and the wine have come from the toil of bodies and land. They have come from the hands that have prepared them and the backs that have been broken in the planting and harvest. Therefore, the actualization of the eucharist as a spiritual and socio-economic act extends to the human bodies and labor found within the eucharistic elements. The eucharist as the *Lord's* Supper enacting God's economy does not neglect the economic ethics involved in the provision of food and the elements. Goizueta calls attention to the necessary

---

9. Ibid. 311.

10. Groody writes, "In the Eucharist, we see in faith not only the body and blood of Christ. In the Eucharist, we also see the body and blood of the migrant, the body of the crucified, who also poured out their lives for their families so that they might eat and that we might eat, so that they might drink and we might drink, even if it cost them their lives. It is in this spirit that the bishops of the United States and Mexico write that we need to 'seek to awaken our peoples to the mysterious presence of the crucified and risen Lord in the person of the migrant and to renew in them the values of the Kingdom of God that he proclaimed." Ibid., 301.

unity between the sacramental character of the eucharist and the economic and political justice which it also encompasses.[11] While the eucharistic elements are understood as gifts of God in Christ (as well as gifts of seed, soil, sun, and water), they also are understood as economic products grown and produced by persons and socio-economic structures. Goizueta notes how, "worship and celebration are always aesthetic and ethical-political relationships mediated by economic products and structures. Before the bread and the wine are the body and blood of Christ they are the body and blood of the poor persons; the bread was kneaded by some-*one* and the grapes were picked by some-*one*."[12]

In this sense, the church's witness to God's glory and beauty has everything to do with its witness to God's love and justice.[13] The church's table manners learned in the eucharist meal cannot be neatly separated from the land and the hands that have provided the grapes and grain. Similarly, worship at the table is not separated, but intimately wedded to the socio-economic lives of community members.

Goizueta makes these connections by drawing upon the sixteenth century historical example of the conversion of Bartolomé de las Casas. Las Casas, a Spanish priest who came to "the Indies" in 1502, also served the Spanish crown as an *encomendero* (holder of land) who owned indigenous persons. In 1517, however, his life was radically changed through the eucharist liturgy.[14] In preparing to celebrate mass, Las Casas came to realize that the bread of the eucharist was "ill-gotten" through the exploitation of indigenous people. In this realization Las Casas began to see the problematic nature of his role as both priest and *ecomendero*. Goizueta notes,

> The key to Las Casas' conversion was in his sudden recognition, in the light of the Scriptures, that the eucharistic bread is "the bread of the poor," and that, in turn, "the bread of the poor is their life." In light of this recognition, he is forced to reconsider "his position in the nascent colonial system," and "forsakes his condition as a member of an oppressive system, whose contrariety to all justice and to God's will he has not until now perceived."[15]

11. See Goizueta's chapter 5: "Popular Catholicism as Human Action," in *Caminemos con Jesús,* 100–131.

12. Ibid., 131.

13. Ibid., 125.

14. Ibid., 123. For a comprehensive account of Las Casas' conversation, see Gutiérrez, *Las Casas,* 47–51.

15. Goizueta, *Caminemos con Jesús,* 124. Also see Gutiérrez, *Las Casas,* 47–48.

In the eucharistic meal, Las Casas came to recognize the bread as not just a symbol, but rather the everyday bread of someone's labor. Goizueta notes how this experience illustrates the connection between the mediation of worship in the eucharist and the economic production of bread. Las Casas also came to see that the bread was acquired unjustly. It was taken from the indigenous persons, while they often were left without food. This led Las Casas to challenge his own participation in Spanish colonization through his economic function as an overseer of the land and indigenous peoples therein.[16]

In turn, Goizueta challenges Christians to recognize how eucharistic worship must address the church's complicity in economic systems that oppress the poor. Building upon his challenge, I argue that the eucharist, as well as meal sharing together as expressions of hospitality, direct the church community to greater responsibility in its journeying with and among migrants. Christian hospitality built on a theology of the eucharist calls the church to repentance and action. The church is responsible for raising consciousness of the economic struggles migrants face and for calling its members to actions of advocacy and justice with and among migrants. For example, there are occasions when the eucharist requires abstinence from grapes and grain in recognition of the inhumane working conditions many farmworkers endure daily. Being guests at God's table and recipients of God's continual provision demands that Christians act as responsible stewards who refuse to separate the political and economic realities of daily life from their worship of God and participation of God's work in the world. The church does not reflect God's eucharistic formation when the church turns a blind eye to suffering and to divisions in its midst.[17] Groody warns against a eucharistic celebration that ignores the call for justice:

16. See Goizueta, *Caminemos con Jesús*, 124–25.

17. Also espousing a high sacramental theology of the eucharist, Eastern Orthodox theologian John Zizioulas expounds upon how the church becomes a reflection of the eschatological community of Christ. He writes, "In terms of human existence this mainly means one thing: the transcendence of all divisions, both natural and social, which keep the existence of the world in a state of disintegration, fragmentation, decomposition and hence of death. All cultures in one way or another share in this fallen and disintegrated world, and therefore all of them include elements which need to be transcended. If the Church in its localization fails to present and image of the Kingdom in this respect, it is not a Church. Equally, if the eucharistic gathering is not such an image, it is not the eucharist in a true sense." Zizioulas' footnote of this section reads: "A eucharist which discriminates between races, sexes, ages, professions, social classes etc. violates not certain ethical principles but its eschatological nature. For that reason such a eucharist is

> The memory of Christ is institutionalized in the Eucharist, and it tells the story of salvation, of freedom, and of liberation in ritual form. . . . If our Eucharistic celebration is not intimately connected to the larger liturgy of life, to the larger search for justice, to fighting to free those who are enslaved, then it has no meaning, and singing "alleluia" has no significance. . . . If Christians hunger to receive the bread of life at liturgy but have no hunger to feed those whose lives are threatened and who are in need of bread today, they ignore Christ.[18]

Through the practice of the eucharist the church is challenged to welcome *in* those who are in need of bread and justice, as well as to go *out* and embody the good news of God's justice for the world. The bodily performance of the eucharist challenges ecclesial community to embody a journeying hospitality that accompanies migrants in their the daily needs and struggles.

There is an integral connection between daily sustenance, the eucharist elements, and a sacramental calling to the world. As Inge writes, "Having been fed with the sacramental elements of bread and wine, through which Christ nourishes us with his body and blood, we are to go out to find Christ in the people and places of our everyday life."[19] The eucharist forms the people of God into sacrament by which God's followers are given a new vision of seeing and acting in the world. Eastern Orthodox theologian John Zizioulas echoes this sentiment. He writes, "The eucharist is the moment in the Church's life where the anticipation of the *eschata* takes place. The *anamnesis* of Christ is realized not as a mere re-enactment of a past event but as an *anamnesis of the future,* as an eschatological event. In the eucharist the Church becomes a reflection of the eschatological community of Christ, the Messiah, an image of the Trinitarian life of God."[20] The celebration of the eucharist also is a sign of the coming eschatological community of Christ wholly manifested in the everyday realities of peoples' lives and struggles. The relationships and community formed at and by the table give rise to material hope amidst these struggles.

---

not a "bad"—i.e. morally deficient—eucharist but not eucharist at all. It cannot be said to be the body of the One who sums up all into Himself [sic]." Zizioulas, *Being as Communion,* 254–55. Also see the entirety of chapter 7 "The Local Church in a Perspective of Communion," 247–60.

18. Groody, *A Promised Land,* 310–11.

19. Inge, *The Christian Theology of Place,* 62.

20. Zizioulas, *Being as Communion,* 254–55.

Eucharist and Economic Life in the Church

By virtue of being a meal and performing an ethic of sharing, the celebration of the eucharist is a central act of hospitality. In fact, the eucharist continually transforms hospitality as strangers become friends in the welcome embodied in sharing meals together. In the next pages, I unpack the economic formation of the church through the practice of the eucharist in order to discuss implications for the church's "political" gathering as God's people, sharing in God's table. I suggest that through acts of eating together the eucharistic community learns how its witness to God's economy can manifest itself within the economic realities of a transnational migration context.

M. Douglas Meeks discusses the early church as household (*oikos*) patterned after the economy of God (*oikonomia tou theou*).[21] He suggests, "every Christian should be prepared to think about economics and to participate in economic life according to the criterion of God's righteousness in Jesus Christ."[22] Unpacking the household metaphor, Meeks expounds upon how the church critically appropriates God's household and economy in light of other economies in the world.[23] In addition to understanding *oikos* as both household and household management, Meeks describes it as access to livelihood. Translating *oikos* imagery into today's economic context, he elaborates:

---

21. Meeks, *God the Economist*, 33. He notes: "Recent research has shown the pivotal theological, liturgical, and social implications of the concept of *oikos* for the primitive Christian communities." He cites numerous examples, which include, Wayne A. Meeks, *The First Urban Christians*; Elliott, *A Home for the Homeless*; Schüssler Fiorenza, *In Memory of Her*. See Meeks, *God the Economist* (33 n. 9) for further sources. Meeks continues: "'The *oikos* or household constituted for the Christian movement as well as for its environment a chief basis, paradigm and reference point for religious and moral as well as social, political, and economic organization, interaction, and ideology.'" Elliot, *Home for the Homeless,* quoted in Meeks, 33. The language of God's household, in contrast to images of God's kingdom, is an important image in feminist ecclesiology because of how it evokes communal representations of God's eschatological restoration, not to mention drawing attention to often neglected everyday realms of household. For example, Letty Russell employs this household imagery in *Church in the Round*. Here, however, I focus specifically on the economic dimensions of household management in *oikos* rather than focus on the place of household.

22. Meeks, *God the Economist*, 3. He adds, "the faith in the God of the Bible has economic implications that derive from who God is and from God's own redemptive history with the world."

23. Ibid., 33.

> The household living relationships of the *oikos* are the institutional relationships aimed at the survival of human beings in society. *Oikos* is the way persons dwell in the world toward viability in relation to family, state, market, nature, and God. *Oikos* is the heart of both ecclesiology and political economy.[24]

This description helps to expand the understanding of household beyond a *place* and its connotation as a static location. Rather, *oikos* as "the way persons dwell" incorporates the fluctuating means of survival, such as labor, upon which a community must rely. While the place of household is valuable, I focus on the ethics, exchanges, relationships, and ways of life shaped therein. Russell's use of household imagery in her "church in the round" ecclesiology similarly reflects the dynamic nature of household economy. As discussed in previous chapters, she incorporates the "sweaty tasks" of daily living, relationships centered around a household table, and "kitchen table solidarity."

According to Meeks, God's economy is egalitarian, communal, and characterized by abundance or even superabundance.[25] Building upon Meeks's economic theological reflection, it is possible to see the eucharist as a central practice that guides the church in living toward God's economy amidst the world's economy. God's economy cannot be separated from witness because it teaches the church how to live and understand its place in the local and global economies.[26] Meeks describes the important role the sacraments of baptism and eucharist play for the church in revealing and living into God's economy for the sake of the world:

> Baptism is entrance into God's economic work through the death and resurrection of Jesus Christ. Those who are baptized receive preveniently God's gracious promise of forgiveness and of power against death. In that promise they hear God's call to participate in God's own history of distributing righteousness.
>
> God creates a new home for those who have heard this promise and this commission by calling a meal. Like all households, God's household is structured around a table. *The Eucharist is God's economic act par excellence in the household of Jesus Christ.* In it

24. Ibid., 33.

25. See ibid., 9–13.

26. Meeks notes, "Because the church exists for the sake of God's love of the world (John 3:16), there can be no sound teaching about the church that does not include the relationship of the church to our society's economy and the world's economy." Ibid., 33.

is made present God's own self-giving, God's own economy by which God intends to make the world into a home.[27]

As the community gathers to share in God's continual provision at the table, it learns what participation in God's abundant economy means for itself and for the world. The eucharist is God's economic act as it demonstrates God's self-giving and provision of daily sustenance in bread and in salvation through Jesus Christ. This orientation to God's abundance stands in contrast to the fear of economic scarcity in the global market that dominates persons' lives. While the world's economy is predicated upon competition for scarce resources, especially for poor and vulnerable populations, God's economy is grounded in abundance and characterized by love and sharing.

Meeks's theological elaboration of how economy and livelihood (*oikos*) are derived through eucharistic practice is instructive. Just as understandings of home and household have been stretched and even contested because of transnational migrants' border passage and perpetual displacement and movement, so too can the economic imagery of household be stretched to new provisional locations. Seeking to build relationships and community with persons whose bodies are marked by wandering means that ecclesial communities must venture out to new spaces and allow church to happen in new ways. Above we saw how the church can move outside of walls and pews and relocate its movable eucharistic feast to the borderlands. This relocation and the new spatial imagination found in eucharistic meals on the borderlands offer the possibility of God's good news breaking in afresh in new places and contexts.

Yet, even as eucharistic meals venture toward new patterns and places, it is important to observe that the church's ongoing practice of the eucharist originates with the simple practice of meal sharing in community. The eucharist is first and foremost patterned after Jesus' Last Supper with his disciples before his death. Mennonite theologian John Howard Yoder relates Jesus' Last Supper with his disciples to sharing a common meal. He writes, "The meal Jesus blessed that evening and claimed as his memories was [the disciples] *ordinary* partaking together of food for the body. . .That direct connection with ordinary eating together is reinforced by the connection we see in the Gospels between food and the appearance of the risen Lord."[28] The correlation between Jesus' Last Supper and a common meal is confirmed in Luke 24:30 when the Emmaus-bound disciples who had not

27. Ibid., 44, 45; italics original.
28. Yoder, *Body Politics*, 16.

recognized Jesus journeying with them, suddenly saw who he was when they sat together at the table and Jesus gave thanks for the bread.[29]

Both sacramental and non-sacramental expressions of the eucharist encompass actions around a table and meal sharing practices which form the community toward a particular economic expression in the world. Yoder also relates early Christian communities' sharing of meals in the post-Pentecost church with enacting a new economic way of life together as described in Acts 2:44–47a:

> All who believed were together and had all things in common; they would sell their possessions and goods and distribute the proceeds to all, as any had need. Day by day, as they spent much time together in the temple, they broke bread at home and ate their food with glad and generous hearts, praising God and having the goodwill of all people. (NRSV)

How the eucharistic community shares material resources—like bread—is a sign of its trust in, faithfulness to, and worship of God as provider. Reflective of God's economy, the eucharistic community cares about providing for one another's needs, not neglecting when this need surfaces as daily bread. Yoder describes ecclesial formation in the sharing of bread through sacramental realism. For Yoder, *all* bread and *all* acts of eating together are eucharistic. He writes, "It is that bread *is* daily sustenance. Bread eaten together *is* economic sharing. Not merely symbolically, but also in fact, eating together extends to a wider circle the economic solidarity normally obtained in the family."[30] He continues, "In short, the Eucharist is an economic act. To do rightly the practice of breaking bread together is a matter of economic ethics."[31] The formation that happens in the breaking of bread and sharing of the cup together shapes communities to differently perceive economic systems and structures and concern themselves with the persons who have grown, harvested, and produced this provision. As an economic ethic, the eucharist in both formal and informal manifestations of a shared meal demands the change and transformation of the community so that the church's meal of thanksgiving is not ill-gotten, but reflects the justice and love of God.

---

29. Yoder notes the same correlation in Acts 1:4 and John 21:9–13. Ibid.

30. Ibid., 20.

31. Ibid., 21.

REVOLVING GUEST-HOST RELATIONSHIPS: GIVING AND RECEIVING

The formation of Christians through guest/host relationships within table-fellowship is equally central to the expression of hospitality as the practice of shared meals. The church learns its table manners through a eucharistic practice in which the community experiences being both guest and host. The eucharistic meal trains its participants to be both guests of God in Christ and hosts to Others. Below I explore the value of cyclical role reversals surrounding guest/host and giving/receiving dynamics in the church as instructive for re-shaping relationship-building and community through contemporary hospitality practice. Koenig develops how this eucharistic formation originates in Jesus' actions in Christian Scripture. By virtue of Jesus' continual serving of his disciples at the table, his followers first learn the most basic economic and relational acts—how to give and receive as both guests and hosts at the table. Koenig draws attention to the servant-ethic Jesus modeled for his disciples during his lifetime. In Luke 22:24–30, for example, Jesus requires his own disciples to be guests in his presence so they can learn to be servant hosts for others.[32]

Koenig goes on to describe how the early Judeo-Christian communities in Acts and the Pauline epistles enact an alternative ethic of sharing so that material resources are fairly distributed and community members are treated with equality regardless of their socio-economic status in society.[33] The commitments demonstrated in caring for one another's socio-economic and spiritual needs, especially the needs of those with less economic means in the community, involve the nurturing of relationships and growth together in community as followers of Christ. Koenig points to this commitment to giving and receiving in relationships when he writes, "Grace abounds because God multiplies both the giving and receiving (2 Cor. 9:8–11). From the perspective of New Testament hospitality the Spirit calls less for a 'solidarity with victims' than for a commitment to work alongside those who suffer grave injury or injustice in the expectation that all of us will bring gifts to one another (Rom. 1:11–12)."[34] This commitment to relationships infiltrates far deeper than initial welcome exchanges that guest/host language insinuates, and even extends beyond standing with the victim.

32. Koenig, *New Testament Hospitality,* 118–19.

33. See ibid., 110–11.

34. Ibid., 134–35.

Reflective of journeying in relationship, hospitality embraces the ebb and flow of relationships born out of an initial meeting that extend into deeper friendships and imply long-term commitment. In order for these relationships to be shaped into Christian community, each person drawn together through acts of hospitality and friendship must recognize the Other and receive from the Other. Each must perceive her or his own strangeness before the Other and move evenly toward one another in hospitality. The relational journey progresses into friendship as the host and guest come to recognize the gifts the Other brings and the two continue to share gifts. In order for true relationship and community to be embodied, the guest and host habitually switch roles and extend the welcome in new directions. The commitment to work alongside one another requires a commitment to receive from another and to be willing to change to make space for of the Other. In summary, though the language of guest and host implies certain roles and tasks, eucharistic formation transforms traditional guest and host roles into ongoing guest/host reversals, catalyzed by the ongoing exchange of giving and receiving as the two become friends. In turn, as relationships are transformed into Christian *koinonia,* they contribute to the broader shaping of life together in the church.

Koenig unpacks *philoxenia,* the Greek word for hospitality, not simply as meaning love of strangers but delight in the guest-host relationship. He highlights the complexities within relationships found "in the mysterious reversals and gains for all parties which may take place."[35] For Christians, Koenig continues, delight in the guest-host relationship is fueled by the expectation that the Triune God will play a role in every hospitable encounter and action.[36] Encounters are transformed into relationships and economies of friendship as two persons move beyond the confines of traditional guest/ host roles and become intertwined in the gift and reception cycle that characterizes strong relationships. Ward's words are fitting:

> In such an economy, to give hospitality also requires us to recognise how we are receiving hospitality: the reception of what is given is also a hosting in oneself of the other. There is no superiority between host and guest. For to host is to allow the guest to be as oneself; and to be a guest is to receive the host as oneself. True justice only operates in obedience to the economy of friendship that recognises the question in every encounter, "Who is the

35. Ibid., 8. Also referenced in Russell, *Church in the Round,* 173.

36. Ibid., 8. Koenig also cites Heb 13:2 and Rom 1:11–12 as examples.

stranger?," and realises the answer is: "Neither of us—while we have each other."[37]

Thus, the practice of hospitality reflects shared engagement and reciprocal interaction between strangers who have become friends under God's purposes.

For Ward, this economy of friendship is predicated upon the gracious and inexhaustible economy of God. The relationships of the Trinity demonstrate unending possibilities through God's superabundant giving and receiving. This emphasis echoes back to Yong's Trinitarian logic of abundance that he deems necessary in order for Derrida's absolute hospitality to function discussed in chapter 4. Because of power dynamics and violence at play within any encounter with the Other, the Christian who welcomes another is continually opened to relinquish control to the Other and give herself or himself away—in effect, give the keys to the house—to the Other. In order to escape tendencies toward self-annihilation, it is important to reiterate that the Christian's giving of the self originates in the abundance she or he continually receives in God. Ward writes that such giving, "can only come from that which is continually being given such that what I am being emptied of is that which I am being given. That is, such sociality, which moves beyond ourselves and into a permanent journeying towards the other, is only possible within an economy of the gift in which I am constituted in the transit of grace."[38] The gracious, continually given gift of God that Ward identifies is both provided and received anew in the eucharist.

As new friendships are born in ecclesial communities, the community's life together and its ecclesiology continually emerge from these interactions shaped by the eucharist. When new persons are encountered, they become gifts to the community and potential agents of transformation. Hospitality practice in the church also demands the community to change and adapt in ways that are reflective of the journey of relationship-building and community formation. Journeying with new friends and strangers continually offers the church potential encounters with God's good news manifesting itself anew. The relationship between a community and its

37. Ward, "Hospitality and Justice toward 'Strangers,'" 7.

38. Ibid., 6. He continues, "Only then can my desire for the other not be an appetite—that having the other would satisfy, but an infinite generosity, beyond appetite and beyond even attraction. There are alternatives economies of the gift that do not figure mutuality in terms of a return to the same." Additionally, Ward notes this caution: "While we cannot handle Trinitarian relations and the eucharist as magic wands nevertheless these teaching structure the character of Christian hope." Ibid., 4.

practice of hospitality is never static. Each encounter with the Other, each deepening of friendship through the offering and reception of gifts, each participation in the eucharist and every shared meal re-forms the community itself. In turn, the newly re-formed community is situated to discover new expressions of hospitality.

The ecclesial community shaped by the eucharist is continually prompted to give by virtue of what it has received in Jesus Christ. In fact, the practice of hospitality appropriated to context is a necessary outgrowth of a community's eucharistic practice, and must be continually and intentionally nurtured. Hospitality draws the community out to encounter, share, and receive from Others. Meeks aptly notes, "The economy of grace depends on who is invited to dinner. If we do not eat with the stranger, we will never be able to establish *oikic* relationships with the poor in any conceivable way that approximates the intention of the Triune Community's righteousness/justice."[39] The welcome of the stranger offers the mystery of salvation back to the church. In fact, as Groody reminds us, the church as the body of Christ welcomes the Other as Jesus Christ.[40] Yong's theological engagement of the Derridean reversal introduced earlier is not far off—the guest holds the host's salvation, redemption, and liberation. Ecclesial communities extending hospitality are thus transformed by the reception of the guest and the continued giving and receiving that characterize friendships.

LOVE FEASTS CELEBRATED AT THE SAN DIEGO/TIJUANA BORDERLAND

In 2008, a Christian ecumenical group began gathering where the border fence meets the Pacific Ocean at Border Field State Park and *Playa de Tijuana* (Tijuana Beach) to share in a eucharistic meal joining brothers and sisters in Mexico and the United States. Each Sunday afternoon for two years following, Christians continued to gather and celebrate a Love Feast,

39. Meeks, "Peace and Justice," 20.

40. In this spirit, the *Conferencia del Episcopado Mexicano* and the United States Conference of Catholic Bishops joined to write a pastoral letter concerning migration by which they "seek to awaken our peoples to the mysterious presence of the crucified and risen Lord in the person of the migrant and to renew in them the values of the Kingdom of God that he proclaimed." Groody, ibid., 311. The entire pastoral letter is documented in *Strangers No Longer: Together on the Journey of Hope*, United States Conference of Catholic Bishops, 2002.

representative of the Agape feasts of the early church (1 Cor 11:17–34).[41] Not seeking to challenge differing theologies and liturgies of the eucharist, the group decided to share in the Love Feast as a eucharistic, but non-sacramental meal. Through the wire fence, they passed tortilla and sometimes sweet bread, as well as *tamarindo* juice, foods representative of Mexican culture. The site in which the community gathered represented a historical place of meeting known as Friendship Park where only a thin iron fence marked the U.S.-Mexico border, allowing families and friends to gather on both sides of the border to talk, touch, or pass friendly exchanges.[42] The park was especially important for families after family members had been deported or were unable to cross the border. The group joined these

41. Gates, "Communion at Friendship Park. He writes, "On June 1, 2008 Methodist minister Rev. John Fanestil and I, a minister in the Church of the Nazarene, led a bi-national prayer vigil and a Lovefeast at Friendship Park. We planned to share a 'love feast,' rather than enter into the complicated liturgical issues of how to share Communion with the spectacularly ecumenical crowd that turns out for our border gatherings.' With its roots in the Agape feasts of the early church (1 Corinthians 11.17–34) and developed into a regular community practice by the German Moravians in the 18th century, a Lovefeast is a simple meal shared in a spirit of humility and peace that Christ is present in our lives. Although mostly practiced among the faithful, the Lovefeast often extended to all who gathered as a witness to the love found in Christ. Early Methodists and Nazarenes embraced this tradition and it was out of these deep roots that we shared sweetbread and tamarindo juice in prayer and Christian solidarity. . . After this initial Lovefeast, we decided to move to regular Sunday communion. For eight months Rev. Fanestil took the lead to continue to offer communion through the fence at the monument every Sunday. Rev. Fanestil committed to serving communion regularly at this site until physically prevented from doing so." Ibid., 5–6. Also see John Fanestil, "Border Crossing Communion at Friendship Park," *Christian Century*, October 7, 2008. http://www.christiancentury.org/article_print.lasso?id=5330 2/24/2009.

42. The history of Friendship Park is described as follows on the Friends of Friendship Park Website: "Friendship Park is located within the Border Field State Park (http://www.parks.ca.gov/?page_id=664) in San Diego, California. Established in 1974, the park encompassed four hundred eighteen acres of land in the Tijuana Estuary to enhance public access to its natural and cultural features. Lying along the Pacific Coast and adjacent to Mexico, the new development allowed access to the beach and more importantly historic Monument Mesa. On top of the Coastal Mesa rests border marker 258, originally marker 1, observing the U.S. Mexico boundary, established in the Treaty of Guadalupe Hidalgo in 1849. Over one hundred fifty-nine years ago the Boundary Joint Commission met at that exact location in San Diego to survey the land and divide their countries. In the 1880's a monument was placed to commemorate the initial point of the boundary and celebrate a friendship between the two nations. In 1971 Pat Nixon, the wife of President Richard Nixon, commemorated this beautiful spot as friendship park or parque de amistad, a place where friends and family could meet, despite nationality." http://friendshippark.org/html/History/.

families to call for God's peace and provision, to gather in support of their brothers and sisters who were suffering in family separation, and to listen to the stories of those around them. The Love Feast symbolized the unity and reconciliation the body of Christ seeks across national dividing lines. The group's ongoing gathering, however, soon came to be viewed as a controversial act in which the politics of the church challenged the politics of nation-state.

Early in 2008, before the group starting meeting and despite much dispute and opposition from San Diego residents, the U.S. government's Department of Homeland Security solidified its plans to close public access to Friendship Park and erect a triple-fence between the United States and Mexico.[43] That same year concerned community members led by the American Friends Services Committee formed the Friends of Friendship Park coalition. Motivated by concern for decisions made regarding the U.S.-Mexico border and immigration that adversely affect migrants, the coalition hoped to preserve the park. In the spirit of the corporate and communal partnerships discussed in the previous chapter, the coalition joined with other ecumenical groups: Border Angels, Border Encuentro/ Border Meetup, Center for Justice and Reconciliation (Point Loma Nazarene University), Ecclesia Collective, Foundation for Change, Interfaith Coalition for Immigrant Rights, Peace Resource Center of San Diego, as well as other organizations, various individual members, and community residents.[44] Many of the ecclesially affiliated groups regularly joined in the weekly Love Feast across the border fence, as well as the annual celebration of *La Posada Sin Fronteras*.[45]

43. Gates details some of the longer history of this development: "As a response to increasing levels of immigration from Mexico and increasing fears about immigrants from Mexico, the US federal government launched Operation Gatekeeper in 1994, doubling the amount of funding and the number of Border Patrol agents patrolling the San Diego sector by 1997. US Border Patrol commissioned a study that claimed a 'three-fence barrier system with vehicle patrol roads between the fences and lights would provide the necessary discouragement.' Funding for increased US-Mexico border security infrastructure doubled at least three times since the implementation of Operation Gatekeeper. The Illegal Immigration Reform and Immigrant Responsibility Act (1996) provided a mandate for the completion of fourteen miles of triple layer fence, but the construction across Border Field State Park and the Tijuana Estuary was stalled by community resistance, principally the California Coastal Commission (2004)." Gates, 3.

44. For a comprehensive list of a number of community members, organizations, foundations, businesses, and faith groups in San Diego County that are part of the coalition, see: http://friendshippark.org/html/About.html.

45. See chapter 5's discussion about *La Posada Sin Fronteras*.

In February of 2009, Friends of Friendship Park came together to worship on the U.S. side of the border in peaceful resistance to Homeland Security's closure of Friendship Park and commencement of the construction of the fence.[46] The coalition extended a community-wide invitation to the gathering, open to anyone and publicized through local media and e-mail networks. A couple dozen participants on the Tijuana side of the border joined the more than 150 people gathered on the San Diego side. The peaceful resistance comprised of a cross-border singing of Gabriel Faure's *Requiem* and prayer, as well as the familiar celebration of a eucharistic meal through the border fence.[47] The peaceful resistance expressed the unity the church seeks that transcends nation-state, socio-economic, and power divisions. Those who gathered sought to embody *one* church gathered *without borders*, which opposed U.S. political decisions that perpetuated division. Countless disruptions arose during this act of peaceful resistance from persons seeking to challenge the group's gathering. First, the U.S. Border Patrol stopped the group 25 feet from the border fence prohibiting the physical sharing of the eucharistic elements with those on the Mexico-side of the border because of what they claimed was a violation of customs laws. Second, individuals claiming to be representatives of "the Minutemen," who refer to themselves as anti-illegal immigration group, arrived seeking to disrupt the gathering by shouting racist insults, blaring whistles and bull horns during the group's singing, and trying to penetrate the circle the group formed to celebrate the eucharistic feast.[48] Despite

46. Additionally, other Christian churches, immigrant advocacy organizations, professors, students, and immigrants joined in the peaceful resistance.

47. Providing background on Fraure's *Requiem,* Gates notes: "As perhaps the most famous music written for a *"Missa pro defunctis"* (Mass for the Deceased), the liturgical significance of this ½ hour masterpiece extends well beyond the life of this particular setting and event. Sung in Latin on this day, Christians on both sides of the border were mourning the loss of life and fellowship in neither Spanish nor English, but in the historic language of the (Catholic) Church. While there is much to critique about the colonial use of Latin as the medium of instruction in the history of the church . . . in this setting the Latin seemed to serve a far more conciliatory function. It provided a common language that was the language of the faith, a language that united Spanish and English speaking Christians without ignoring, destroying or subordinating either. Lost in the use of Latin, of course, is the significance of the words for those who don't know this piece or understand Latin. Somehow, in this setting, the music communicated far more than enough." Gates, 7.

48. Gates describes, "Although there was no evidence that they were supported by Jim Gilchrist's Minuteman Project (http://www.minutemanproject.com/), some of them overtly identified themselves as Minutemen and as American patriots in the spirit of the

these disturbances and the enforced distance from the actual border itself, the singing and performance of the liturgy continued—prayers were offered in both Spanish and English, and Holy Communion was celebrated. Border Patrol, however, later detained the clergy who presided over Holy Communion, as he attempted to approach the border fence to serve communion to those waiting on the Mexico side.

What had been a Christian worship service (singing, prayer, and communion) that had been repeated many times prior, morphed into a political act of resistance. Jamie Gates, pastor, professor, and co-leader of the worship gathering, recounted:

> As we neared the place where the border fence runs out into the ocean, for the first time in eight months of border communions, the Border Patrol prevented us from. . . coming right up to the fence. A heavily armed line of Border Patrol officers and 4x4 quads . . . halted the procession on the beach about 50 feet from the vertical iron beams that serve as part of the primary fence that runs into the ocean. They claimed that this was space now under federal control. We now stood at the border of state and federal government jurisdictions. This was a new line in the sand.[49]

As a result, the worship participants questioned the nation-state's right to disrupt the gathering of the church, which professes to be held in by no border.[50] The group's performance of worship in this space contested the political lines of citizenship and socio-economic ownership of land. Despite all the actions of the day that reminded those gathered on both sides of the border of the differences between them, their gathering witnessed to a unity that transcended lines, borders, or boundaries of nation-states.

The acts of worship formed a bridge joining those who gathered on both sides of the border in the love of God. Though no church walls housed the group that afternoon, church took place *on the move*. While migrating persons' lives are marked by forced displacement and perpetual mobility dictated by outside forces, the community of believers enacted a different movement. Church *on the move* happened through the community's

---

Minuteman Project." Gates, 7.

49. Gates, 7. Also see the article: Penni Crabtree, "Meeting Place Sealed Off: Border Patrol Agents Prohibit Access to Friendship Park," *San Diego Union Tribune,* February 22, 2009 http://www3.signonsandiego.com/stories/2009/feb/22/1m22park23590-meeting-place-sealed/?metro.

50. See Gates, 22, Appendix 1: "A reflection emailed to friends the day after the border communion and requiem."

voluntary relocation to the borderland and their patterning their worship in the spirit of journeying with and alongside persons whose lives are marked by displacement and wandering. In turn, the celebration of Holy Communion gathered and united a group of strangers across borders in order to enact the way of Jesus and witness to God's coming reign. Such gathering in eucharistic worship at the border embodied new ecclesial patterns of a journeying hospitality and a journeying ecclesiology. The church that extends beyond borders is fashioned together by liturgies, performances, and partnerships—however simple or complex—that welcome, journey with, and gather people into the body of Christ so they may together to live into God's reign.

Formation of a New Community

Building on Augustine's imagery of the City of God and its political implications for ecclesiology today, William Cavanaugh directs us toward the visible witness the church enacts in the world precisely through its gathering and performance of liturgy. The acts of peaceful resistance and worship of the San Diego/Tijuana ecumenical community described above visibly performed an alternative economics and politics within the public space of Friendship Park. Yet, from a broader theological perspective, the church itself—by virtue of its baptism and eucharistic formation—lives out an alternative. Drawing attention to the economic and political origins of the early church, Cavanaugh points to the unity between Greek images of *oikos* and *polis* in Scripture together with the Hebrew understanding of being gathered as God's people. Cavanaugh writes,

> Ephesians 2.19 uses both "public" and "private" language simultaneously: "you are citizens (*sympolitai*) with the saints and also members of the household (*oikeioi*) of God." . . . In using the term *ekklesia* the Church understood itself as the eschatological gathering of Israel. In this gathering those who are by definition excluded from being citizens of the *polis* and consigned to the *oikos*—women, children, slaves—are given full membership through baptism.[51]

The dimensions of *oikos* and *polis* enacted in the church are distinguished from the first-century Greek cultural understanding of economic and

51. Cavanaugh, *Theopolitical Imagination*, 86–87.

political formation because the church is oriented toward God's eschatological gathering. The church throughout history up to today is called to God's vision even as it continually re-appropriates cultural understandings of citizenship, household, and gathering. The church is formed into a distinct gathering in the world in which all persons—especially those previously excluded in society—are now welcome. This new economic and political gathering, called *ekklesia,* manifests itself on earth in continuing response to the coming eschatological gathering in Christ. A new community, born in baptism and nurtured in the eucharist, continues to call the church to new embodiments of faithfulness and love that point to God's reign.

Ecclesial practices such as hospitality, not to mention the central practice of the eucharist or love feast, help to gather and direct the church to offer alternatives in the world. The shared eucharistic meals across the border described above enacted alternatives to the geopolitical and socio-economic divisions of national borders. Additionally, more broadly speaking, the church's continual celebration of God's abundance and love in the eucharist embodies an alternative to scarcity, fear, and competition in the world. Alternative ways of life in the church manifest themselves as good news particularly in the face of persons displaced or forced to migrate because of political and economic forces of globalization. Through these practices the church is shaped into a community of refuge or welcome as well as accompaniment and friendship in journeying. As Jesus Christ shaped the disciples by his service in the Last Supper, this supper continues to shape Jesus' followers into servants and hosts, though they are always guests at God's table. Sharing in the eucharist shapes the community into the new humanity called by virtue of baptism as citizens of God's reign on earth and in heaven.[52]

The political formation of a new social body or new society is initiated in baptism. This new society unites a people amidst all of its differences into one body of Christ. Baptism builds relationships and community in the name of Christ that bridge the differences which previously separated people, such as gender, ethnicity, servitude, etc.[53] Koenig's description of Paul's views on baptism and the new humanity is fitting:

> For him, life in the church is always a matter of becoming as well
> as being. Nevertheless, one dare not underestimate the being.
> Something transformative has happened to those who believe

52. Koenig, *New Testament Hospitality,* 70.
53. Ibid., 29–30.

and are baptized. They have found themselves drawn into a new form of life where there is "neither Jew nor Greek, . . . neither slave nor free, . . . neither male nor female" (Gal 3:28). Out of diverse individuals one organism is being formed. Yet this is a corporate life that does not destroy the identities of its member but honors them, more than they have ever been honored before, as receivers and givers of divine gifts (1 Corinthians 12–14).[54]

The church is continually called to embody this new society that joins peoples together in the name of Christ. In *Body Politics*, Yoder astutely observes that this joining of all kinds of people in baptism is not an individual change but a specifically communal one.[55] Baptism draws the Jews and Gentiles—representing many peoples, cultures, and histories—into *one* creation. Communally, baptism inaugurates a new inter-ethnic social reality.[56] This new social reality—a new creation—comes with a confession of Jesus Christ, new forms of relationship, and new social practices in community.

The formation of a new people is particularly illuminating in the context of ecclesial communities relocating themselves to celebrate the eucharist on the border. Reflecting on meal practices in early Christian communities, Koenig adds,

54. Ibid., 57.

55. Yoder writes, "In all three epistles [2 Corinthians, Galatians, and Ephesians], then, in different language, the functional affirmation is the same: Baptism celebrates and effects the merging of Jewish and Gentile stories. A people with the law and a people without, a people walled off from the world and a people open to it, become a single community, melding the legacies of both. The several expressions "new humanity," "peace," and "new creation," which we have noted, and the contrast between being and knowing "in Christ" (*en Christo*) and being and knowing "ethnically" (*kata sarka*) may well have figured in the baptismal ritual as equivalent ways of describing the changed status of one who becomes publically a confession believer. The new status is a new kind of social relationship, a unity that overarches the differences (Jew/Gentile, male/female, slave/free) that previously had separated people." Yoder, *Body Politics*, 29–30.

56. Yoder's elaboration is fitting, "It is not enough to say that each of us is individually born again and baptized, with the result that all the born-again individuals are collected in one place, commanded by God to love one another and plant churches, with no more reason for discrimination. Paul says more than that; he says that two peoples, two cultures, two histories have come to flow into one new humanity, a new creation. The order is the reverse of our modern expectations. There is a new inter-ethnic social reality into which the individual is inducted rather than the social reality being the sum of the individuals. This new belonging provokes subjective faith, but it is not the product of the individual's inward believing. It will move history. It will create cultures and institutions. Yet its truth is not dependent upon those effects for its verification." Ibid., 30.

the kingdom of God is like a movable feast, a roving banquet hall that seeks the people of Israel as guests and hosts. At this table they may find reconciliation with one another, as well as a true home and a plenty that fills them up and propels them toward sharing relationships with their neighbors . . .

By joining Jesus and his followers, especially at meals, one begins to live from the present blessings of the kingdom and offer up one's work to the final restoration of human community which is already underway.[57]

The church's gathering across borders and divisions to share in God's movable feast enacts a different communal and political formation than that perpetuated by national borders and divisions of race and class. The church, in turn, seeks to bridge border divisions and bring people together in unity. Yet, this unity that the new community seeks does not form people into uniformity that destroys or covers over difference. Rather, carefully preserving irreducible otherness in human relationships is central to the formation of a hospitable community. Accompaniment and journeying with and among Others involves the risk of allowing oneself to be confronted and changed by the Other. Ecclesial practices, like hospitality, must be critically examined and continually reformed by these relationships. Through practices of sharing meals in new spaces, journeying with one another and the stranger on the margins, as well as continually being challenged to be both guest and host, both giver and recipient despite different socio-economic locations, the church continually learns how to live as a hospitable community amidst new contexts.

CONCLUSION

The practices of baptism and eucharist reveal dynamics of formation that instruct the church how to live in community. Our exploration of eucharist, baptism, and other performative dimensions of hospitality in the church have illustrated that the re-conception of hospitality as a practice untaken *with* and *among* migrants arises out of ecclesial practice and a new ecclesial spatial imagination. The practices of the early church continue to direct ecclesial communities of today in how to welcome and journey with Others. Yet, creative and intentional re-appropriation of these practices must take shape in each time and place.

57. Koenig, *New Testament Hospitality*, 43–44.

The embodied expressions of hospitality I have referenced illustrate how hospitality is a living, evolving expression of the Reign of God in the church, not a static and sterile set of prescribed practices. In fact, these lived examples present possibilities for the re-imagination of hospitality and ecclesiology. They demonstrate how both must be continually discerned and imagined anew amidst ever-changing contexts. The process of discernment, negotiation, and contextual re-appropriation of hospitality and ecclesiology is itself a journey of faithfulness, though the ecclesial community does not neglect the value of place and taking up residence at times. It is a journey of coming to know when to take root and when to be uprooted to journey farther for the sake of the gospel.

The church, precisely in the context of migration, is called to embody what it means to be a hospitable, inter-ethnic community. At the same time, the church often does not live into the calling it accepts in baptism.[58] In light of our failures, it is important to remember that baptism signifies repentance and cleansing. It is always possible to begin again in the spirit and hope of baptism.[59] The eucharist too presents the community with the opportunity to be confronted by its failures, to repent, and to fully give itself away for the sake of the world. This work is never done; the church is always reforming its life and practices toward deeper faithfulness to God's vision. My investigation of hospitality is but one example of challenging and reforming ecclesial communities' understandings and performances of hospitality in the complex contexts of the twenty-first century.

The next chapter will draw together the questions and insights explored up to this point through the four moves that have structured this book: 1) surveying contemporary theological reflection on hospitality and current hospitality practice within congregations in the United States, 2) examining the complex context of twenty-first century migration, particularly U.S. Latino/a migration, 3) critically analyzing hospitality practice in light of this context through U.S. Hispanic and postcolonial theologies with

---

58. Healy emphasizes the limits of the church in its humanness even as it is constituted by God and oriented toward God's ultimate truth. He seeks to, "maintain the tension between claims for the church's orientation to the ultimate truth on the one hand and, on the other, acknowledgement of ecclesial sin and of the church's dependence upon the challenges and insights of those religious and non-religious bodies that are orientated primarily to other truths." Healy, 20. Additionally, on page 22 he notes that the church's response to ever-shifting contexts should be to reconstruct its concrete identity so as to embody its witness in truthful discipleship.

59. Yoder, *Body Politics*, 41.

the aim of re-shaping hospitality practice, and, finally 4) constructively re-imagining hospitality practice in light of U.S. Latino/a migration. This concluding chapter will reflect on further ecclesiological implications found in re-imagining hospitality in light of migration. I also offer final considerations regarding spatial and temporal ecclesial imagination directed toward how the identity and mission of the church are shaped through hospitality practice re-conceived as journey and accompaniment with and among persons who migrate.

7

Journeying Somewhere through Hospitality Practice
Renewed Imagination and Praxis

THIS FINAL CHAPTER WILL address how the challenges to hospitality examined in this book deepen ecclesiology. I take further steps to discuss hospitality *as* ecclesial ethics. That is to say hospitality is ecclesial ethics lived out.[1] First, however, I expound upon a larger ecclesiological understanding of space and time that underlies my investigation of hospitality and migration. The people of God are sojourners, journeying toward the heavenly kingdom, yet also making God's reign visible on earth. Hospitality practice re-conceived as journey and accompaniment with those deemed "other" directs ecclesial communities toward deeper faithfulness in their identity and mission in the world. In the spirit of Russell's spatial construction of "church in the round," I suggest a new spatial imagination for a church *on the way* that journeys with migrants. I conclude by offering several strategic practical theological suggestions for congregations in reforming hospitality practice toward a journeying hospitality.

The practice of the eucharist—which includes the formal and informal manifestations of this meal—plays a central role in shaping ecclesial communities toward a journeying hospitality with and among migrants. Baptism and eucharist together gather individuals into a community and

---

1. See Keller, "The Love of Postcolonialism," 226.

mark their citizenship in heaven even as they are simultaneously residents on earth. The imagery and language of "citizenship in heaven" and "resident alien" are held in tension in the nature and mission of the church as a community that dwells in the balance between the present and the eschatological Reign of God in Christ. As citizens of heaven, Christian disciples look toward the hope of God's coming reign while creating a space in the world where God's reign can appear materially. Hospitality is a bodily manifestation of the church's identity and witness before the world. Rooted in baptism and the eucharist, hospitality practice reminds the church of its identity and heritage as a pilgrim people and points it forward to go out, encounter Others, and build relationships along the way. What makes the church's journeying unique and hopeful is that to which it is journeying. The church is journeying *somewhere* and must discern its praxis in light of that destination.

Focusing on how the church forms bodies in the world, Cavanaugh describes the church as "a performance enacted liturgically in time."[2] Naturally, the language of performance ties back to chapter 5's description of expressions of a journeying hospitality with and alongside migrants through *Las Posadas* rituals and Holy Thursday liturgical processions. Sharing in eucharist and love feasts on the borderlands challenge the church toward unique manifestations of hospitality in new spaces and places. As ecclesial communities extend welcome in celebrating Holy Communion across geopolitical borders, their actions also create a space of ecclesial unity across border divisions. Cavanaugh ties the performance of the church to the narrative of God that begins in the Judeo-Christian Scriptures and continues into the present and future faithfulness of the church. Thus, performances of liturgy become "spatial stories" because they direct the church toward life together in light of God's revelation. For Cavanaugh, the preeminent "spatial story" is found in the eucharistic forming of the body of Christ.[3] As the church gathers to continually remember Jesus' Last Supper with his disciples before his death, the community's sharing in this meal also "re-members," or gathers, them into one communal body in the name of Christ. Cavanaugh describes the eucharist as "an operation performed on matter and place—in this case by God, with human cooperation—which produces a different kind of space."[4] Thus, in celebrating the eucharist in a

2. Cavanaugh, *Theopolitical Imagination*, 93.
3. Ibid., 93.
4. Ibid., 92.

particular place, God transforms the community into a space for enacting God's restoration on earth.

Similarly, the alternative formation of space in the eucharist enacts a different conception of time. The eucharistic liturgy incorporates temporal acts of remembering, living in the present, and looking forward into the eschatological Reign of God. Cavanaugh writes, "The Eucharist not only tells but *performs* a narrative of cosmic proportions, from the death and resurrection of Christ, to the new covenant formed in his blood, to the future destiny of all creation."[5] The eucharistic community is not confined by the operations of space and time of the world, but rather this practice re-orients Christian lives toward the space and time of God's coming reign. Through the performance of the eucharist, the church is perpetually gathered in the name of Jesus to receive the gifts of God and to go out into the world by the power of the Holy Spirit to witness to God's coming restoration of the world.

The eucharistic worship at the U.S.-Mexico border described in the previous chapter illustrates how the enactment of church politics conflicts with the political spaces and stories of the world. Additionally, living out the spatial story of the eucharist shapes the community to be self-critical in ways that draw out confession, repentance, and change. Cavanaugh's argument regarding the church enacting an alternative space is particularly pertinent to common misperceptions about immigration in the U.S. ecclesial landscape. Unfortunately, the difference between nation-state political orientations and the Christian political orientation toward God's reign is often confused in the U.S. church when questions of citizenship surrounding immigration are raised. Inexcusably, congregations can preoccupy themselves with national citizenship, as evidenced by church members who question an immigrant's legal status before welcoming her or him into the community

---

5. Ibid., 118. Cavanaugh distinguishes between how the church understands space as opposed to the space created in the modern nation-state. He writes, "A space takes into account the vector of time, such that different spaces are created by the ensemble of movements and actions on them. Space is produced by people performing operations on places, using things in different ways for different ends. According to Certeau it is stories that 'organize the play of changing relationships between spaces and places.' . . . In theological terms we can think of Certeau's work here as a gloss on Augustine's conception of the two cities. They do not exist beside each other on a territorial grid, but are formed by telling different stories about different ends, and by thus using matter and motion in different ways. . .The Eucharistic liturgy can be understood as what Certeau calls a 'spatial story,' an operation performed on matter and place—in this case by God, with human cooperation—which produces a different kind of space." Ibid., 92.

as a sister or brother in Christ. Cavanaugh connects political orientations found in the church to the community's understandings of space and territory. The lived examples of the church negotiating identity and faithfulness on the borderlands illustrate Cavanaugh's point well. Questions of territory and citizenship are heightened in the geopolitical spaces of borderlands.

It is helpful to return to the earlier discussion drawing from Michel de Certeau's spatial distinction between maps and itineraries. Cavanaugh builds upon Certeau's delineation between how space is mapped in modernity and pre-modern conceptions of space marked by pilgrim itineraries. He describes Certeau's distinction as follows:

> Pre-modern representations of space marked out itineraries which told 'spatial stories,' for example, the illustration of the route of a pilgrimage which gave instructions on where to pray, where to stay the night, and so on. Rather than surveying them as a whole, the pilgrim moves through particular spaces, tracing a narrative through space and time by his or her movements and practices . . . By contrast, modernity gave rise to the mapping of space on a grid, a 'formal ensemble of abstract places' from which the itinerant was erased. A map is defined as a 'totalizing stage on which elements of diverse origin are brought together to form a tableau of a "state" of geographical knowledge.' Space itself is rationalized as homogeneous and divided into identical units. Each item on the map occupies its proper place, such that things are set beside one another, and no two things can occupy the same space. The point of view of the map user is detached and universal, allowing the entire space to be seen simultaneously.[6]

The spatial construction of the nation-state is pertinent to common misperceptions regarding migration and treatment of immigrants in the United States. Interestingly, the modern nation-state's "dominant overcoding of the map" depends on "establishing its own place, its own territory to defend."[7] When national consciousness is predicated upon a need to defend territory against those who would overtake it, this sentiment can more easily materialize into fear and acts of hatred toward "foreign" immigrants, particularly undocumented immigrants. Additionally, the national map portrays the nation as a homogenous unit so that difference and distinction are interpreted as threats. Often the differing histories, backgrounds, ethnicities, languages, and practices of migrants are interpreted as "disrupt-

6. Ibid., 110–11.

7. Ibid., 117.

ing" the whole. This understanding of space as both territory to defend and homogeneous unit has infiltrated the church in the United States.

In contrast, the "spatial story" enacted in the eucharist resists such perceptions and actions. Cavanaugh notes how instead of the overarching map, a eucharistic spatial story "moves on pilgrimage through the places defined by the map and transforms them into alternative spaces through its practices."[8] This spatial formation challenges the church to understand territory and space differently. Space is more fragile, temporal, and even borrowed. Participating in the eucharistic spatial story can direct the community toward a different understanding of space embodying the welcome, justice, peace, and love of God. Rather than understanding space as a territory to defend, the church embodies God's abundance and love in sharing space. The Christian story is a perpetual movement toward God's commonwealth that enacts an alternative economics and politics in the world. Members of the church develop relationships with migrants and journey with them as they make a living in the United States because, as Christians, they follow the story of Scripture and the spatial story of the eucharist that teaches the value of sharing the table with the stranger. In this vein, Cavanaugh challenges Christians to not reinforce the borders of the national territory defined by "citizenship," but instead build up the body of Christ that transcends these borders, and is offered to all.[9] In sum, the practices and performances of the church challenge the community's understanding of citizenship, borders, economic responsibility, and ethics, shaping them as an alternative community within the world.

The mapping of space in the modern nation-state is extended in globalization. The "territory" to defend still relates to national territory, but it is rooted in the less visible and less tangible control of money and power. Globalization enacts a universal mapping of space that perpetuates detachment from any particular localities.[10] Detachment from particular times and places means that local concerns and interests are subordinated to global agendas. The exploitation of vulnerable persons concealed under the false pretenses of global expansion and human progress is one result of the broad scope of globalization.[11] This pattern is clear in the phenomenon of forced economic migration that leaves people vulnerable to danger

8. Ibid.

9. Ibid., 93–94.

10. Ibid., 98.

11. Ibid.

and exploitation as they seek economic means of survival. As was noted in earlier chapters, undocumented migrant farmworkers or factory workers, desperate for means of survival and without laws to protect them, often fall victim to such exploitation.

In contrast to the spatial story of globalization characterized by hypermobilization as well as detachment, Cavanaugh returns to the configuration of space and time for the church set out in the eucharist. The eucharist is celebrated in local communities scattered over the earth as they are simultaneously gathered up into one. Thus, the identity of each Christian community and each person in the local is not lost or subsumed in the overarching space of the global. In fact, the spatial story of the global church is not understood, except through the particular, valued place and time of the local congregation.[12] Cavanaugh writes,

> The City of God makes use of this world as it moves through it on pilgrimage to its heavenly home. But this pilgrimage is not the detachment from any and all spaces, the sheer mobility of globalism. The Eucharist journeys by telling a story of cosmic proportions within the particular face-to-face encounter of neighbours and strangers in the local eucharistic gathering. In an economy of hypermobility, we resist not by fleeing, but by abiding.[13]

The eucharist, however, is not an anecdote to globalization. Rather, it is the spatial story by which the eucharistic community participates in God's transforming of particular places, daily lives, and bodies into spaces where God's reign is revealed. The eucharistic formation of the body of Christ displays God's eschatological hope in the material and concrete.

A journeying hospitality is one manifestation of this alternative spatial story. As Christians build relationships with migrants and accompany them through the challenging situations they face, the community enacts a different way of journeying together in the name of Christ. God's eschatological story offers good news as it unfolds an alternative to the ways of life globalization prescribes. The church orients its life toward the story of God begun in Israel, continuing in Christ, and leading to the eschaton. This is a story of God's provision, salvation, and restoration for the world. The

12. Ibid., 115. Cavanaugh describes the eucharistic community as not *part* but the *whole* body of Christ, what he calls a true *Catholicity* on p. 114. The eucharist is a spatial story in which the universal church resides *within* each local embodiment of the body of Christ.

13. Ibid., 117.

Christian spatial story guides Christians not only for the future, but also in the present as they are welcomed by and journey with a community in Christ. The eucharistic community enacts God's hope for the world as it journeys toward the *telos* of its heavenly home. It is in this sense that the eucharist tells and performs a narrative of cosmic proportions.[14] At the same time, this is not a journey of detachment or fleeing, but remaining and dwelling. New stories and lives merge and join as the church continually welcomes Others, all the while learning how to identify and pattern its life after God's story unfolding in the world.

The practice of the eucharist displays God's abundance in the world and nurtures eucharistic communities toward alternative ways of sharing life together. In effect, the spatial stories ecclesial communities perform in practices, such as baptism and eucharist, are maps or itineraries that teach Christians how to live. Inge notes how stories organize and instruct people how to live in certain places. He notes, "the spatial story is not simply descriptive but prescriptive. *Stories give us a way to walk*."[15] Ecclesial communities whose hospitality practices are shaped by the eucharist and sharing meals together exude the abundance of God's *oikonomia* in their life together. As Cavanaugh notes above, when they continually gather and celebrate the feast of the Lord's Supper, they are tracing God's narrative through space and time by their movements and practices and manifesting God's story anew in concrete time and space.

"NOT QUITE" SUSPICION

Kwok Pui-lan picks up and retools the Augustinian imagery of the city of God and the city of humans in quite a different sense than Cavanaugh. Awakening suspicion, Kwok's spatial and temporal imagination questions how the church interprets God's eschatological vision particularly in light of twenty-first century migration. Kwok writes,

> The city of God and the city of humans are always in tension with one another. The true invisible church is always at odds with the church that wields so much power and cooperates with the crown. Throughout the ages, the pilgrims and the monks who have gone out to the desert to form communities on the border and other

14. Ibid., 118.
15. Inge, 107; italics mine.

alternative base communities have created important sites of re-sistance and renewal.[16]

Kwok develops how theology tied to the history and destiny of a people—Israel and the church—is always about time and space, but a dialectical time and space. Journey, passage, and crossing always relativize and disrupt space of kingdom, nation, or temple. Israel as a people on a journey is "the foundation for providing spaces for others who are strangers, aliens, and immigrants." She continues, "the church has never been fully incorporated into world history."[17] According to Kwok, the time and space of "not quite" is internally transgressive because "it troubles the national, racial, ethnic, class, gendering, and ecclesial tales that homogenize difference, suppress the minorities, and coerce everyone to be the same."[18] In this sense, Kwok plays off of the temporal unknown of "not yet" in Christian eschatology, and calls for further suspicion of how the church is manifested "already" on earth. Because minority voices have been covered over and made to fit within the dominant majority, Kwok argues for the misfit of "not quite" to always persist in the church. Her spatio-temporal imagination resists as-similation and she challenges the church to always work out its theology on borders and in-between spaces, not seeking to grasp the holy.[19]

Survival in this world requires the necessity of a hope materialized for vulnerable peoples, and therefore resists the tendency to jump too quickly to an eschatology of "not yet." Particularly in light of the sufferings many migrating women endure, Kwok's articulation of concrete realization of hope on earth is a necessary corrective to the abstract:

> The hope for some of the disenfranchised women may be a place to dry their fish on the beach, enough seeds for next spring, or money enough to send their children to school. The future is not a grand finale, a classless society, or even a kingdom of God, but more immediate, concrete, and touchable. It may be the pooling of communal resources, of living better than last year, or of see-ing grandchildren grow up healthy and strong. It is a historical

---

16. Kwok, "A Theology of Border Passage," 115.

17. For Kwok, theology reflects these tensions because it is "a story that is not fin-ished, a body that is not fixed, and a story that resists final closure." Ibid., 114–15.

18. Ibid., 115.

19. Ibid.

imagination of the concrete and not the abstract, a hope that is more practical and therefore not so easily disillusioned . . .[20]

There is a need for new voices, particularly ones shaped by diaspora, to speak of the tangible realization of hope and to remind the church to always see itself as "not quite." Residing in the "not quite" propels the church to continually seek new, concrete forms of resistance and renewal.[21]

Postcolonial theologians astutely question *how* the concrete church identifies God's narrative, reign, and eschatological vision without risking perpetuating an image of itself. An image perpetuating sameness that suppresses and silences the voices of the margins has plagued the church throughout history. They demand that the church be confronted by new voices and perspectives. The journeying patterns of church that I have been exploring further illustrate the "not yet" of eschatology and the "not quite" of its manifestation in the church. The church's search for God's reign is never-ending, resisting closure and uniformity. The ecclesiological tension of "already/not yet" exposes the church's failures to live up to its calling and demands the church's humility, self-critique, repentance, and transformation. While the church is always journeying toward God's eschatological vision, it never possesses the vision. In turn, God's eschatological plans propel the Christian community outwardly to venture out and encounter the Other in the concrete contexts of everyday life. The church's knowledge of and embodied witness to God's vision is always provisional and incomplete, though it will be mediated by the tangible practices of a local community. The people of God must continue to search for where church is happening anew.

Postcolonial theological imagination challenges the church to recognize borders and margins and allow itself to be confronted by what happens in the interstices and in-between places and the people encountered there. In the spirit of the church's perpetual searching for something more, Rivera's rhetorical questions serve as a guide: "What refuses enclosure? What *crosses* over? What revels and reveals itself in the many tongues of many peoples? What is dis/closed in the shifting borderlands?"[22] Building upon

20. Kwok, *Postcolonial Imagination and Feminist Theology*, 37–38.

21. Kwok writes, "A diasporic consciousness, which is located from here and there, reads back metropolitan history and regimes of knowledge from multiple vantage points because people in diaspora are 'outsiders' from within." Ibid., 49.

22. Rivera, "Alien/nation, Liberation, and the Postcolonial Underground," 14.

postcolonial challenges, the church's capacity to speak meaningfully in its context depends on its lived witness in response to history.

Cavanaugh's theology of the eucharist juxtaposed with Kwok's postcolonial imagination bring together the tension between memory and suspicion in Christian faithfulness. Cavanaugh's detailing of space and time in the church becomes valuable in light of how people's lives are bound to perpetual wandering in globalization. Evoking the *memory* of "storied place" in Scripture reveals conflicting allegiances and raises suspicion of globalization's control over bodies and places. This memory is also central to guiding the church toward God's *telos*. The church does not offer hope or good news if it journeys aimlessly or in perpetual questioning; rather, hope and good news are born of the purpose and direction the church receives in seeking God's reign on earth as it is in heaven. Such hope can be found in ecclesial communities' embodiments of alternatives that enact new possibilities in the face of the competition, scarcity, fear, and fragility of life determined by global market forces and the power dynamics of "empire."

The church comes to understand that to which it is headed eschatologically while it journeys on earth. Ecclesial communities journey from one concrete manifestation to another like a pilgrim journeys from place to place. The hospitality practice of the church and the new friends it encounters and is encountered by along the way form and inform the church in its journey. Thus, the tangible manifestations of the church's hopes for its context are not separate from its eschatological hope. Signs of eschatological hope are made manifest in the material. Possibilities of resistance and renewal and their realization arise in ecclesial communities that prophetically call the church back to its place of being "not quite" at home in human history. At the same time, the immediate and concrete elements of hope found in stored seeds or the pooling of communal resources are hope for the living. Small tactics of survival are hope, and they embody tangible, albeit momentary, glimpses of the hope to come. Such hopes guide and instruct the church in its movement forward.

The ongoing meal sharing practices in communities demonstrate this dynamic between the church's historical and eschatological manifestation. Ed Loring of the Open Door Community in Atlanta writes: "We understand that every meal we eat is related to the Eucharist, to the eschatological banquet—that promise by which we live that there is enough for everybody, and that when we obey God's Spirit who is moving across the earth there will be no hunger."[23] The community enacts the eschatological hope of God's abundant provision for all within its daily sharing of meals. Likewise, the church practicing hospitality through eucharistic meals enacts the ways of God's eschatological restoration on earth. The cosmic proportions of Holy Communion are discovered within the particular face-to-face encounter of neighbors and strangers in the local eucharistic gathering.[24] In the local community, the people of God learn how to enact this cosmic story in the everyday. Such ecclesial performances and practices of hope continually instruct and challenge the church in how to embody a journeying hospitality with new friends. New manifestations of hope in the world mean that the church community also will look and feel different. The people of God must deliberately orient themselves to look for new signs of the Reign of God breaking in through the concrete experiences of everyday life.

JOURNEYING SOMEWHERE WITH OTHERS

This investigation intentionally focuses on material and bodily manifestations of church extended through hospitality practice reconfigured on the borderlands. Material manifestations of hospitality, however, do not preclude the significance of eschatological time and space as the church is oriented by its story and by its core practices toward the Reign of God. The church's proclamation and embodiment of this hope is the good news for the sake of the world. While hypermobility of globalization often leads a sense of aimlessness and rootlessness, the people of God profess to be going *somewhere*. Patterned by pilgrimage, the people of God are journeying toward the hope of the resurrection and seeking to materially embody this hope in the everyday. In turn, the actions of welcoming and journeying with and among migrants continue to challenge the church to live into its own pilgrimage heritage, as well as to venture into new territories and horizons with those it encounters. In one sense, this book has illustrated an "ethic of hospitality" in light of lives marked by wandering. Yet, as Catherine Keller reveals, the language of "ethic" and "hospitality" is a tautology.[25] In reality, ethics *is* hospitality. More specifically, hospitality is ecclesial

---

23. Loring, *I Hear Hope Banging at My Back Door*, 6, in Pohl, "A Community's Practice of Hospitality," 135.

24. Cavanaugh, *Theopolitical Imagination*, 117.

25. Keller, "The Love of Postcolonialism," 225.

ethics. Hospitality is central to shaping the church *on the way* in light of twenty-first century migration.

Acts of hospitality are opportunities for the church to learn and embody the good news afresh. In order for the gospel to be relevant and meaningful it demands always to be born anew as it is continually re-told, re-appropriated, re-created in ever-shifting contexts. Rivera's postcolonial challenge is again appropriate:

> Within the imperial centers, a church ministering among recent immigrants and long-term diasporas—among people with an increasingly complex ethnic identity, with wildly varying combinations of traditional faith and plural, "syncretistic," religious formations—cannot rely on inherited "rules of recognition." It is challenged to ever greater flexibility in its community building. It hears again the ancient, underfulfilled command—corrective of any idolatry of identity—to love the alien/stranger/immigrant *as yourself.*[26]

Rivera disrupts the inherited "rules of recognition" of orthodoxy, which historically have set the boundaries of who is "in" and who is "out" within Christian tradition. Yet, she also returns to ancient and underfulfilled command to love the immigrant as yourself. This book has wrestled with the broader ecclesiological tension Rivera exposes above in that hospitality practice and the church may not look the same as they traditionally have been conceived. Still, even allowing for contemporary, contextual appropriation, there will be expressions of early Christian hospitality such as meal sharing that remain formational. The church cannot detach itself from its own history and roots, even while they are complicated and conflicted; such failures are part of the "storied place" of the church. Nor can it remain bound to old forms. The challenging contexts of transnational migration summon new forms of church not seen before. And so, we journey forth with both courage and humility.

Michael Nausner's postcolonial engagement of territory, itinerancy, homeland, and borderland holds together the dialectic of place and pilgrimage. Nausner wrestles with the tension between Christian identity and territoriality, questioning how Christian practice *takes place* somewhere but cannot be tied to a *fixed* territoriality.[27] Building upon Tanner's observation

26. Rivera, "Alien/nation, Liberation, and the Postcolonial Underground," 15; italics in original.

27. Michael Nausner, "Homeland as Borderland," 121.

that Christian social existence is "without a homeland in some territorially localizable society," he argues that while territory and its relation to religious practice are important, Christians must never understand territory as a fixed place.[28] Rather, Nausner points toward the concept of Christians' continuous negotiation of spatiality that has been so central to my investigation of alternative spatial imagination for the church and its practice of hospitality.[29] Not unlike Certeau's engagement with pre-modern itineraries, Nausner draws from cultural anthropological themes of indigenous, nomadic itinerancy and its relationship to routes, space, and ancestors so that "land is defined in accordance with journeys undertaken by ancestors. An intricate web of tracks as envisioned between the places these ancestors visited."[30] These observations lead him to challenge how institutionalized religion, specifically Christianity, relies on sedentary culture.[31] Homeland and territory must be re-imagined as dynamic borderland where itinerancy is a guiding theme. At the same time, the value of ancestors and history— or what Nausner identifies as "roots"—lies in how they shape identity and subjectivity. "Roots," however, do not solely shape Christian identity. Rather, the traces of the "roots" that remain are placed in dialogical relationship to the "routes" one is traveling. Ecclesial roots cannot be discarded as they have unquestionably fed and nurtured identity, *and yet* they must be challenged and disrupted by what is encountered *en route*. The "rules of recognition" Rivera contests above remain important as the theme of journeying challenges them to greater fluidity. Indeed, as we look back on

28. Ibid., 121–22. Also see Tanner, *Theories of Culture*, 103.

29. Nausner, "Homeland as Borderland," 121–22.

30. Nausner draws from Gill, "Territory," 299. He writes, "Inspired by his fieldwork among Aborigines in Australia, anthropologist Sam Gill gives an account of an understanding of territory that is not that of a solid plane but rather of tracks across the land. A net of tracks rather than a sealed territory becomes the identifying image of the land." Nausner, "Homeland as Borderland," 127.

31. Ibid., 128. Here Nausner notes how Susan Stanford Friedman, "does not oppose *routes* to *roots* as privileged metaphor for the development of subjectivity. Rather, she talks about a 'dialogic relationship' between the two with 'roots' 'signifying identity based on stable cores and continuities' and 'routes suggesting identity based on travel, change, and disruption.'" Friedman, *Mappings*, 151, quoted in Nausner, 128. Nausner continues, "In terms of boundaries, this means that a *dialogic* is 'constituted by the bipolar pull between the erection of borders delineating difference and the dissolution of those boundaries in the formation of permeable borderlands of exchange, blending, and transformation.'" Friedman, 153, quoted in Nausner "Homeland as Borderland," 129.

the journey of Christian history, "roots of recognition" may be the more apropos metaphor.

I close pointing to the process of transformation within the Presbyterian Church of the Ascension in East Harlem when the community exchanged its rectangular eucharist table for a round one and relocated the eucharist to the center of the congregation.[32] Russell narrates the beauty and challenge of the transformative process:

> That summer we decided to leave the benches 'in the round' and enjoyed the chance to worship while sitting only a few feet from one another. Having eliminated both the back pews and the 'high altar and pulpit,' we created a huge round table by cutting the largest piece of plywood we could find and placing this circle on the old rectangular table base. When fall arrived, people remembered their old tradition and wanted to move back to the customary separation of chancel, pews, and people. But I didn't forget how wonderful it was to divide word and bread in the midst of the people, and I managed to talk the elders into moving around the table again the next summer. By the time the second fall had arrived, the new tradition stuck and was considerably reinforced when no one wanted to help move the pews back! Thus was born a round table that symbolized our table talk and table sharing as we gathered in community.[33]

Inspired by how space, performance, and community affect the identity and mission of ecclesial communities, this book has engaged the question: *How can ecclesial communities develop new patterns of journeying and embody new spatial imagination amidst the challenging context of twenty-first century migration?* I have referred to this process of negotiation as a journey of faithfulness amidst ever-changing circumstances. My re-imagination has

---

32. Russell narrates this transformation in her church as follows: "The Presbyterian Church of the Ascension in East Harlem is an old 'brick Gothic' structure built with arches of stucco and brick in a style that is supposed to be similar to some Waldensian churches in Italy. Its many floors provide spaces for persons of all ages to gather so that it can serve as a center for many community activities. One year in the early 1970s we decided to create a sanctuary that in itself symbolized our connection to one another as a family that gathered across racial lines. The opportunity came for this move when we decided to refinish the floor and took up the pews in time for a special Pentecost celebration that would begin in the basement and then move in procession to the 'upper room' as we waited for the Spirit. For this occasion we placed all of the benches in a square, with a large space in the center around the table where we could crowd together for the breaking of bread." *Church in the Round*, 20.

33. Ibid.

centered on the formation of the eucharist and other ecclesial practices as "roots" that must be placed in dialogical relationship with new "routes." Russell claimed that the "table community is a major image of the church that links the community of Christ to the breaking of bread as well as to sharing with the poor."[34] In this exploration, we have held tightly to the formative nature of the eucharist table and the meal sharing practices and postures it shapes in ecclesial communities, even as these communities manifest the table in a number of different ways. One might say we have journeyed alongside the "roots of recognition" at the eucharist table and in the movable feast. Again, Russell's words are fitting, "Because Christ is present in the world, especially among those who are neglected, oppressed, and marginalized, the round table is also connected to the margins of both church and society, always welcoming the stranger to the feast or sharing the feast where the 'others' gather."[35]

Hospitality re-imagination is carried forth by the theology of the eucharist to invite, and at times demand, recognition of where church is happening and opened to new possibilities. New ways of being and doing church manifest themselves in *the borderlands, in-between places*, and *bridge-building activities*. Moreover, followers of Christ are invited to discover themselves being gathered into the body of Christ *on the margins* and *on the move* in ways that stand in contrast to displacement, perpetual involuntary movement, and other negative consequences of forced migration. Church happens and hospitality is extended in new places and territories through community organizing and networking, through open air eucharistic celebrations across chain link fences, in liturgical performances down city streets, in communal enactments of scriptural migration and hospitality stories, in meal sharing, and in strangers coming to recognize one another as friends. In the years to come the church will take on new forms we cannot yet imagine as ecclesial communities inhabit the "not yet" between their contexts of fear, scarcity, and competition and the superabundant economy of God. Still, one thing will not change. Faithful hospitality after the pattern of Christ will always lead us *out*, beyond our familiar communities, into the liminal spaces at the cultural, economic, and geopolitical borders imposed by empire to participate in the re-formation of the church as a community of Others that receives itself in looking *back* to the roots of the journeying church of history and *forward* to the in-breaking Reign of God.

34. Ibid., 18.
35. Ibid.

Bibliography

Aalen, Sverre. "'Reign' and 'House' in the Kingdom of God in the Gospels." *New Testament Studies* 8 (1962) 223–33.

Abraham, Susan. "What Does Mumbai Have to Do with Rome? Postcolonial Perspectives on Globalization and Theology." *Theological Studies* 69 (2008) 376–93.

Ahmed, Sara. *Strange Encounters: Embodied Others in Post-Coloniality.* Transformations. New York: Routledge, 2000.

Anzaldúa, Gloria. *Borderlands/La Frontera: The New Mestiza.* San Francisco: Aunt Lute Books, 1999.

Augustine, Saint. *City of God.* Translated by H. Bettenson. London: Penguin, 1972/1984.

Bacon, David. *The Children of NAFTA: Labor Wars on the U.S./Mexico Border.* Berkeley: University of California Press, 2004.

Badillo, David A. *Latinos and the New Immigrant Church.* Baltimore: Johns Hopkins University Press, 2006.

Bass, Dorothy C., ed. *Practicing Our Faith: A Way of Life for a Searching People.* San Francisco: Jossey-Bass, 1997.

———. "Ways of Life Abundant." In *For Life Abundant: Practical Theology, Theological Education, and Christian Ministry,* edited by Dorothy C. Bass and Craig Dykstra, 21–40. Grand Rapids: Eerdmans, 2008.

Betcher, Sharon V. *Spirit and the Politics of Disablement.* Minneapolis: Fortress, 2007.

Bhabha, Homi. *The Location of Culture.* New York: Routledge, 1994.

Bond, Gilbert. "Liturgy, Ministry, and the Stranger: The Practice of Encountering the Other in Two Christian Communities." In *Practicing Theology: Beliefs and Practices in the Christian Life,* edited by Miroslav Volf and Dorothy C. Bass, 137–56. Grand Rapids: Eerdmans, 2002.

Bourdieu, Pierre. *Outline of a Theory of Practice.* Translated by Richard Nice. Cambridge Studies in Social Anthropology 16. Cambridge: Cambridge University Press, 1977.

Bowe, John. "Nobodies: Does Slavery Exist in America?" *The New Yorker.* April 23, 2003.

Brah, Avtar. *Cartographies of Diaspora: Contesting Identities.* Gender, Racism, Ethnicity. New York: Routledge, 2002.

Bretherton, Luke. *Hospitality as Holiness: Christian Witness amid Moral Diversity.* Burlington, VT: Ashgate, 2006.

Browning, Don S. *A Fundamental Practical Theology: Descriptive and Strategic Proposal.* Minneapolis: Fortress, 1991.

———, ed. *Practical Theology: The Emerging Field in Theology, Church and World.* San Francisco: Harper & Row, 1983.

Bibliography

Brueggemann, Walter. *The Land: Place as Gift, Promise, and Challenge in Biblical Faith.* 2nd ed. Overtures to Biblical Theology. Minneapolis: Fortress, 2002.

Cavanaugh, William T. *Theopolitical Imagination.* London: T. & T. Clark, 2002.

―――. *Torture and Eucharist: Theology, Politics, and the Body of Christ.* Challenges in Contemporary Theology. Malden, MA: Blackwell, 1998.

Certeau, Michel de. *The Practice of Everyday Life.* Translated by Steven Rendall. Berkeley: University of California Press, 1984.

Chauvet, Louis-Marie. *Symbol and Sacrament: A Sacramental Reinterpretation of Christian Existence.* Translated by Patrick Madigan and Madeleine Beaumont. Collegeville, MN: Liturgical, 1995.

Chomsky, Aviva. *"They Take Our Jobs!" and 20 Other Myths about Immigration.* Boston: Beacon, 2007.

Conference of Catholic Bishops, United States. *Strangers No Longer: Together on the Journey of Hope.* Washington, DC, 2002.

Costen, Melva Wilson. *African American Worship.* Nashville: Abingdon, 1993.

Crabtree, Penni. "Meeting Place Sealed Off: Border Patrol Agents Prohibit Access to Friendship Park." *San Diego Union Tribune.* February 22, 2009. http://www3.signonsandiego.com/stories/2009/feb/22/1m22park23590-meeting-place-sealed/?metro/.

Day, Dorothy. *Dorothy Day: Selected Writings.* Edited by Robert Ellsberg. Maryknoll, NY: Orbis, 2009.

De La Torre, Miguel A. "For Immigrants." In *Church and Public Life: An Agenda for Change,* edited by Rebecca Todd Peters and Elizabeth Hinson-Hasty, 73–84. Louisville: Westminster John Knox, 2008.

―――. *Trails of Hope and Terror: Testimonies on Immigration.* Maryknoll, NY: Orbis, 2009.

Derrida, Jacques. *Adieu to Emmanuel Levinas.* Translated by Pascale-Anne Brault and Michael Naaz. Stanford: Stanford University Press, 1999.

―――. *Politics of Friendship.* Translated by George Collings. New York: Verso, 1997.

Derrida, Jacques, and Anne Dufourmantelle. *Of Hospitality.* Translated by Rachel Bowlby. Stanford: Stanford University Press, 2000.

Dodson, Jualynne, and Cheryl Townsend Gilkes. "'There's Nothing Like Church Food': Food and the U.S. Afro-Christian Tradition: Re-Membering Community and Feeding the Embodied Spiritual(s)." *Journal of the American Academy of Religion* 63 (1995) 519–38.

Douglass, James. "Dorothy Day and the City of God." *Social Justice Review* 54 (May 1961) 40–43.

Dube, Musa, W. "Go Therefore and Make Disciples of All Nations." In *Teaching the Bible: The Discourses and Politics of Biblical Pedagogy,* edited by Fernando F. Segovia and Mary Ann Tolbert, 224–46. Maryknoll, NY: Orbis, 1998.

―――. *Postcolonial Feminist Interpretation of the Bible.* St. Louis: Chalice, 2000.

―――. "Postcoloniality, Feminist Spaces, and Religion." In *Postcolonialism, Feminist, and Religious Discourse,* edited by Laura E. Donaldson and Kwok Pui-lan, 100–122. New York: Routledge, 2002.

Dulles, Avery. *Models of the Church.* Expanded ed. New York: Image Books Double-day, 2002.

Dussel, Enrique. *Invention of the Americas: Eclipse of "the Other" and the Myth of Modernity.* Translated by Michael D. Barber. New York: Continuum, 1995.

Bibliography

Eiesland, Nancy L. *The Disabled God: Toward a Liberatory Theology of Disability.* Nashville: Abingdon, 1994.

Fanestil, John. "Border Crossing Communion at Friendship Park." *Christian Century,* October 7, 2008. http://www.christiancentury.org/article_print.lasso?id=5330 2/24/2009.

Freire, Paulo. *Pedagogy of the Oppressed.* Translated by Myra Bergman Ramos. New York: Continuum, 1986.

Elizondo, Virgilio P. *Galilean Journey: The Mexican-American Promise.* Rev. ed. Maryknoll, NY: Orbis, 2007.

Elizondo, Virgilio P., and Timothy M. Matovina. *Mestizo Worship: A Pastoral Approach to Liturgical Ministry.* Collegeville, MN: Liturgical, 1998.

————. *San Fernando Cathedral: Soul of the City.* Maryknoll, NY: Orbis, 1993.

Elliott, John H. *A Home for the Homeless: A Sociological Exegesis of 1 Peter, Its Situation and Strategy.* Philadelphia: Fortress, 1981.

Gates, Jamie. "Communion at Friendship Park: Liturgy and Politics at the U.S.-Mexican Border." Presented at annual meetings of the Society of Christian Ethics, San Jose, CA, January 9, 2010.

Gill, Sam. "Territory." In *Critical Lens for Religious Studies,* edited by Mark C. Taylor. Chicago: University of Chicago Press, 1998.

Gittens, Anthony J. "Beyond Hospitality? The Missionary Status and Role Revisited." *International Review of Missions* 83/330 (1994) 397–416.

Goizueta, Roberto S. *Caminemos con Jesús: Toward a Hispanic/Latino Theology of Accompaniment.* Maryknoll, NY: Orbis, 2003.

————. *Christ Our Companion: Toward a Theological Aesthetics of Liberation.* Maryknoll, NY: Orbis. 2009.

González Justo L., *Mañana: Christian Theology from a Hispanic Perspective.* Nashville: Abingdon, 1990.

Gonzalez, Michelle A. "Who Is Americana/o? Theological Anthropology, Postcoloniality, and the Spanish-Speaking American." In *Postcolonial Theologies: Divinity and Empire,* edited by Catherine Keller, Michael Nausner, and Mayra Rivera, 58–78. St. Louis: Chalice, 2004.

Griffin, Mark, and Theron Walker. *Living on the Borders: What the Church Can Learn from Ethnic Immigrant Cultures.* Grand Rapids: Brazos, 2004.

Groody, Daniel G. *Border of Death, Valley of Life: An Immigrant Journey of Heart and Spirit.* New York: Rowman & Littlefield, 2002.

Groody, Daniel G., and Gioacchino Campese, eds. *A Promised Land: A Perilous Journey: Theological Perspectives on Migration.* Notre Dame: University of Notre Dame Press, 2008.

Guarnizo, Luis Eduardo, and Michael Peter Smith. "The Locations of Transnationalism." In *Transnationalism From Below,* edited by Michael Peter Smith, Luis Eduardo Guarnizo, 3–34. New Brunswick, NJ: Transaction, 1998.

Gutiérrez, Gustavo. *Las Casas: In Search of the Poor of Jesus Christ.* Translated by Robert R. Barr. Maryknoll, NY: Orbis, 1993.

————. *A Theology of Liberation: History, Politics, Salvation.* Revised ed. Translated and edited by Sister Caridad Inda and John Eagleson. Maryknoll, NY: Orbis, 1973.

Hagan, Jacqueline, and Helen Rose Ebaugh. "Calling upon the Sacred: Migrants Use of Religion in the Migration Process." *International Migration Review* 37 (2003) 1145–62.

Bibliography

Hallie, Philip. *Lest Innocent Blood Be Shed.* New York: Harper & Row, 1979.

Hauerwas, Stanley. *The Peaceable Kingdom: A Primer in Christian Ethics.* Notre Dame: University of Notre Dame Press, 1984.

———. *Sanctify Them in the Truth: Holiness Exemplified.* Nashville: Ignatius, 1991.

———. "The Servant Community." In *The Hauerwas Reader,* edited by John Berkman and Michael Cartwright, 371–91. Durham, NC: Duke University Press, 2001.

Hauerwas, Stanley, and William H. Willimon. *Resident Aliens: Life in the Christian Colony.* Nashville: Abingdon, 1989.

Healy, Nicholas M. *Church, World, and the Christian Life: Practical-Prophetic Ecclesiology.* Cambrige Studies in Christian Doctrine 7. Cambridge: Cambridge University Press, 2000.

Inge, John. *The Christian Theology of Place.* Explorations in Practical, Pastoral, and Empirical Theology. Burlington, VT: Ashgate, 2003.

Isasi-Díaz, Ada María. *En La Lucha: Elaborating a Mujerista Theology.* Minneapolis: Fortress, 1993.

———. *Mujerista Theology: A Theology for the Twenty-First Century.* Maryknoll, NY: Orbis, 1996.

———. "The New *Mestizaje/Mulatez*: Reconceptualizing Difference." In *A Dream Unfinished: Theological Reflections on America from the Margins,* edited by Eleazar S. Fernandez and Fernando F. Segovia, 203–19. Maryknoll, NY: Orbis, 2001.

Isasi-Díaz, Ada María, and Yolanda Tarango. *Hispanic Women: Prophetic Voice in the Church.* Minneapolis: Fortress, 1993.

Keller, Catherine, "The Love of Postcolonialism: Theology in the Interstices of Empire." In *Postcolonial Theologies: Divinity and Empire,* edited by Catherine Keller et al., 221–42. St. Louis: Chalice, 2004.

Koenig, John. *New Testament Hospitality: Partnership with Strangers as Promise and Mission.* Overtures to Biblical Theology. Philadelphia: Fortress, 1985.

Kwok, Pui-lan. *Postcolonial Imagination and Feminist Theology.* Louisville: Westminster John Knox, 2005.

———. "Theology and Social Theory." In *Empire and the Christian Tradition: New Readings of Classical Theologians,* edited by Kwok Pui-Lan et al., 15–39. Minneapolis: Fortress, 2007.

———. "A Theology of Border Passage." In *Border Crossings: Cross Cultural Hermeneutics,* edited by D. N. Premnath, 103–17. Maryknoll, NY: Orbis, 2007.

Lee, Michael E. "The Galilean Jesus as Faithful Dissenter: Latino/a Christology and the Dynamics of Exclusion." In *Jesus in the Hispanic Community: Images of Christ from Theology to Popular Religion,* edited by Harold Joseph Recinos and Hugo Magallanes, 16–37. Louisville: Westminster John Knox, 2009.

Lévinas, Emmanuel. *Entre Nous: On Thinking-of-the-Other.* Translated by Michael B. Smith and Barbara Harshav. European Perspectives. New York: Columbia University Press, 1998.

———. *Time and the Other and Additional Essays.* Translated by Richard A. Cohen. Pittsburgh: Duquesne University Press, 1997.

———. *Totality and Infinity: An Essay on Exteriority.* Duquesne Studies. Philsophical Series 24. Pittsburgh: Duquesne University Press, 1969.

Lindbeck, George A. "The Church." In *The Church in a Postliberal Age,* edited by James J. Buckley, 145–65. Grand Rapids: Eerdmans, 2002.

Bibliography

———. *The Nature of Doctrine: Religion and Theology in a Postliberal Age*. Louisville: Westminster John Knox, 1984.

Lohfink, Gerhard. *Does God Need the Church? Toward a Theology of the People of God*. Translated by Linda M. Maloney. Collegeville, MN: Liturgical, 1999.

Loring, Ed. *I Hear Hope Banging at My Back Door: Writings from "Hospitality."* Atlanta: The Open Door Community, 2000.

Lugones, María, ed. *Pilgrimages/Peregrinajes: Theorizing Coalition against Multiple Oppressions*. Lanham, MD: Rowan & Littlefield, 2003.

MacIntyre, Alasdair. *After Virtue: A Study in Moral Theory*. 2nd ed. Notre Dame: University of Notre Dame Press, 1984.

Massey, Douglas S. "Closed-Door Policy: Mexico Vividly Illustrates How U.S. Treatment of Immigrant Workers Backfires." *American Prospect,* July 1, 2003. http://prospect.org/cs/articles?articleId=6824.

Matsuoka, Fumitaka. *Out of Silence: Emerging Themes in Asian American Churches*. Cleveland: United Church Press, 1995.

Meeks, Douglas M. *God the Economist: The Doctrine of God and Political Economy*. Minneapolis: Fortress 1989.

———. "Peace and Justice: The Eucharistic Community of Gifting." *Liturgy* 13/1 (1996) 16–21.

Meeks, Wayne A. *The First Urban Christians: The Social World of the Apostle Paul*. New Haven: Yale University Press, 1983.

Metz, Johann Baptist. *Faith in History and Society: Toward a Practical Fundamental Theology*. Translated by David Smith. New York: Seabury, 1979.

Milbank, John. *Theology and Social Theory: Beyond Secular Reason*. 2nd ed. Malden, MA: Blackwell, 2006.

Miller, William D. *Dorothy Day: A Biography*. San Francisco: Harper & Row, 1982.

Minow, Martha. *Making All the Difference*. Ithaca, NY: Cornell University Press, 1990.

Moessner, David. *Lord of the Banquet: The Literary and Theological Significance of the Lukan Travel Narrative*. Minneapolis: Fortress, 1989.

Moraga, Cherríe, and Gloria Anzaldúa, eds. *This Bridge Called My Back: Writings by Radical Women of Color*. New York: Kitchen Table, 1983.

Nanko-Fernández, Carmen M. "Beyond Hospitality: Implications of Im/migration for Teología y Pastoral de Conjunto." *Perspectivas: Hispanic Theological Initiative Occasional Papers* 10 (Fall 2006) 51–62.

———. *Theologizing in Espanglish: Context, Community, and Ministry*. Maryknoll, NY: Orbis, 2010.

Nausner, Michael. "Homeland as Borderland: Territories of Christian Subjectivity." In *Postcolonial Theologies: Divinity and Empire*, edited by Catherine Keller et al., 118–33. St. Louis: Chalice, 2004.

Newbigin, Lesslie. *The Open Secret: An Introduction to the Theology of Mission*. Rev. ed. Grand Rapids: Eerdmans, 1995.

Newman, Elizabeth. *Untamed Hospitality: Welcoming God and Other Strangers*. Grand Rapids: Brazos, 2007.

Niebuhr, Richard H. *Christ and Culture*. New York: Harper & Row, 1951.

Nouwen, Henri J. M. *Reaching Out: The Three Movements of Spiritual Life*. Garden City, NY: Doubleday, 1975.

Oden, Amy G., ed. *And You Welcomed Me: A Sourcebook on Hospitality in Early Christianity*. Nashville: Abingdon, 2001.

Bibliography

———. *God's Welcome: Hospitality for a Gospel-Hungry World.* Cleveland: Pilgrim, 2008.

Ogletree, Thomas W. *Hospitality to the Stranger: Dimensions of Moral Understanding.* Philadelphia: Fortress, 1985.

One Border One Body: Immigration and the Eucharist. DVD. directed by John Carlos Frey. Notre Dame: Gatekeeper Productions, 2008.

O'Shea Merriam, Brigid, OSF. *Searching for Christ: The Spirituality of Dorothy Day.* Notre Dame: University of Notre Dame Press, 1994.

Palmer, Parker J. *A Company of Strangers: Christians and the Renewal of America's Public Life.* New York: Crossroad, 1986.

Passel, Jeffrey S., and D'Vera Cohn. "A Portrait of Unauthorized Immigrants in the United States." Washington DC: Pew Hispanic Center, April 2009. http://pewhispanic.org/reports/report.php?ReportID=107.

———. "Trends in Unauthorized Immigration: Undocumented Inflow Trains Legal Inflow." Washington DC: Pew Hispanic Center, October 2008.

———. "Unauthorized Immigrant Totals Rise in 7 States, Fall in 14: Decline in Those from Mexico Fuels Most State Decreases." Washington, DC: Pew Research Center's Hispanic Trends Project, November 2014.

Pohl, Christine D. "A Community's Practice of Hospitality: The Interdependence of Practices and of Communities." In *Practicing Theology: Beliefs and Practices in the Christian Life,* edited by Miroslav Volf and Dorothy C. Bass, 121–36. Grand Rapids: Eerdmans, 2002.

———. *Making Room: Recovering Hospitality as a Christian Tradition.* Grand Rapids: Eerdmans, 1999.

———. "Welcoming Strangers: A Socio-ethical Study of Hospitality in Selected Expressions of the Christian Tradition." Ph.D. diss., Emory University, 1993.

Pohl, Christine D., and Pamela J. Buck. *Study Guide for Making Room: Recovering Hospitality as a Christian Tradition.* Grand Rapids: Eerdmans, 2001.

Premnath, D. N., ed. *Border Crossings: Cross-Cultural Hermeneutics.* Maryknoll, NY: Orbis, 2007.

Public Citizen Product ID 9013, *Another America is Possible: The Impact of NAFTA on the U.S. Latino Community and Lessons for Future Trade Agreements.* Washington DC, 2004. http://www.citizen.org/documents/LatinosReportFINAL.pdf.

Richard, Lucien, OMI. *Living the Hospitality of God.* New York: Paulist, 2000.

Rieger, Joerg. *Christ and Empire: From Paul to Postcolonial Times.* Minneapolis: Fortress, 2007.

———. "Christian Theology and Empires." In *Empire and the Christian Tradition,* edited by Kwok Pui-lan et al., 1–14. Minneapolis: Fortress, 2007.

Rivera, Mayra. "Introduction: Alien/Nation, Liberation, and the Postcolonial Underground." In *Postcolonial Theologies: Divinity and Empire,* edited by Catherine Keller et al., 1–21. St. Louis: Chalice, 2004.

———. *The Touch of Transcendence: A Postcolonial Theology of God.* Louisville: Westminster John Knox, 2007.

Russell, Letty M. *Church in the Round: Feminist Interpretation of the Church.* Louisville: Westminster John Knox, 1993.

———. *Just Hospitality: God's Welcome in a World of Difference.* Edited by J. Shannon Clarkson and Kate M. Ott. Louisville: Westminster John Knox, 2009.

Russell, Letty M. et al., eds. *Inheriting Our Mothers' Gardens: Feminist Theology in Third World Perspective.* Philadelphia: Westminster, 1988.

Bibliography

The Rutba House, ed. *School(s) for Conversion: 12 Marks of New Monasticism.* Eugene, OR: Cascade Books, 2005.

Sanders, Cheryl Jeanne. *Saints in Exile: The Holiness Pentecostal Experience in African American Religion and Culture.* New York: Oxford University Press, 1996.

Schiller, Nina Glick, et al. "From Immigrant to Transmigrant: Theorizing Transnational Migration." *Anthropological Quarterly* 68 (1995) 48–63.

Schmemann, Alexander. *For the Life of the World: Sacraments and Orthodoxy.* Crestwood, NY: St. Vladimir's Seminary Press, 1988.

Schüssler Fiorenza, Elisabeth. *In Memory of Her: A Feminist Theological Reconstruction of Christian Origins.* New York: Crossroad, 1983.

Segovia, Fernando F., "Biblical Criticism and Postcolonial Studies: Toward a Postcolonial Optic." In *The Postcolonial Bible*, edited by R. S. Sugirtharajah, 33–44. Bible and Post-colonialism 1. Sheffield: Sheffield Academic, 1998.

———. *A Dream Unfinished: Theological Reflections on America from the Margins.* Maryknoll, NY: Orbis, 2001.

———. "Interpreting beyond Borders: Postcolonial Studies and Diasporic Studies in Biblical Criticism." In *Interpreting beyond Borders,* edited by Fernando F. Segovia, 11–34. Bible and Postcolonialism 3. Sheffield: Sheffield Academic, 2000.

———. Two Places and No Place on Which to Stand." In *Mestizo Christianity: Theology from a Latino Perspectives,* edited by Arturo J. Bañuelas, 28–43. Maryknoll, NY: Orbis, 1995.

Segundo, Juan Luis. *The Liberation of Theology.* Translated by John Drury. Maryknoll, NY: Orbis, 1976.

Smith, Gregory A. "Attitudes toward Immigration: In the Pulpit and the Pew." In *Pew Forum on Religion and Public Life* (April 26, 2006). http://pewresearch.org/pubs/20/attitudes-toward-immigration-in-the-pulpit-and-the-pew.

Smith, James K. A. *Desiring the Kingdom: Worship, Worldview, and Cultural Formation.* Grand Rapids: Baker Academic, 2009.

Souza Josgrilberg, Rui de. "Wesley e a experiência cristã." *Revista Caminhando* 11/18 (Jul-Dec 2006) 41–54.

Stanford Friedman, Susan. *Mappings: Feminist and the Cultural Geographies of Encounter.* Princeton: Princeton University Press, 1998.

Stone, Bryan P. *Evangelism after Christendom: The Theology and Practice of Christian Witness.* Grand Rapids: Brazos, 2007.

———. "The Missional Church and the Missional Empire." *Didache: Faithful Teaching* 13/2 (2014). http://didache.nazarene.org.

———. "Wesleyan Ecclesiology—Part 1 & 2." Presented at the Oxford Institute for Wesleyan Studies, Oxford, June 2007.

Sugirtharajah, R. S. *Asian Biblical Hermeneutics and Postcolonialism: Contesting the Interpretations.* Biblical Seminar 64. Maryknoll, NY: Orbis, 1998.

Tanner, Kathryn. *Theories of Culture: A New Agenda for Theology.* Guides to Theological Inquiry. Minneapolis: Fortress, 1997.

Taylor, Charles. *Modern Social Imaginaries.* Public Planet Books. Durham, NC: Duke University Press, 2004.

Turner, Victor. *The Ritual Process: Structure and Anti-Structure.* Ithaca, NY: Cornell University Press, 1969.

Vanier, Jean. *Community and Growth: Our Pilgrimage Together.* Rev. ed. New York: Paulist, 1989.

Bibliography

———. *Essential Writings.* Edited by Carolyn Whitney-Brown. Modern Spiritual Masters Series. Maryknoll, NY: Orbis, 2008.

———. *Images of Love, Words of Hope.* Edited by Susan Morgan, Richard Nielsen, and John Sumarah. Hantsport, NS: Lancelot, 1991.

———. *Our Journey Home: Rediscovering a Common Humanity beyond Our Differences.* Translated by Maggie Parham. Maryknoll, NY: Orbis, 1997.

Vasconcelos, José. *Obras Completas.* 4 vols. Mexico: Libreros Mexicanos Unidos, 1958–61.

Vergote, Antoine. "Symbolic Gestures and Actions in Liturgy." In *Liturgy in Transition,* edited by Herman Schmidt, SJ, 40–52. New York: Herder & Herder, 1971.

Volf, Miroslav. *Exclusion and Embrace: A Theological Exploration of Identity, Otherness, and Reconciliation.* Nashville: Abingdon, 1996.

Volf, Miroslav, and Dorothy C. Bass, eds. *Practicing Theology: Beliefs and Practices in Christian Life.* Grand Rapids: Eerdmans, 2002.

Ward, Graham. "Hospitality and Justice toward 'Strangers': A Theological Reflection." Paper presented at the 'Migration in Europe: What Are the Ethical Guidelines for Political Practice?" Symposium, Katholische Akademie. Berlin, November 2003.

Watts, Jill. *God, Harlem U.S.A.: The Father Divine Story.* Berkeley: University of California Press. 1992.

Whitney-Brown, Carolyn. "Introduction." In *Essential Writings,* by Jean Vanier. Modern Spiritual Masters Series. Maryknoll, NY: Orbis, 2008.

Wolfteich, Claire. *Lord, Have Mercy: Praying for Justice with Conviction and Humility.* San Francisco: Jossey-Bass, 2006.

Yoder, John Howard. *Body Politics: Five Practices of the Christian Community before the Watching World.* Nashville: Discipleship Resources, 1992.

———. "See How They Set Their Face to the Sun." In *For the Nations: Essays Public and Evangelical,* 51–78. Grand Rapids: Eerdmans, 1997.

Yong, Amos. *Hospitality and the Other: Pentecost, Christian Practices, and the Neighbor.* Maryknoll, NY: Orbis, 2008.

———. *Theology and Down Syndrome: Reimagining Disability in Late* Modernity. Waco: Baylor University Press, 2007.

———. *The Bible, Disability, and the Church: A New Vision of the People of God.* Grand Rapids: Eerdmans, 2011.

Young, Iris Marion. *Justice and the Politics of Difference.* Princeton: Princeton University Press, 1990.

Zizioulas, John. *Being as Communion: Studies in Personhood and the Church.* Crestwood, NY: St. Vladimir's University Press, 1997.

Zwick, Mark, and Louise Zwick. *The Catholic Worker Movement: Intellectual and Spiritual Origins.* Mahwah, NJ: Paulist, 2005.

———. *Mercy without Borders: the Catholic Worker and Immigration.* Mahwah, NJ: Paulist, 2010.

Index

Index

Index